BRITISH HIGH POLITICS AND A NATIONALIST IRELAND:

CRIMINALITY, LAND AND THE LAW UNDER FORSTER AND BALFOUR

Margaret O'Callaghan

CORK UNIVERSITY PRESS

First published in 1994 by
Cork University Press
University College
Cork
Ireland

British Library Cataloguing in Publication Data
A CIP catalogue record for this book is available from the British Library.

ISBN 1 85918 001 9 hardback
1 85918 002 7 paperback

Typeset by Phototype-Set Ltd, Dublin
Printed by Colour Books Ltd, Dublin

For James and Beulah

CONTENTS

Acknowledgements   ix
Abbreviations   xi

INTRODUCTION   1
    The Shadow of an Obsession

1   WHAT THE LIBERALS SAW: IRELAND UNDER GLADSTONE'S   11
    SECOND MINISTRY
      Definitions
      Law and Order versus Relief
      Defining 'the Irish Problem': Painting the Devil on the Wall

2   LIBERAL PARALYSIS   31
      Rehearsing the Arguments
      War to the Knife

3   A LIBERAL DILEMMA   61
      A State Trial
      The Protection of Person and Property (Ireland) Act, 1881
      From Detention to Politics

4   FREEHOLD IN VICTORIAN IRELAND   95

5   PARNELLISM AND CRIME: CONSTRUCTING A CONSERVATIVE
    STRATEGY OF CONTAINMENT, 1887–90   104

6   THE FORMATION OF CONSERVATIVE POLICY, 1886–87   122
      The Case of Kerry Stated
      Unwelcome Analysts: Tories out of Step – Hicks-Beach and
        Redvers Buller
      Conservative Policy: The Post-Home Rule Bill Hiatus

7 THE TRANSFORMATION OF THE LAND QUESTION 145

CONCLUSION 153

Notes and References 155
Appendix I 182
Appendix II 185
Appendix III 188
Bibliography 191
Index 209

ACKNOWLEDGEMENTS

When I was eight my father stopped the car at the end of an interminable annual drive from the suburbs of Dublin to the pilgrimage site of his family home near Kilfelim, Farranfore, Co. Kerry and said, telling me that the place was called Lisheenbawn Cross, 'That's where they shot Herbert'. I would like to thank him, Jeremiah O'Callaghan, and my mother Miriam O'Callaghan, for permitting me to know that the past matters.

For permission to quote from the Balfour, Campbell-Bannerman and Gladstone papers I am indebted to the named copyright holders and the staff of the British Library; for the Crewe papers I am indebted to the Cambridge University Library; for the Harcourt and Sandars papers to the Bodleian Library, Oxford; and for the papers of Sir Michael Hicks-Beach, Earl of St Aldwen, to the Gloucestershire County Record Office. The staff in the Manuscripts and Official Publications Rooms in the Cambridge University Library have been consistently helpful, as have the Manuscripts Room staff in the British Library, those at the Bodleian, the National Library of Ireland and most particularly the National Archives in Dublin in its past incarnation in Dublin Castle and in its new environs.

This book began as a Cambridge PhD, supervised by Professor Peter Clarke. I would like to thank him for his help, stimulation and confidence. The research was funded by the Master and Fellows of St John's College, Cambridge who elected me to a Laski Research Studentship and by the Master and Fellows of Sidney Sussex College, Cambridge, where I was a research fellow. To these I express my thanks. I would also like to express particular thanks to Professor Derek Beales for his constant encouragement. My colleagues in the Department of Politics at the Queen's University of Belfast, in particular Professor Cornelius O'Leary, Professor Paul Bew, Dr Richard English and Dr Graham Walker, have provided a congenial atmosphere in which to write on Irish history and politics.

I have incurred many intellectual debts to those who taught me as an undergraduate and postgraduate at University College, Dublin, particularly the late Professor Desmond Williams, Professor Ronan Fanning and Professor Dónal McCartney. I would also like to thank the original examiners of my PhD, Professor Roy Foster and Dr K. Theodore Hoppen, also Professor

ix

Oliver MacDonagh, Dr Brendan Bradshaw, Dr Christopher Andrew and the late Professor Nicholas Mansergh for crucial advice at different times.

My closest intellectual companion in thinking about late-nineteenth century Ireland, among other things, has been my ever-stimulating great friend, Frank Callanan.

The earlier chapters of this book are particularly indebted to the work of Alan Warren and Richard Hawkins and to Colin Matthew's superb edition of the Gladstone diaries. All of the rest of the book rests on the work of an extraordinarily prolific generation of historians of late-nineteenth century Ireland.

My further thanks must be to Maurice Biggar, Catherine Whistler, Rory Montgomery, Éamon O'Flaherty, Kitty Shields, Mary Short, Seán Hawkins, Elaine Sharland, Dorothea Barret, Vibike Sorenson, Ewen Green, Terry Jenkins, Richard Darrah, Tom McGurk, Martin Kemp, Clem McIntyre, Anita Herle, George Reid, Patrick Healy and James Ferris. Betty Donnelly and Marita Jaschob have provided splendid assistance.

Finally, and most importantly, my greatest thanks are to my husband and scholarly fellow-traveller, James McGeachie, who has taught me most of what I know about England and suggested the title for this book.

Margaret O'Callaghan
Belfast
June, 1994

ABBREVIATIONS

LPRO   London, Public Record Office, Kew

CSORP   Chief Secretary's Office Registered Papers

NAD   National Archives, Dublin

PRONI   Public Records Office, Northern Ireland

NLI   National Library of Ireland, Dublin

BL   British Library, London

CUL   Cambridge University Library

INTRODUCTION

This book focuses on the nature of the relation between British high political decisions, crime, nationality and the law in Ireland in the period that started with the so-called Land War of 1879. Works by historians of Ireland over the past twenty-five years have dramatically altered perceptions of the social and economic realities of post-famine Irish society. Traditional nationalist accounts presented the period of the 1880s as one during which an undifferentiated peasantry rose spontaneously under the leadership of the Irish parliamentary party to throw off the oppression of a predatory landlord caste, the concrete manifestation of the power of English government in Ireland. This interpretation has been dismantled in almost every particular. The studies that have most radically ripped the old story apart are economic. By establishing, through studies of individual estates, that Irish landlords were not in fact generally absentee and wealthy, by establishing the existence of variations within the rural tenantry, by questioning the economic correctness of Gladstone's willingness to legislate on the basis of nationalist tenurial analysis, many aspects of the truth behind what Anna Parnell called 'the tale of a great sham' have been illuminated. David Fitzpatrick's clarion call to historians of Ireland to 'let statistics be the hammer with which to shatter the myths' is both salutary and bracing.

But there is another story to be told. And that is the story of how new myths were constructed in these years. While the basis of myths ought certainly to be laid bare, their political potency ought not to be denied. This work starts from the supposition that political action and governmental decisions alter the nature of popular consciousness. On closer examination of the period it seemed that there was little inevitability in the course that events took, and that their direction was determined by the interaction of Nationalist political organisation in Ireland, and governmental policy in London made manifest through the actions of Dublin Castle. The study that follows is centred around two crucial periods – the years from 1880 to 1882 and the years after the defeat of the 1886 Home Rule Bill. It is contended that the direction of Liberal policy was clarified in the former, and that of the Conservatives was clarified in the latter. Both policies, moreover, developed in response to Nationalist manipulation, and conversely the nature of those respective policies determined the internal politics of Ireland itself.

1

This work begins with a study of the response of the Liberal government to the economic collapse and the breakdown of law and order in the west of Ireland, in 1880. It attempts to show that the structure of the administration at Dublin Castle – and more specifically the dependence of that administration on an extraordinary network of direct communication from resident magistrates and police – created the framework within which the problem was perceived. The structure of the framework was thus in itself potent. The reason for concentrating on the exceptionally detailed observation to which the population was exposed, is to emphasise that this structure helped to generate what it was predicated upon – rural disorder. The complex reality of local disorder was transmuted into statistical information on every aspect of outrage, eviction, legal process and action. This in turn was transmitted to London for political analysis. In London there was an Ireland composed of this information, but denied context. W. E. Forster, as Chief Secretary for Ireland under Gladstone, encountered a problem encountered by Chief Secretaries before and after him: an attrition of his political intimacy with those who appointed him by tainting his London 'Ireland' with the unassimilable complexities of the real one.

The constraints within which the Liberal administration operated in 1880–81 are examined in the parliamentary response to Forster's proposal to introduce a Compensation of Disturbances Bill to mitigate the evils of what he saw to be unjust evictions in times of depression. By initially adopting this proposal with the support of his own party, Forster was in fact displaying a Liberal willingness to recognise that there was some justice in the demands of the poorest tenants of the west. There was, of course, a base Liberal propensity to fail in sympathy with Irish landlords, whom they perceived as undifferentiated. This had been true from the time of the report of the Devon Commission of the 1840s, which made the Irish landlords the economic scapegoats for all the evils of Irish life. The Compensation for Disturbances Bill was defeated, and the degree of rural disorder remained the same. Forster and Gladstone's Liberal ministry were then in possession of few political choices. There was a clamour for a restoration of order from Tories, Irish landlords and many Liberals. The commissions appointed to investigate the agricultural crisis (the brief of the Tory Richmond Commission) and the tenurial situation (that of the Liberal Bessborough) were not due to report for some months. The only remaining option seemed to be a gradual concentration on the political base that was seen to have orchestrated the disorder, the Irish National Land League.

Throughout these chapters there is an attempt to consider the nature of the connection between high and low politics as manifested in administration and law, though the focus is on government. The language of the Irish National Land League, the structure of their mobile organisers and verbal proponents, acted as a constant counterweight to Forster's well-intentioned attempts to 'solve the problem'. The extent to which that governmental fossilisation of the complexity of rural disorder mirrored the position of the Parliamentary Party and Land League is interesting. Thus Joseph Biggar, in jubilantly shouting, 'time for a state trial' in sarcastic anticipation of the government's obvious next move was in a sense colluding with just such an outcome. For London, or rather the London represented by Gladstone, it was a return to the precedents of all Irish rural disorder and political dealings through the nineteenth century, while for Nationalist MPs and organisers it opened yet another chapter in an old story.

The state trial of late 1880 is counterposed with what has gone before in the correspondence of Gladstone and Forster. For, despite the subtlety of Liberal discussion, often sympathetic, of Irish political options, the trial sealed the public image of the Forster administration. Publicly, the forces of the law in the 'disturbed areas' had been seen to back the landlord interest, and publicly again, through the trial, the administration was seen to underline that commitment. The nature of the charge contradicted the earlier Liberal interpretation of the problem, and crystallised a fluid and volatile collection of local responses to distress. Nationalist organisers had already sought to harness much of that dynamism to their own ends by generalising local issues and pinning them beneath a unified language, but the state trial decisively confirmed impressions of their directive role. The trial is also interesting for revealing an urban world and context utterly at variance with the image of Ireland that Irish Nationalist politicians required for an American audience, and that Forster consolidated in the Commons by focusing discussion on his crime statistics and tales of rural horror.

Clearly, the prototypical tenant promulgated by the Land League did exist, despite recent economic-historiographical revisions. As both the Bessborough and Richmond Commissions revealed, there was grinding poverty in many areas. But, as the action of the Land League intensified in early 1881, the internalisation of that image of the prototypical oppressed tenant by all Nationalist gatherings proceeded apace. Thus, superimposed on the green flags, banners and vague misspelt rallying cries in the Irish language characteristic of all popular march-outs since O'Connell, there was a new vocabulary of resistance.

In moving from a state trial to the suspension of habeas corpus Gladstone reluctantly acquiesced in a policy repugnant to his Liberal principles, but strategically irresistible. Because his cabinet had to be carried with him on the proposed Land Bill, coercion was a price that he was willing to pay. Moreover, it is clear from examining Forster's analysis in Dublin, that the country literally was what he proclaimed it to be – ungovernable under the ordinary law. The discrepancy in analysis of the problem that opened up between Gladstone and Forster in the discussion of the basis of what they both persisted in seeing as a single fossilised problem is crucial. For Forster gradually moved, under pressure of perpetual Nationalist goading, to a view of conspiracy by a handful of activists. Gladstone, on the other hand, seems to have accepted the Nationalist self-representation of the breakdown of relations between the rural classes as universal.

The Land Bill of 1881 marks Gladstone's first willingness to enter into the conceptual framework of his declared Nationalist opponents. The Kilmainham episode demonstrates his willingness to deal with them politically. To the Liberals, after 1882, the 'problem' was what Irish Nationalist politicians proclaimed it to be: legitimate, historically conditioned economic and political grievance. To the Tories it was a case of opportunistic Irish politicians providing a veneer of dubious ideology to cover greed and ignorance. Liberal commitment to Home Rule in 1886 was thus merely the logical extension of a willingness to enter into a Nationalist representation.

Since the land was the issue around which politics took place, the second section of this study begins with an analysis of the development of, and reasons for, the evolution of Liberal and Conservative policy in such different directions. The decision of the Liberals to maintain the structure of the 1881 Act was a consequence of Gladstone's stubborn adherence to his own desired analysis. The policy of land purchase, except in the contest of a Home Rule parliament, was anathema to Gladstone. Tories, on the other hand, had ideological objections to what they proclaimed to be the undermining of the status of property in the 1881 Act – an analysis for which they found economic justification.

Since the subsequent cultural impact of these years has been popularly read through the 'success of the land struggle', the historiography against which recent social and economic historians have battled is a constant sub-text. For the success of the on-circuit Nationalist performers in subsuming individual and disparate economic self-interest into a unified rhetoric made the next field and an independent Ireland synonymous in popular perception. The outcome of these years then was not only the economic transfer of land but also the consolidation of a cultural determinism in which to be truly Irish one had to conform to a stereotype of peasant resistance.

The chapter on 'Parnellism and Crime' analyses the process whereby the Conservative administration of Arthur Balfour, sought after 1887, to reassert absolute standards of law and order, and to cease a relativism that was viewed as ideologically dangerous. After the arrival of Balfour in Ireland the country was proclaimed to be in a state of chaos orchestrated by the National League. As is demonstrated in the chapter on Kerry and the Hicks-Beach and Redvers Buller interlude from mid-1887 to Balfour's arrival, the National League was powerful but it in no way controlled every aspect of disorder, every private vendetta pursued within a peasant society. Clearly, both Land and National League rhetoric created an atmosphere of uncertainty and opportunity, but few politicians in 1887 believed the National League to be in control of every local act. They were in control of the Plan of Campaign, which never extended beyond certain target estates. But the nature of Balfour's approach was determined by a desire to claw back ground politically conceded to Irish nationalism by the Liberals before and during 1886. Despite the earlier recommendations of Hicks-Beach for a mild measure of coercion to cope with the Plan of Campaign, allied to an adjustment to the Land Bill of 1881 to accommodate the renewed agricultural depression, Balfour, on succeeding Hicks-Beach in 1887, proclaimed Ireland to be in a state of undifferentiated social disintegration. Through his restructuring of the machinery of outrage returns, statistics on boycotting and categorisations of crime, he reformulated the politics of the preceding near-decade. Recognition of Irish rural poverty, as manifested in his policies on the Congested Districts, was ideologically acceptable to Tories provided such poverty was depoliticised and seen as structural. Even the Irish Landowners Convention displayed, until 1902, no great desire for the rescue of a landlord class by a system of state-aided land purchase. Yet throughout Tory correspondence in these years runs a desire to rescue Irish landlords from a dilemma in which Tory rhetoric proclaimed them to be enmired.

'The Shadow of an obsession'

The popular historiography of the Irish Land War consists of hundreds of locally written popular accounts, countless ballads, a surviving rural agrarian language of excoriation that confined and determined the policies of independent Irish governments after 1921.[1] A language of excoriation and repudiation – of land sharks, gombeen men, blow-ins and grabbers survived independence as a lexicon into the embrace of which only the most foolhardy politicians would dare to enter.

Twentieth-century writers like John B. Keane, John McGahern and Tom Murphy, ostensibly glorifying aspects of the intimacy of Irish rural society, reveal a world where passion is cold, feelings are deep, and 'the land' is the god of all.[2] People kill, lie and die for it; ancient bachelors cling on in squalor and penury rather than die and let it go to others. Patrick Kavanagh saw the land and its constraints as the enemy of all gestation and fertility:

O stony grey soil of Monaghan
the laugh from my love you thieved,
you took the gay child of my passion
and gave me your clod conceived.
You clogged the feet of my boyhood,
and I believed that my stumble
Had the poise and stride of Apollo,
and his voice my thick-tongued mumble.[3]

The anti-hero of his epic *The Great Hunger* (1942) is the archetype of the rural Irish bachelor, unloved and loveless, intimate only with his own soil.[4]

Ireland is a demographic aberration in western Europe. That uniqueness is determined by the revised marriage patterns that followed on the famine.[5] The prime social concern for the surviving rural population after 1850 was the preservation or consolidation of a holding. Seen as protection against starvation, and as a guarantee of security, all other interests were subordinated to it. The Harvard anthropologists Arensberg and Kimball, who studied Irish rural society in the 1930s, found 'the land' to determine almost every social relationship.[6] The sexual moral sanctions of the Irish Catholic Church had material reinforcement insofar as female virginity was a vital bargaining-counter in the movement to better land. Children born out of wedlock were repudiated, as they too could present threats to property.

To be truly 'Irish', then, one should preferably be rural, Irish speaking and Catholic. While the role of the Irish language in deliberately fostering, and the role of the Catholic religion in implicitly permeating the sense of identity of twentieth-century Ireland have been acknowledged,[7] the pervasive agrarian rurality of the idea of Irishness has been taken for granted, if challenged.

In the years from 1970 to 1990 prodigious research was done into the period called the Land War.[8] That work has attempted to disentangle from the mass of propaganda, polemic and hyperbole the economic 'truths' of the period. The historiography had a twofold thrust: on the one hand to disentangle from surviving evidence and statistics the true state of agrarian wealth and poverty,[9] and on the other hand to discover the nature of the internal politics of the Land League. In essence the latter point, a 1960s Marxist perspective which hit Irish historiography in the 1970s, hinges on the issue of the conflicting class interests of the surviving labourers, the small teetering farmers of the west, the substantial urban-based journalists and shopkeepers who often controlled the movement locally, the substantial and large tenant farmers of the east and midlands, and the large tenant farmers who were frequently wealthier than many landlords, who comprised the Land League.[10] Any study of contemporary documents makes it clear that such internal divisions were manifest to all parties involved, and politically self-conscious at the time. Their suppression, rather than their existence, is politically significant. Their detection can scarcely be greeted with intellectual rapture, though it does serve to clarify the other, and more essential, pursuit of the economic 'truths'. For it renders a nonsense the premise on which even the more scholarly of early studies[11] were based, i.e. that the Irish tenant farmer was invariably a half-starving creature with the green grass-stains of the famine upon his lips. In such a feast of revisionism it should, however, be noted that the statistics of the number of persons living in one-roomed mud cabins collected by the impeccable methods of Professor Hancock do not paint a picture wildly at variance with the original.[12] The brushstrokes are perhaps more sharply shaded.

The other question, the economic one, and the 'why' rather than the 'who', is more important. The first revised lesson was that economic conditions improved for the surviving population in post-famine Ireland.[13] The latest economic work conclusively revises that revision. This potentially negates the most potent current 'explanation' of the reason for the outbreak of the Land War; that it was a revolution produced by a frustration in rising expectations.[14] If conditions did not improve, it is difficult to see how expectations were revised, though some shred of the argument can be retained if expectations are related not to actual conditions, but to rising literacy and knowledge of better conditions elsewhere, in this case the USA. The other substantial economic revision relates to the economic position and paternalistic habits of Irish landowners. Studies of landlord indebtedness suggest that many lived close to the economic edge.[15] The caricature of the absentee Irish landlord creaming off the fat of the land does not stand up to scrutiny. Landlord refusal to adjust rents in 1879–80 was not then due to a desire to exterminate by emigration their most unproductive tenants, but was a *necessary* economic response to recession. Eviction statistics are unreliable, since a large percentage of those evicted were subsequently readmitted as caretakers.[16] Those evicted, even nominally, nonetheless experienced a glimpse of the precipice.

Most pressingly, the revised historiography presents the case that the Conservative economic analysis of the 1880s was correct; that 'the problem' was not tenurial but structural.[17] In other words, the problem of Irish agriculture was not what Nationalist politicians proclaimed it to be, but was one of economic insufficiency. Ireland could not economically sustain the surviving rural population. Conservative policies which advocated following the economic logic of the market-place were economically 'correct'. The Liberal administration was economically 'wrong' in legislating tenurially. The line is derived from the perspective of the Harvard economist Barbara Solow.

All of these revised positions have opened up the debate possible on the Land War. They are all, however, committed to getting 'behind the surface' to the truth. This is occasionally described, with a lack of linguistic and intellectual felicity, as 'stripping away the myths'.[18]

This book suggests that the most significant aspect of the Land War was the construction of new myths through the language and imagery used by Irish Nationalist organisers; that, though the preconditions and catalysing agents of the agitation were economic, the significant transformation it wrought is comprehensible only by reference to the political. The Land War can only very partially be understood in terms of local action. All significant transformations wrought were due to central leadership and control, most particularly the diffusion of a central language that acted as a vehicle for transforming mentalities. It was this central language, reported on and gathered from throughout the country, that the London government most acutely responded to – because it was a language of challenge and simplicity. The nature of British governmental response was as generative as Nationalist action.

The existence of rural combinations in nineteenth-century Ireland is well documented. Defenderism in the late eighteenth century appears to have been the most widely distributed, linguistically coherent movement of popular protest. It is no coincidence that its coherence related not merely to the defining opposition of the then newly founded Orange Order, but more specifically to the existence of the skeletal ideology and political structure of the United Irishmen.[19] In other words, a movement essentially local and concerned with specific grievances acquired a coherence through the existence of a small group of linking individuals. Though the aims of Defenderism were narrow and specific rather than national and ideological, the pasted threats and curses of the movement were made in a 'confused language of nationalism and excoriation'. This trend lay rather uncomfortably on the bloody sectarianism of 1798, but the language of ambiguity did endure into the early years of the nineteenth century.

The Dublin authorities in 1795 saw the Defender movement as essentially organised. They arrested, for instance:

> . . . two fellows who travelled as beggar men, and were confidential envoys from the chief promoters of this mysterious and unaccountable plot, who carried the correspondence between the *banditti* of different counties, and went about recruiting partisans, and founding the sentiments of the peasantry.[20]

The Whiteboys and urban Ribbonmen, Carders, Threshers, Rockites, Terry Alts, Molly Maguires, who operated in the decades before the famine, were violent, brutal, exclusionary, murderous and verbal. In 1846 the Deputy Inspector General of the Royal Irish Constabulary told the Devon Commission that:

> . . . when a district becomes disturbed we find that the recollection of bygone transactions relating to land (in which the arrangements of the proprietor had been peaceably affected at the time) are revived, and the occupying tenant, who had hitherto perhaps been unmolested, becomes the object of persecution – even after a lapse of years. *The circumstances of each case of the letting of ground seem to be engraved on the minds of the rural population.*[21] [my emphasis]

Dislocations, or evictions, or indeed any ripple in 'the stagnant pool of rural life' precipitated such crises. Resistance to change is posited as an explanation, but an underlying ground swell of dissatisfaction is noted by every social commentator from Nassau Senior[22] to Paulett Scrope.[23] The evidence of establishment witnesses before enquiries from Norbury[24] to Devon[25] attest to the same fundamental rural dissatisfaction. Recent research shows that the tensions and the violence were frequently between middlemen and farmers, or between labourers and tenants.[26] At the same time the literature from Edgeworth to Carleton purveys the nature of tenant and landlord relations as a comedy of duplicity.[27] The tenant, egregiously deferential on the surface, retaining a studious care for the possible sanctions of his overlord, is invariably depicted slyly scheming through anonymous barbs or secret conspiracy to bring his man down. Edgeworth's Thady Quirk strokes while he stabs, pities what he destroys, but essentially pursues vengeance and vindication.[28]

This then is the background, however loosely sketched, to the events of the 1880s. It perhaps serves to show that the politically constructed protest of the 1880s had a pre-history in behaviour and attitudes throughout the century. More significantly, the famine took place within the living memory of the generation who acted after 1879. A youth of ten years of age in 1847 was just 33 in 1880. The survival of the famine as a living spectre in the society was not the product of the memories of the old and tired but also of individuals in their prime whose recollections were fresh and first-hand. Those who led the Land League nationally were young – mostly individuals in their early or mid-thirties.

In attempting to assess *why* the Land League proved so effective a weapon, several explanations have been advanced. The original explanation was that of the 'New Departure': the decision of the Fenians under John Devoy to commit their limited number of committed men and their considerable Irish-American network to an alliance with the 'advanced' wing of parliamentary nationalism, which they had formerly excoriated, in a directive union with the Irish National Land League.[29] As an explanation, or at least a political one, this line cannot be refuted. Matt Harris and O'Connor Power in Mayo had constructed a potent weapon for the defence of the local tenantry in the creation of the Land League of Mayo. In itself it would hardly have amounted to more than yet another local defence union. It was the nationalisation of the issues of Mayo through the organisation of the Irish National Land League, which was controlled nationally by the Irish Parliamentary Party, that rendered the movement politically potent – that is not to accept a governmentally inclined 'conspiracy theory' on Land League protest. Local protest was locally determined and locally organised, but after mid-1880 that protest was channelled into the structures created by a centrally controlled movement. The local movement was frequently, as the Liberal Chief Secretary Forster suspected, out of the control of the central movement, and a multitude of local squabbles, immemorial disputes and recalcitrant grievances found expression within and through the local branches of the League. Nonetheless, structuring the underlying diversity of aims and intent stood a central formal organisation and a touring circus of stable performers – parliamentarians, paid League officials, urban journalists, providing a directional impetus to what would otherwise have been another chapter in an old story. Thus, many of the questions, apparently culled from 'the international anthropological literature', render complex matters that are exquisitely clear. Asking the eternal 'why' on the Land War, when the superficial accident of surface politics answers all, seems deliberately obtuse. And why the Land War *started* does not seem to be the interesting question.

Parnell's Ennis speech of September 1880[30] was the proscriptive text of the Land War, the defining handbook of a rural behaviour that was designed to be impenetrable to external sanction. It drew upon the informal regulatory rituals inherent in the society – or the brutal cruelties of control if one wishes to put it differently – and formalised them. In so doing it attempted to set against the official law of the land a separate, intimately sanctioned behavioural code which defined self and other within rural society. It was a text of inclusion and exclusion, of community and pariah. The Ennis speech was a manual guide to the analyses inherent within the texts that had proceeded it in the Land League lexicon: the original Land League charter and Davitt's text 'Paudeen O'Rafferty on the Landlords' Ten Commandments'.[31]

Formal Land League statements were published in the press, as were reports of many local meetings. Ironically, however, to recreate the language and milieu of the Land League in Ireland we are drawn back to the minute reports of the notetakers of the Royal Irish Constabulary, and the less frequent and full accounts of the stipendiary magistracy. The constabulary monthly reports were largely based upon the information derived from such notetakers. Thus the police recommendations, supplemented by the frequently unreliable network of paid petty informers who at all times covered the country, were based upon an assessment of 'the climate' derived in this way. Together with the crime statistics, which were minutely monitored and correlated in Dublin Castle, such information provided the raw material out of which government policy was formulated. In the case of the Queen vs Parnell and Others of 1880–81 and in the Parnell Commission of 1888, the actual reported speeches printed by the Dublin Castle authorities (in the later 1880s often preserved in large bound volumes) constituted the Crown brief in the case of the former and *The Times* brief in the latter.

1 WHAT THE LIBERALS SAW:
IRELAND UNDER GLADSTONE'S
SECOND MINISTRY

Why is an Ireland the special lot of this country, so philanthropic, so popular and liberal in its sentiments of government, so anxious to divest its policy of even the suspicion of egotism? . . . And yet the possession of an Ireland is our peculiar punishment, our unique affliction, among the family of nations. What crime have we committed, with what peculiar vice is our national character chargeable, that this chastisement should have befallen us?

Lord Salisbury, 'Disintegration', *Quarterly Review* no. 312,
October 1883

There is the Church of Ireland, there is the land of Ireland, there is the education of Ireland: there are many subjects, all of which depend on one greater than them all: and that trunk is the tree of what is called Protestant ascendancy . . . It is still there, like a tall tree of noxious growth, lifting its head to heaven and darkening and poisoning the land as far as its shadow can extend; it is still there gentlemen and now at length the day has come when, as we hope, the axe has been laid bare to the root of that tree, and it nods and it quivers from its top to its base.

W.E. Gladstone, Hengler's Circus, 23 October 1886

Definitions

The stipendiary magistracy of Ireland were described by Lord Rosse in the late 1840s as 'a collection of elderly roués with broken fortunes and damaged reputations'.[1] This was not quite the case in 1880, but it still contained some truth. The system of the law in Ireland was anomalous by English standards, in legislative content and administrative practice.[2] Both had evolved historically because of 'the singular condition of Ireland'. This euphemism, together with a small army of equally unrevealing catchphrases, was deemed politely to convey a reality morbidly agreed upon by all parties and interests in English politics.

The Irish were, allegedly, obsessed by history. The occurrence of any new 'problem' therefore sent English politicians reaching for the history books. Such administrative or legal problems as that part of the United Kingdom known as Ireland presented were, throughout the nineteenth century, described as *the* Irish problem. The 'Irish problem' was therefore always the

11

same thing in different guises. It was, however, always recognisable because it had certain distinguishing characteristics.

Its initial existence was marked by the extent to which the subject of Ireland encroached on the attention of the literate English public in the form of parliamentary time occupied, or newspaper column inches filled. This was its public profile. Its private life was determined in tandem with this public face, by the number of letters exchanged by the current Prime Minister and his Chief Secretary for Ireland. When both of these were at a high watermark the 'Irish question' was alive, well and kicking in English political culture. When neither of these parallel linguistic processes were at work it did not exist. Thus, though the complex mesh of life lived on the island of Ireland always went on, the 'Irish question' existed only when the noise of that lived life spilled over into English political culture.

The agricultural depression of the late 1870s provoked such a reaction. The initial reports of extreme poverty and distress in the west of Ireland, a result of two successive bad harvests, had resulted in the charitable endeavours of two conflicting relief agencies.[3] But by late 1879 it was apparent to Disraeli's government that the potential political consequences of the economic squeeze were to present problems greater than those of mere relief.[4] Under the Peace Preservation Act, however, the administration at Dublin Castle felt confident of controlling agitation that was seen as in any case endemic within the culture.[5] The last serious 'outbreak' had been in the early 1870s in Westmeath, and that had been effectively dealt with by a swift application of 'extra-ordinary' legal measures.[6] The return of Gladstone to office threatened the calm consensus that up to then prevailed.

In August 1879 the Conservative government had appointed, under the chairmanship of the Duke of Richmond and Gordon, a special enquiry into the 'depressed condition of the agricultural interest and the causes to which it is owing; whether those causes are of a permanent character, and how far they have been created or can be remedied by legislation'.[7]

The Commission was not exclusively Conservative. It included John Poyntz Spencer, the Earl Spencer, Henry Chaplain and Joseph Cowen, as well as George Joachim Goschen, the Duke of Buccleuch and Queensberry, and Baron Vernon.[8] As a measure of how politically seriously the noise of agitation in Ireland was viewed, it was agreed that the Irish enquiry should produce a preliminary report at the earliest possible date.[9] Two selected individuals, Professor Baldwin, Inspector of Agricultural Schools based at Glasnevin, and Major Robertson, a land agent of Abbeyview in Boyle, should supplement the evidence given directly to the Commission by touring the country and interviewing the largest number of people in the time available. As Baldwin and Robertson reported in January 1881 they succeeded in interviewing, according to their own account, 'over fifteen per cent of those under £8 valuation'.[10]

They gave evidence directly to the Commission in the premises of the Royal Dublin Society in Kildare Street, in the intervals between their neo-anthropological peregrinations through the country. As they said, 'We have found the occupants of a large number of these (smallest farms) in so deplorable a condition that we feel unable to describe it in a way which would enable His Grace to appreciate it fully.'[11]

The greater part of the Commission's formal hearing of evidence in Dublin took place in June 1880, after the fall of the Tory government and its replacement by Gladstone's Liberal ministry. Spencer resigned from the Commission, but its investigations were not suspended. It proceeded, however, on an anomalous basis. Appointed by a Tory government, for the purpose of making recommendations on the basis of which policy could be constructed, it now operated under a ministry with no such commitment. The Irish witnesses interviewed by the central Commission were prominent land agents, large landowners like the Marquis of Lansdowne,[12] the Earl of Dufferin[13] and Arthur MacMurrough Kavanagh.[14] The Commission also interviewed Colonel Richard Dease, a director of the Bank of Ireland and the owner of Celbridge Abbey in Kildare,[15] Charles Hare Hemphill, the Chairman of the Civil Bill Courts for fourteen years until 1878[16] (eight of those years spent in Kerry where some of the worst distress and disorder was later found), Samuel Murray Hussey, Justice of the Peace for Cork, Kerry and Limerick, a land agent for thirty years for over 5,100 tenants on estates with a total rental of over £90,000 a year,[17] and Stephen Woulfe Flanagan, a Judge of the Chancery Division of the High Court of Justice in Ireland.[18] Also interviewed was John Ball Greene, the Commissioner of Valuation in Ireland,[19] and a crucial witness in view of the fact that much of the ostensible dispute about rents hinged on the question of the accuracy or inaccuracy of land valuation.

The questioning of the Commission focused on a cluster of central concerns: the nature and satisfactoriness of the tenurial arrangements under which land was held, the efficiency of Irish agriculture, the stranglehold exerted by the Cork butter market on dairy farming in the south-west, the question of landlord absenteeism and the question of the extent to which reports of Irish distress were real or exaggerated.[20] The large tenant farmers interviewed seemed dissatisfied with tenurial arrangements, *not* from the point of view of threatened eviction, but because of fears that their often massive financial investment on rented farms would not be recompensed at the end of their tenancy. Agents reporting conditions on their managed estates agreed that the *ostensible* fear of summarily raised rents was used by tenants to justify *not* improving their farm buildings or the efficiency of their farming. Together with an obsession with 'holding on' to their land, however unproductive, this was seen among smaller tenants to be a core cause of worry. As Bence-Jones, an 'improving' Scottish landowner of 1,000 acres at Lisselan in Cork demonstrated, their obsession was almost comical:

> The landlord proposed to give them leases for 1,000 years, but it was not
> thought long enough, and he said that as it did not make much difference
> to him, he agreed to give it to them for 2,000 years and that satisfied
> them. They have not reclaimed the land or done anything to it on that
> account.[21]

Since the questions asked by the mostly Conservative Commissioners were
not value free, it is not surprising that they chose to focus much of their
attention on the ostensibly pernicious effects of the Land Act of 1870. It was
agreed by all of the 'respectable' witnesses interviewed by the central Commission that this had a catastrophic effect on the always weakly developed
sense of thrift of the small tenant. Banks, credit houses, gombeen men and
loan sharks of all descriptions had been, it was alleged, spirited into existence
by the Act. Tenants were up to their ears in debt to local shopkeepers, banks,
one another and minor lending agencies. Also, as Bence-Jones commented,
they displayed a reckless willingness to go surety for one another, considering
it to be 'the decent thing to do' if a neighbour was in difficulties. Bence-Jones
attributed this to their lack of moral courage. There were exceptions to the
rule of ramshackle teetering on the brink. From the evidence of John Corbett,[22]
a tenant on the Duke of Devonshire's estates at Lismore in Waterford, it was
clear that on the larger estates with long established aristocratic owners, the
tenants' condition seemed more in keeping with an English norm. Charles
Uniacke Townshend[23] had come to Ireland as agent to the Marquess of Bath
in 1851, the total rental of whose estates in Down, Antrim, Tyrone, Monaghan,
Westmeath, Longford, Tipperary, Waterford, Wexford, Kilkenny and Kildare
was in excess of £80,000 annually. Henry Augustus Dillon[24] was agent for
Lord Talbot of Malahide and for the Cork estates of Lord Kinsale and the de
Courceys. They both agreed with the agent of Lord Portsmouth at
Enniscorthy, and the evidence of the Marquess of Lansdowne,[25] that tenants
fared better on the estates of those who held land and property on both sides
of the Irish Sea. According to this consensus the 'culprits' on the landlord side
were those new men who had purchased modest estates under the easy sales
permitted by the Encumbered Estates Act of 1849.[26] They had purchased land
as a commodity, and treated it as such. They lacked the economic resources
to pursue a 'live and let live policy', allegedly dear to the hearts of hereditary
landowners. But over and above this conclusion the message that most clearly
emerged from the witnesses interviewed was the incapacity of the country to
sustain its existing population, the existence of a generalised financial collapse
among the lowest class of the rural population, and the historic barriers to
efficient agriculture presented by the persistent desire of uneconomic smallholders to cling on to patches of land which could sustain them only at the
very margins of existence. This seemed to be borne out by the findings of
Baldwin and Robertson. As they reminded the Commission, of 592,590 tenant
holdings on the island of Ireland 433,287 were of properties of under thirty

acres. More significantly, 123,257 of these were properties of under five acres. 155,675 mud cabins of one room, built by the tenants since Irish landlords made no capital investment in their property, were occupied by 227,379 families.[27]

> The tales told to us by small farmers of their indebtedness seemed so incredible that we took the trouble wherever we could to verify them by reference to the books of shopkeepers. In a few cases we found they understated the sums they owed; and in no case have we been able to detect wilful exaggeration. This may seem strange to many intelligent persons whose knowledge of the Irish people is derived from hearsay. In many cases we found that the real state of the small farmers in the south and west is not known to their landlords, or to the land agents, or to the very bailiffs on the estates which we have examined.[28]

The evidence presented by witnesses before government enquiries is by definition suspect. It is partial, it must be read in the light of the political bias of the enquiry as structured and the subjective interests of the witnesses concerned; in short, it must be read like any other historical source. It reveals at the very least how people saw, or wished to present, their situation, a focus at least as valid as the ostensible 'reality' of what it is proclaimed to have been by economic historians. All the witnesses who appeared before the Richmond Commission agreed on one point: that Ireland was in the grip of an economic crisis in 1880.

Law and Order versus Relief

The permanent Under-Secretary in the Dublin Castle administration was Thomas Henry Burke. The son of a small Catholic landowner from Galway, he began his career as a clerk in the Castle in the worst year of the famine, 1847. He was then eighteen years old. He was appointed Under-Secretary in 1869, a position that he held without interruption until his murder in the Phoenix Park in May 1882.[29] He was the administration's senior and most experienced civil servant. Chief Secretaries were frequently influenced by his procedural expertise and prior experience, though it is absurd, if profitable to certain Liberals, to paint him as the dreaded 'Castle hand', intent upon enticing pure Liberals from their faith. He was, above all, an administrator. When difficulty arose, he looked to precedent. Chief Secretaries who came to Dublin knowing next to nothing about Ireland, derived much of their knowledge of life on the ground from conversations with Burke and the permanent Law Officers at Dublin Castle. As the story of Gladstone and his Chief Secretary William Forster reveals, things looked different in Dublin. As political appointees like Forster grew aware of crevices opening between them and their political masters in London, their alternative analyses, in part derived from instinct and in part from an awareness of how remote the language of London seemed as they disembarked at Kingstown, found a clarity in the administrative imperatives voiced by these permanent officials. Under Marlborough and Lowther policy was unproblematic. The usual Tory rules applied: relief for distress and the suppression of violence. A decision on the issue of the renewal of coercive powers was postponed by Beaconsfield, as his manifesto of 18 March 1880 reveals, probably for electoral reasons.

The nature of the administrative complexities imposed upon Dublin Castle in their attempts to maintain order are revealed starkly by a letter from Burke to the Admiralty in January 1880:

> I am directed by the Lord Lieutenant to acquaint you for the information of the LC of the Admiralty that His Excellency received this morning from the Inspector General of the RIC a report from the County Inspector of Galway requesting that a gunboat might be sent to Galway not later than the 21 inst., to convey constabulary to certain places along the coast of Galway, as owing to the difficulties of communication it would be difficult to transport by any other means the large number of constabulary that have to be sent for the protection of individuals and for the due enforcement of the law in the present very disturbed districts.[30]

But, as Burke admitted, the Castle had *already* telegraphed direct to the Rear-Admiral at Queenstown requesting the gunboat, 'since time was so short'. Three days later, on 20 January 1880, Burke wrote again to the Admiralty. This time it was:

> . . . to acquaint you, that in consequence of the disorderly conduct of the inhabitants of Clare Island off the coast of County Mayo it has been found necessary to establish a police station temporarily there.[31]

The Royal Irish Constabulary, he reported, found themselves in the less than heartening position of depending on the islanders for transport to and from the mainland. As Burke delicately put it, 'There is some danger that the islanders might under certain circumstances altogether refuse to cooperate in transportation.'[32] He knew the required language for London.

Sanction for a boat was required. The gunboat 'Goshawk' was moored in Galway Bay, 'attending to the threats posed by certain fishermen from Clifden to Relief Committee boats carrying meal to the islands'. He meticulously, faultlessly, explained – realising the rephrasing necessary. More revealing is Burke's letter to the Secretary of the Treasury, enclosing a letter from the Inspector General of the Royal Irish Constabulary 'recommending for the reasons stated therein that the revolvers and pistols now in possession of the constabulary should be cased and replaced by superior weapons and that the number at present distributed amongst the force should be increased'.[33]

The Dublin Castle Irish 'government' consisted of the Lord Lieutenant, the Law Advisers and the Inspector General of Police. The Chief Secretary, with the Solicitor and Attorney-General, spent most of his time in London during parliamentary sessions. Final executive decisions were ostensibly in the hands of the Chief Secretary, when he was in cabinet. If the Lord Lieutenant was a politician of the stature of Marlborough or Spencer, he held the real power and was in cabinet. At any one time therefore, either the Lord Lieutenant or the Chief Secretary was a cipher.

Gladstone, as Lord Aberdeen put it, had a succinct description of his view of the realities of Irish government: 'the cabinet for policy, the Lord Lieutenant (or Chief Secretary) for administration'.[34] This is perhaps the most important line to remember for an understanding of the two-tier dialogue that lay at the heart of ostensible communication between Dublin and London.

The courts of local jurisdiction were administered as in England by Justices of the Peace. They were drawn from the best of county society, though in the early years of the century the Justices of the Peace of Cork were described as 'brewsters, maltsters, distillers and rack rent landlords'.[35] In general, however, they were country gentlemen: landlords, solicitors, land agents and other worthies. In 1886, of 5,000 justices only 1,200 were Catholic, a reasonable reflection of even the revised balance of 'better society'. From the early years of the nineteenth century these local Justices of the Peace had been supplemented by a paid magistracy who administratively evolved over time into the paid County Court judges. Another category of supplementary magistrate, originally designated as a magistrate of police, was appointed in the disturbances of 1814. His role initially was to take command of an area proclaimed by the Lord Lieutenant to be in a state of disorder.

This category of magistrates was ended by the police reforms of 1836, and in its place the Lord Lieutenant was empowered to appoint categories of magistrates to reside in such districts as he saw fit.[36]

> These magistrates, who were to report regularly to the Chief Secretary on the state of their districts, were not to hold office in the constabulary, and this separation of the resident magistracy from the police inspector was emphasised in 1853, when it was enacted that the superannuation certificate for the former was to be given by the Chief Secretary and not by the Inspector General of the constabulary.

They were to attend petty sessions and fairs, to take 'informations' or make reports. They were to observe and analyse all 'developments' within their areas, and to ensure that Dublin Castle was 'acquainted with the whole of the duties performed by the stipendiary magistrates even to their minute detail'. To this end they were to keep a diary, which was to be forwarded to the Chief Secretary at monthly intervals, for his information. By 1879 there were seventy-two such stipendiary magistrates, in constant communication with the Castle.

The Royal Irish Constabulary was a centralised force, responsible for the peace of the country outside Dublin, which was under the control of the

Dublin Metropolitan Police.[37] The men of the constabulary were mostly farmers' sons. Before the famine they had usually been the sons of labourers. There was little promotion from the ranks and most of the officers were from Irish county society, though, as Clifford Lloyd, one of the most notorious resident magistrates remarked 'in the last few years many young English gentlemen from the English universities and English public schools have joined this noble force'.[38] They were, as a contemporary observer put it, 'thrown much in contact with the gentry of their counties both socially and in the performance of their duties'. Discipline was strict, promotion slow. Clifford Lloyd described the force in the following way:

> The Royal Irish Constabulary can best be described as an army of occupation, upon which is imposed the performance of certain civil duties . . . Candidates are obliged to undergo a physical as well as an educational test, having qualified in which they join the depot in Dublin where a course of discipline and instruction in both military training and civil duties is imposed upon them. The organisation at the depot (which is situated in the Phoenix Park) may be said to be purely military, for it constitutes not only a school for recruits but a reserve of both cavalry and infantry, from which the force is maintained at its proper strength and from which sudden demands for men are met.[39]

Once trained, recruits were never allowed to serve in their own county, or in its immediate vicinity. As Lloyd again commented:

> The transformation that takes place, apparently in every characteristic, is very remarkable, and, I may add, very wonderful, showing, on the one hand, the natural weakness of the Irish character, and on the other, the facility with which it can be moulded and turned to good account. The recruit joins the depot a wild Irishman; he leaves it a steady, loyal, respectable, thoughtful, and disciplined member of society, forming one of a body of men unequalled among nations in character and physique, of which the people of the United Kingdom might well feel proud. It is left to designate themselves 'leaders of the people', to apply to their brethren in the Royal Irish Constabulary such terms as 'liveried scoundrels' and 'curs' of low degree.[40]

The RIC was a force of about 9,000 men, commanded by the Inspector General and his Deputy, both of whom were based in Dublin. Under this central authority were County Inspectors, who were in turn reported to by sub- or district inspectors. These sub-inspectors wrote detailed monthly reports for their county inspectors, who in turn wrote detailed reports for the Inspector General. These were studied in Dublin Castle in a process paralleling the Chief Secretary's scrutiny of the Resident Magistrates' reports. There was a network of information from the extremities to the core. Each county had a given quota of men in relation to population, known as the 'free force'. If extra men were required, a requisition was signed by a Resident

Magistrate which was forwarded by the local officer to the Inspector General.

The role of the stipendiary magistrate becomes clear when it is appreciated that the bill for extra men was presented to the local jury at the next assizes. This was raised on the rates and returned to the government. Thus every district paid for any disturbance generated in the area. The smallest area that could be proclaimed was a barony. In cases of sustained disturbance, a condition that could be said to exist if deemed necessary on the basis of the 'Notes' prepared monthly for the Chief Secretary's information, the government paid half when the district was so 'proclaimed'. So local officers 'submitted' to county officers who 'submitted' to the Inspector General. No decisions were made locally, as Lloyd bitterly comments: the Inspector General 'passed such orders upon them as his complete ignorance of local requirements might suggest'.[41] There was little scope for co-operation between magistracy and police, though both engaged in a crippling process of 'keeping one another informed'.

> The fact that one Resident Magistrate's petty sessions district comprised portions of two or three sub-Inspector's police districts, and of two or more counties, and that different portions of one police district were within the jurisdiction of more than one resident magistrate, will show how extremely difficult, indeed impossible, it was to exercise authority or to fix ability when the urgent necessity of doing both became evident.[42]

Armed with rifles and sword bayonets, attired in military uniform, the Royal Irish Constabulary were a body of men impotent in all immediate respects.[43] They could do nothing without instructions from Dublin, given the potential political sensitivity of their actions. As a force they were neither flexible nor innovative.

Defining the Irish Problem: Painting the Devil on the Wall

The real problem confronting the Liberal ministry of 1880 was the problem of deciding what the problem was. Clearly it was the Irish problem. It appeared on the surface to be two things. On the one hand it was an economic problem. That might be initially doubted since that was what political agitators proclaimed it to be. But apart from their suspect description there was the independent evidence of sources sympathetic to the government.[44] In the most isolated and removed areas of the west people were starving. They were not starving in the centres near towns like Westport, where the agitation of the newly formed Irish National Land League was organised.[45] However, in those areas where they were not starving, they were certainly experiencing a severe economic squeeze. So the problem was economic. Or, was it?

Agitators were clearly attempting to make it political. That, from the vantage point of London, was a predictable farce. It was the standard manifestation of a handful of Irish political opportunists. But there *was* another problem. That problem was growing daily more manifest. It was the existence of a widespread, violent resistance to paying rent. It was made violent by the physical resistance of large groups of tenant farmers and rural riff-raff to the serving of processes by bailiffs, or attempted evictions of those who failed to pay rent.[46]

In short, it was a problem of law and order, or rather the diminished power of the law, and the increasing difficulty of maintaining order. And what were 'the people' hearing? Stirring stuff. In June 1880 the executive of the Irish National Land League published an address, signed by Parnell, Joseph Biggar, William H. O'Sullivan, Patrick Egan, A. J. Kettle, Michael Davitt and Thomas Brennan. It was grandiloquently addressed 'To the people of Ireland' and posted throughout the country. It was published in full in the *Freeman's Journal*, but like almost every other piece of Nationalist propaganda published in the next decade, a copy of it remains intact in the papers of the Chief Secretary. It had been forwarded to Dublin Castle by a diligent local magistrate or police constable, and it bears marks and notes of the purposes to which it was subsequently put: as 'evidence' of Land League vice in the case of the Queen vs Parnell and Others of 1880–1,[47] and in the Special Commission into Parnellism and Crime of 1888. This is important, as will be seen.

> Again . . . as long ago, when famine was rampant in the land, again the Emigrant ship is offered as a remedy for your ills. A race that cannot be conquered must be exterminated, and beasts are preferred to men.

The creation of a rhetoric of power that united individual economic self-interest with the fate of an independent Ireland – the merging of the politics of the next field with the politics of the idea of the land of Ireland was the central political achievement of those who directed the so-called Land War. The triumph of that vision was not solely the achievement of Nationalist propaganda; rather, its triumph as an interpretation to which most Irish people at least ostensibly subscribed a decade later was the product of an intimate and symbiotic connection between the nature of nationalist manipulation and British government policy. Thus, if the rhetoric of the Land League proclaimed Britain to be engaged in a policy of systematic repression, committed to the extermination of the Irish people, the actions of government in the first years of the Land War effectively appeared to confirm that analysis. How and why that happened is a complex story. The political language of the agrarian agitation was constructed on an extrapolated image of the small, oppressed, near-starving tenant of the west and south, confronted by the might of a vicious individual landowner, enforced by the power of the English state. Thus, for Nationalists there was no need for a complex analysis of economic depression. People starved because landlords were determined to extract the fat of the land, even in times of economic crisis. According to this interpretation the English government, through the power of the Royal Irish Constabulary were prepared to enforce the sectional interests of the landlords in the name of the rights of property.

> Why do your enemies or your miscalled friends exhort you to leave the land of your birth, the land in which you desire to live and die? Is it because there is no room for you? . . . Is it because you are the victims of periodical famines? True, you are. But let the man-made causes be removed and the industry of the people and the fertility of the soil will keep off famine for ever. But as long as landlordism is permitted to cramp your energies, to put penalties on your industry and make the fruit of your labour its own, so long will hunger and rags and misery prevail . . . Irishmen, the land is yours. Here, by the very law and fact of your existence you are entitled to live and die . . . The so called rights of property must yield to the far higher rights of humanity . . . Beware of the suicidal competition for land on which landlordism throws the blame of its own unmeasured wickedness. Beware of the emigration agents who are doing the work of the English government.[48]

Thus the 'problems' which the Gladstone government faced – of hunger, unrest and chaos in Ireland, were compounded by the political reformulation of that complex reality by the appealing simplifications of the Irish Nationalist Party on circuit in Ireland and in the House of Commons, where they made their presence intolerable by their extended practice of obstruction.

On 1 March 1880 Gladstone read articles by Spencer Robinson and the Knight of Kerry in *Nineteenth Century*.[49] The influence of journalistic coverage of Ireland between 1879 and 1882 is important. In many of its London and Dublin manifestations it created another side for the Parnellite coin: beleaguered landlords under siege in a hostile and threatening alien land. In the next days Gladstone corresponded with Arthur MacMurrough Kavanagh, Tory MP for Wexford from 1866-68, MP for Carlow from 1868 to his defeat in 1880.[50]

MacMurrough Kavanagh was an eccentric by any standards. Born without arms or legs, he claimed direct descent from the kings of Leinster. His was one of the few families who had held their estate in Leinster without interruption from the 12th century. He conducted himself in a mannered version of what he deemed to have been the style of an Irish chieftain, receiving his tenants under an oak tree in the courtyard of his mansion, Borris House, in Carlow. For these occasions he dressed in a black cloak and kept his pet bear chained nearby.[51] The outcome of the 1880 general election had been a bitter blow to him. As he returned to his constituency on the night of the 1880 count, he felt sure that the bonfires on the hillsides were there to celebrate his victory. Instead he found that his tenants, 'his children', were, in their torchlit procession, celebrating his defeat. 'It is not so much the defeat or the loss of the seat that I mind,' he wrote to Edward Gibson, Tory Attorney-General for Ireland from 1877-1880, and Disraeli's closest adviser on Irish policy, 'but to feel that almost every one of my own men who met me with kind expressions and cheerful promises were traitors, is the hard part of the burden and the poison of the sting.'[52] MacMurrough Kavanagh saw himself as a patriotic Irishman and a Conservative. He believed in the Union and saw no difficulty in reconciling his sense of loyalty to the Empire with his love of native place. He rebuilt the villages of Borris and Ballyragget, subsidised and managed the railway from Borris to Bagnalstown, and ensured that the New Ross poorhouse was provided with a Catholic chapel.[53] For men like Kavanagh the Land League was a bitter attack on their sense of self. Edith Somerville describes this sense of betrayal in *Irish Memories*, though it lurks as a sub-theme in all of her fictional works with Martin Ross. She begins *Irish Memories* defiantly with a quotation from Lord Dunsany's *Gods and Men*:

> What is this child of man that can conquer Time and that is braver than Love? . . . Even Memory . . . He shall bring back our year to us that Time cannot destroy. Time cannot slaughter it if Memory says no. It is reprieved though banished.[54]

For her, and for others like Kavanagh, the 1880s were 'the years of the locust'.[55]

Kavanagh was merely one of Gladstone's Irish correspondents in these months. According to J. L. Garvin, the balance of the cabinet was upset after Forster's first return from Dublin. 'As earnestly as any of his colleagues he desired reform of the Irish land system, though far from understanding its roots and ramifications' (the implication here clearly being that Chamberlain did):

> . . . but in Dublin 'the Castle' was the citadel of the garrison and could not be anything else. There his staff painted 'the devil on the wall'. Full of their own actual difficulties and alarmed apprehensions in the face of the new spirit and tactics of social revolt, saturated through personal connection and by sympathy with the Anglo-Irish interest, they convinced their ministerial visitor from London the 'order' was the instant and paramount issue . . . Let us be just. What is not discriminate is not history. Forster was not merely swallowed by bureaucrats of reactionary habit. Even enlightened landlords and moderate Liberals in Ireland were self-deceived. Like the O'Conor Don they persuaded the Chief Secretary that he must put down disorder before grappling with reform.[56]

This neat *post hoc* analysis, penned in 1932, was of course a necessary part of the redemption of Chamberlain, the young radical. It is untrue in almost every particular. It misrepresents the basis of Forster's analysis of the situation after his arrival in Ireland in May 1880. It implies that the rest of the Liberal cabinet did not believe that repression should proceed in 1880. It suggests that there was a consensus within the cabinet on the need for a total restructuring of land holding, a view not borne out by contemporary papers. In fact the general views of the cabinet on Ireland could be characterised as being composed of little but ignorance and indifference.[57]

True, Forster was warmly recommended to Burke and the Castle hands by Lowther: 'I am glad that you have got Forster as he is head and shoulders over the head of Shaw-Lefevre, who would have played the deuce and excited the mob with the notion that the days of the Commune were at hand.'[58] The Queen's speech on 21 May 1880 stated the cabinet's official policy on the crisis:

> The Peace Preservation Act for Ireland expires on the 1st June. You will not be asked to renew it. My desire to avoid the evils of exceptional legislation in abridgement of liberty would not induce me to forego in any degree the first duty of every Government in providing for the security of life and property. But while determined to fulfil this sacred obligation I am persuaded that the loyalty and good sense of my Irish subjects will justify me in relying on the provisions of the ordinary law firmly administered for the maintenance of peace and order.[59]

This was the public statement of Liberal policy. The reality was that *no* policy had been formulated. The commitment to the maintenance of the ordinary law was a response to Liberal sensitivities, not a response to conditions in Ireland. In December 1879 the administration had requested the opinion of the Resident Magistrates on the question of renewal of special legislation. Almost all had been convinced of the necessity of retaining *some* powers of an exceptional nature.[60]

The issue before the cabinet was the renewal or non-renewal of the Peace Preservation (Ireland) Act. As Forster put it, there had been exceptional legislation in operation since 1847, and from 1796 to 1840 exceptional acts in relation to the possession of arms. Acts in force in 1880 were less stringent since 1870. He added that even if the cabinet *did* decide to renew exceptional powers 'there would be a break in continuity', therefore, for the first time since 1847, there 'must be a month without exceptional legislation'. Forster emphasised the onus on government:

> By law evictions must be carried out. We have no discretion re humanity or moral justice of evictions. The question is whether the law is to be defied or not and if we refuse to support any legal process we must expect that in the district in which this occurs no rent would be paid or indeed any other debt.

He substantiated his position by quoting figures of agrarian outrages. The five-year average from 1873 to 1878 was 220. For 1878 that figure was 301. And the figure for 1879 was 850. The increase, he claimed, was *marked* after April

1879. He noted that the Tory government had increased military strength by four regiments. To re-enact the Bill would require several sections, i.e. (1) the power of levying on a district cost of police for special protection or repression; (2) the power of levying on a district cost of compensation for murder or other outrage; (3) the power of summoning, and detaining reluctant witnesses; (4) the power of searching house for handwriting as evidence of threatening letters; (5) enactments with regard to secret societies and unlawful oaths; (6) a penalty for arms without licence; (7) the power to search.

Burke and Law had further emphasised that the Fenian secret society was 'mischievous and dangerous in intent and prepared to take advantage of any disturbance: I do not think that it need be considered at present except as an organisation ready to supply arms'. The late government, according to Forster, by not renewing the Act at the beginning of the session, let 'matters come to this pass that we *must* risk non-existence of Arms Act for some weeks. If the cabinet wish myself and Cowper we shall try to do so'. Many, despite wishing for the retention of exceptional powers, saw their districts as quiet, e.g. J. H. Mansfield in Galway East Riding. In Oughterard, Dennehy, RM, reported only one 'incident', that '50 sheep of the hotel-keeper at Maam were shot at night and taken away'. From Gort, D. B. Franks reported that in his district, comprising the Petty Sessions of Gort, Ardrahan, Kinvara in Galway and parts of Ballyvaughan in Clare 'no crimes, disturbances or process serving, non-payment of rent or evictions have as yet taken place'. Landlords in these areas had, however, voluntarily granted very liberal abatements of rent. Forster was scarcely in Dublin a week when he felt threatened by a discussion on Ireland in cabinet: 'Childers writes that you discussed last Wednesday a bill for extending the Bright Clauses. Had I supposed that this was likely I should have put off coming here.'[61]

In fact, Bright, Spencer, Shaw-Lefevre of the 1877 Select Committee and Law had been asked to draw up heads for a reform of the land 'situation' by facilitating an expansion of the land purchase clauses of the 1870 Act.[62] Gladstone was quick, if not entirely honest, in reassuring Forster. His reply is worth quoting in full, since it reveals the complete *lack* of urgency with which he viewed a part of the United Kingdom which, according to daily newspaper accounts, was in the throes of revolution. It is also interesting in revealing his oblique message to Forster on the status of the Lord Lieutenant:

> I think Childers has inadvertently led you to an incorrect impression. Bright introduced the subject of his purchase Clauses, a few remarks explanatory of his meaning were made, and it was agreed that he should get the heads on paper which he thinks might be dealt with during the year . . . Let me take this opportunity of saying another word on a subject of real importance. Ireland has been illegitimately paid for unjust inequalities by an unjust preference in much lavish public expenditure. The Lord Lieutenant is not the real parliamentary officer for Ireland. I

am afraid you may find in the Secretary's office a bad tradition. I do not recollect ever, during nearly ten years for which I have been Finance Minister, to have received from a Secretary for Ireland a *single* suggestion for the reduction of any expense whatever. I hope that with many other honours you will take to yourself the honour of breaking this bad tradition.[63]

Quite how the Irish administration, in the grip of a major economic crisis, with starvation stalking the west and south, and with police and army stretched to breaking point was to save money, he does not suggest. It does, however, reveal how purely academic was Gladstone's view of Ireland. True, he had spent some three weeks touring country houses in the east in 1877 and was, late in 1880, to make a bizarre visit to the Sunday congregation of Christ Church in the course of a cruise.[64] But the prevailing sense that emerges from an examination of his diaries and letters in 1880 is that he viewed Ireland, when forced to turn his attention to it by virtue of its persistence, as an intellectual conundrum to which he had merely to apply his intellect to 'solve'. The final decision *not* to apply coercion was made at the cabinet of 14 May in consultation with O'Hagan, Law, Barry and Sullivan.[65] It was decided that Spencer should withdraw from the Richmond Commission, but that the commission's Irish enquiries should be permitted to continue. Insofar as land reform was considered at this time it appears, despite subsequent representations to the contrary, to have been confined to an extension of purchase clauses in the 1870 Act and to the question of compensation for evicted tenants.

On 28 May O'Connor Power, the Home Rule MP and former Fenian introduced a bill to ensure that evicted tenants would be compensated for disturbance.[66] This was highly controversial since provision for compensation was based on the supposition that the rights of property were not absolute. To Tories and most Whigs it suggested that landlords were to be deprived of their only real sanction against non-paying tenants. Nonetheless the cabinet introduced their own Compensation for Disturbances Bill some days later. Forster's bill, which he reluctantly forced the cabinet to back, was not conceived as a radical revision of the existing land law, but as a temporary measure to limit the number of evictions for non-payment of rent which were leading to chaos and disruption. He felt that the demands made upon the Castle to support summary evictions were stretching the powers of the police and army. Also, as he privately admitted, such evictions were in fact impossible to effect, and the claimed onus upon the administration to enforce what was unenforceable was bringing the law into disrepute.[67]

In deference to the Parnellite articulation of distress and evictions as essentially provoked by insecurity of tenure, lack of compensation for improvements, and the inability of tenants to sell an 'interest' proclaimed by them to be manifest, Gladstone appointed a commission to enquire specifically into the nature of tenurial relationships and the question of how far the 1870 Land Act had gone to accomplish an improvement in the tenants' position.[68] The eviction figures for 1880 appeared to be so high that this was deemed to be warranted, though almost all of those evicted in 1879 and 1880 were evicted for *not* paying rent.[69] The 1870 Act had been intended to protect the solvent, *paying* tenant from arbitrary eviction. Quite why the tenurial position required reconsideration then seems unclear. Essentially, because it was alleged that the machinery of the 1870 Act was inefficient, that the question of land valuation on the basis of which rents were set was the subject of sustained disagreement, and that when disputes arose on rent levels between landlords and tenants they were settled by County Court Judges who invariably represented the landlord interest. The appointment of a commission by Gladstone was partly designed to elicit a wide spectrum of views, but its immediate political purpose was to act as a holding operation to ensure that the land question could be said to be under consideration, while the question of law and order was dealt with. The commission was chaired by a Liberal landlord with estates on both sides of the Irish Sea, Frederick George Brabazon, Earl of Bessborough.[70] The other members were the maverick Tory, MacMurrough Kavanagh, the defeated leader of the Irish Home Rule party, William Shaw, who was politically respectable because of his rejection by his own party, Charles O'Connor, descendant of Charles O'Connor of Belanagare, the historian and antiquarian, who agitated through the Catholic Committee for Catholic Emancipation in the 1780s prior to losing the bulk of his estates to his younger brother who inherited the property by changing his religion,[71] and Richard Dowse, Baron of the Exchequer 'in that part of our United Kingdom of Great Britain and Ireland called Ireland'.

Thus, by June 1880 there were two touring circuses 'investigating' the nature of agrarian trouble: one from an economic point of view, the other from a tenurial one; one merely tolerated by the government and the other appointed by them; both excluding the views of the Home Rule party; and neither having any immediate public profile. But, as Gladstone said, the important point was to 'divide' the problem. Both of these commissions therefore conducted their enquiries in a rarefied and timeless manner. The questioning of the enquirers in both commissions took on the colours of a general-knowledge quiz on Irish history, ranging from clarifications of subletting arrangements during the Napoleonic wars to the complexity of 'native' tenurial practices in the dim and distant past. That all of this muddle had been explored *ad nauseam* in countless previous commissions constituted for similar purposes in the preceding half century scarcely seemed to matter. There was a careful rule of thumb on Ireland: go back to the roots of it. Most of the questioners took on the verbal contours of recent arrivals from another planet. The theatre was remarkably effective, if restricted in terms of audience.

Meanwhile, Gladstone himself was 'reading up' on the problem, mulling over the moral rights and wrongs of the passage of the Act of Union which enabled him to interpret the 'figures' that Forster was repeatedly exhorted to forward:

> Can you inform us before Saturday by figures not only of the graduated increase of evictions but of the counties or districts in which such increase has taken place? And will this not *confirm or confute* the Duke's statement that they are evictions of *men unwilling*, not men unable to pay their rent?[72] (my emphasis)

This was on 10 June, as he attempted to calm the objections of the Duke of Argyll and Lansdowne, on the now highly controversial Compensation for Disturbances Bill.[73]

As Richard Hawkins has shown in his excellent study of the serving of processes in Carraroe in June of 1880, the Dublin Castle administration found themselves in a position that was practically untenable.[74] They were compelled, by the letter of the law, to assist with hundreds of constabulary, certain landlords and land agents in serving processes preparatory to eviction on individuals, who they knew from their own local government board inspector, Henry Robinson, to be on the verge of starvation.

> There is no part of my district that claims a larger part of my attention on the score of a dense and poor population than the neighbourhood of Carraroe. Separated from Oughterard by forty miles of bad road it is probably the most inaccessible and least advantageously situated spot in the whole of Ireland. There is but one post a week, so a letter sent from Dublin a day late would take as long to reach Carraroe as it would to be delivered in Italy.
>
> Leaving the eight miles of wild moorland which divides Moycullen and Spiddal, the road takes a sudden descent over the brow of the hill to the shore of Galway Bay, and three short miles of bog at Castleroe are the only break in one interminable row of cabins nestling under the huge boulders the whole way along the twenty-five miles of road between Spiddal and Carraroe. . . . I have nowhere seen such industry and energy as is here displayed in the working of the holdings, the men and women digging, the girls spreading seaweed, the boys collecting it. Every member of the family is engaged, while on the very small children devolves the duty of keeping house, an important trust which they temporarily abandon at twelve o'clock to carry a lighted sod down to the fields to kindle their fathers' midday pipes.
>
> As to the condition of the people they are at all times an exceedingly poor community and the circumstances which have inclined to impoverish the whole of the west have rendered them doubly poor. At present they are living on their seed, as they find that their wants in this respect are likely to be met through another channel. A few of them have some little money, and some who have boats avail themselves of an occasional fine day to replenish the store from their long lines. These are the means at present and charity is interposing to make them suffice till the crop is down.[75]

These tenants were not political agitators, not until political agitation became their only mode of self-defence. They were unable, not unwilling, to pay. Nonetheless the Castle was compelled to back the landlords up in a violent, expensive and ultimately futile support of agents and process servers. Burke, contrary to the Liberal image of him as a coercionist, was anything but sympathetic to the particular landlords of Carraroe:

> What a sad flood of light this throws on the Irish land question . . . The absentee landlord, . . . the careless sub-agent . . . the fraudulent bailiff and the wretched tenantry striving to maintain 515 human beings upon 1,334 acres of wretched land – of which 110 is under crop – and not a single tenement valued over £4.[76]

Cowper, in a letter to Spencer after the incident on 14 June 1880, writes:

> I suppose you look at the Irish papers now and then, and hear from Forster anything that is to be heard . . . I am very glad the Curraghoroe (sic) notice serving went off without incident. It was an abominable case of tyranny.
> I believe the landlord (Kirwan) is half foolish; and the agent (G. J. Robinson, MP) a great brute.[77]

As Hawkins concludes, the decision to introduce a Compensation Bill related to Forster's desire not to be placed in a position of defending with full police and military might such absurd acts of landlord brutality. As Hawkins quotes, Forster wrote:

> I think that it will tend to convince my colleagues that we cannot leave the ejectment law precisely as it stands, even for this year . . . A few soldiers would probably suffice (i.e. a few soldiers appearing at the scene of the process serving) – there would be an outcry – I should not mind that. It would (1) show that we were determined to have the law obeyed and (2) do much to prove that the law must be altered.[78]

Forster then was seeking to influence the perceptions of the public in Ireland on the one hand, and to influence his cabinet colleagues on the other. The gap between him and London was already opening, a mere month after he had arrived in Dublin. The thrust of the Compensation Bill was to be that if a tenant was evicted for non-payment of rent, and if it were demonstrated to the satisfaction of the County Court judge that he was unable to pay as a result of recent distress and famine, the landlord would then be obliged, on evicting the tenant, to pay him the same level of compensation as he would have been compelled under the 1870 Act to pay to an *unfairly* ejected tenant. This would be a temporary measure, to last in the first instance for a year.

But crucially, as the debate on the Bill proceeded in the House of Commons, the perception of Forster emerging *popularly* in Ireland, derived from actions like Carraroe, was as the ruthless backer of a rack-renting landlord, the icy enemy of a starving tenantry.

In the Commons Forster attempted to reassure the House on the limited nature of the measure proposed:

> No compensation will be given unless the tenant cannot pay his rent; unless he is too poor to pay; and unless his poverty arises, not from sickness, unthriftiness or from his action, but from the special grounds of these three bad harvests. Then, again he must be willing to try his utmost or pay a reasonable rent – that is to submit to pay a rent either reasonably reduced under the circumstances of the year, or with reasonable time given in which to pay, and the landlord must be unwilling to make that reasonable reduction, or to give him that reasonable time. If all these conditions are fulfilled then the tenant comes under the scope of Section 3 of the Land Act.[79]

Forster had worked in Ireland with James Hack Tuke during the famine of 1847, and he read to the House a letter he had received that day, 25 June, from Tuke:

> To nine tenths of the population of Connaught the possession of a bit of land is the sole means of existence. Of manufacture there is none, and the majority of the farms being too small to need hired labour, of agricultural labour there is scarcely any. Take away from the tenant his little holding, and nothing is left to him but the workhouse. Except in some of the towns there is not even an unoccupied house which a man could hire if he obtained work apart from his holding. Hence the tenacity with which the holding is retained and defended . . .
>
> They are like shipwrecked sailors on a plank in the ocean; deprive them of the few inches by which they 'hold on' and you deprive them of life . . .[80]

Forster further quoted from the *Flag of Ireland*, a newspaper which Parnell, rather unnecessarily, said was not a Land League publication:

> A representative of the Land League, at a meeting held last Sunday said that the League 'had in view a set of objects, and if they enabled them to carry out those objects they would make the property of Irish landlords so worthless that they would leave it with them . . .'. To goad an unarmed and helpless people, by thinly veiled enticements like these, to deeds for the attainment of objects which are unattainable – which must bring ruin, swift and sudden upon themselves and their families – is entirely unjustifiable, and the men who do this incur very grave responsibility.[81]

The Liberal party passed the bill in the Commons, but after heated debate in the Lords, where many Irish landlords sat with English landlords who held Irish estates, the Bill was dumped in a verbal carnival yet again depicting the devil on the wall. The view of the *Flag of Ireland*, not that of Tuke, prevailed.

To Tories, the words of Disraeli on the 1870 Act were being fulfilled:

> The argument of the Irish tenant – belonging to the very class that you
> are now setting up by this fundamental violation of the fundamental law
> of the country – *will* be to this effect – I have lost my holding because I
> did not pay my rent; can anything be more flagrantly unjust than that a
> man should be deprived of his contingent right to a third of the freehold
> because he does not pay his rent?[82]

The government justification of the measure, as presented by the Irish
Attorney-General, Law, was statistical necessity[83] – the near doubling of eviction figures in the first six months of 1880 as compared with the last half of
1879. The increase in indictable offences in Mayo was 100 per cent, while the
increase in Donegal, where the Ulster custom applied was minimal. But there
was another interpretation, of which the rising Tory Randolph Churchill
forcibly made himself the spokesman. This was to shift the weight from
economic to political considerations and to assert that the different situation was
due to the political organisation of the Land League in Mayo. This was to be the
text of future battles.

2 LIBERAL PARALYSIS

Rehearsing the Arguments

In June, July and August, while Forster fought to maintain a veneer of control in Ireland, both Houses of Parliament engaged in long and bitter debates on 'the Irish question'. Thus Forster spent his time, when not briefing Gladstone on facts, figures, statistics, relative rises and falls of crime, evictions and controls, justifying his hastily tacked-together policy in the Commons. He was assisted in this task by Law, the Irish Attorney-General, and Johnson, the Irish Solicitor-General. The issues which he was called upon to address were the retrospective sanctioning of Tory provisions for the relief of distress, and the Compensation for Disturbances Bill.

The former was relatively straightforward, though revealing the extent of the gap between the rhetoric of the Union which proclaimed Ireland to be an integral part of that Union, with the practice. The measures proposed by Forster to cope with distress were merely a ratification of those introduced under the Tory administration of Marlborough.[1]

In mid-November 1879 the Treasury, on the application of Marlborough, had authorised the Commissioners of Public Works in Ireland to lend money to owners of land. A circular informing landlords of their right to borrow was issued on 22 November 1879. Little was borrowed. By 12 January 1880 a new circular was issued detailing a loan at more favourable terms of interest. This new loan was financed, not by the Imperial Exchequer, but by drawing on the funds of the Irish Church Temporalities Commissions to facilitate highly attractive interest terms. By 17 June 1880 £1,250,000 had been borrowed by landlords in this way. The other provision which the Liberal administration proposed to sanction was a grant of £30,000 for the construction of fishery piers. Power was given to the Commissioners of Public Works, with the consent of the Treasury, to make loans to railway and other public companies, upon the security of baronial guarantees given at presentment sessions. Thus provision for relief was made through three indirect channels, in a manner that would not interfere with even the most orthodox notions of political economy; more significantly, in a way that cost the London government and the Irish administration nothing.[2]

According to Parnell the bulk of £250,000 was spent in purchasing iron, timber, Portland cement, lime, drainage tiles and in paying the wages of highly skilled workers. He claimed that little, if any, of it found its way into the hands of the most distressed smallholders. He further claimed that wages earned in this way were immediately appropriated by landlords for unpaid rent. He claimed that the government was not relieving distress, but rather relieving 'landlords who could not obtain their rents with the same celerity as formerly they could'. Parnell rejected the measures proposed as beneficial to vested company and landlord interests, and utterly inadequate from the tenant's perspective.

He then articulated, in the debate of 17 June, the Land League's base position in relation to Irish rural poverty and unrest:

> In the judgement of all those who had lived longest in Ireland and had most carefully considered the condition of the people of that country, it always had been apparent that the main cause of periodical famines there was the condition of Irish land tenure . . . It would be his [Mr Parnell's] duty to move certain clauses which would put the question of this distress in Ireland upon its proper footing before the country. They had too long been told that distress in Ireland proceeded from the laziness and want of thrift of the Irish people. They had been too long in the habit of appearing before the nations of the world as beggars for charity and there were many people – in fact the majority of the people of Ireland – who now thought that the time had come when this practice should cease, and that they should have the opportunity of living in their own country, and of obtaining prosperity from the natural riches and resources of the country – an opportunity which the laws of England had denied them for so long a period.

The Liberals had, he claimed, shown themselves to be no different from the Tories who preceded them:

> What was wanted by the Irish people was not so much that they should be relieved from the necessities produced by famine out of Imperial funds, as that they should be put in a position to manage their own business by an Irish parliament, instead of being subject, as was the case under the last parliament, to alien legislation.[3]

The Relief Bill of the present Liberal government was, he claimed, founded on precisely those principles which had condemned a quarter of a million to their deaths a mere thirty years before. The Tory government, warned of imminent distress in May 1879, had done nothing but arrest Michael Davitt on 'a trumped up charge of sedition' which they then shrank from prosecuting.

This was a somewhat disingenuous account of the latter half of 1879, since it failed to mention the existence of the Land League. The first provision of government was then, according to Parnell, a boon to the landlords at the expense of the Irish Church Surplus. The sum in question ought, he said, to have come from the Imperial Exchequer, if Ireland was, as proclaimed, a part of the United Kingdom, and ought to have been assigned to the Boards of Guardians, and lent directly to the occupiers.[4]

The £30,000 promised for harbour piers was, according to Parnell, a pittance. Scotland had received over £1 million for fisheries during the century while for six years Ireland had received nothing at all:

> In fact the Chief Secretary had set his bait with the little sprat of £30,000 to catch the magnificent mackerel of £750,000.

As for the provision for the Commissioners of Public Works to make loans to railways and other companies on the security of baronial guarantees given at presentment sessions it merely ensured that:

> . . . any bubble company sprung up in London, Australia or anywhere else, provided they could obtain an Act of Parliament giving them borrowing powers, without the subscription of a farthing of capital could go to Ireland and obtain a baronial guarantee and carry on works at the expense of the starving ratepayers of Ireland.[5]

Joseph Biggar's response was characteristically abrasive. He had put down a Notice of Opposition to the Bill in order to secure a full discussion of it because it 'was as worthless a measure as could be expected from a right honourable gentleman who knew nothing of Ireland'.[6] In his opinion 'the Irish Church Surplus should be kept for some better purpose than putting money into the pockets of landlords'.

Law, the Irish Attorney-General, confirmed that in fact £1 million had been granted to the landlords. That sum had been applied for between 12 January and 29 February and had been sanctioned before the Liberal government took office.[7]

Gladstone emphasised that the main object of the Relief of Distress Bill was to 'fulfil the engagements and redeem the pledges of the last government'.[8] O'Connor Power pointed out that Mr Gladstone was determined to follow in the construction of the Bill a policy of 'give and take, only that the giving was to the class that was in the least need of it – namely the landlord class'.[9] He also stated that in administering relief to Ireland through Boards it was worth recalling that there was 'not a single official board in Ireland that had learnt the alphabet of its business – not one of them':

> They were simply nominations of individuals who, in the main, had no practical knowledge whatever of the subject with which they had been charged. If the Relief Bill was to bring any advantage of an independent or substantial character to the people of Ireland, *it would be the business of the Right Honourable Gentleman, the Chief Secretary, to see that the provisions of the Bill were properly carried out* by the Board of Works and the other authorities without whose action the provisions of the Bill were useless.[10] [my emphasis]

The language of Forster's communications with Gladstone from the beginning of his time in Dublin was both pedagogic and investigative. The underlying assumption of their exchange is the context of 'the problem'. Investigation and substantiation were the nexus of constructing 'the solution'. Forster was at all times gathering information. In May, when considering the issue of renewal of the Peace Preservation Act, he had hoped to 'be ready next cabinet with as much information as can be got about the Peace Acts but I do not know that I ever had to deal with so difficult a question'. At the end of this letter of 7 May he expresses his preference for the *real* question:

> You will not wonder that I find the land question *the* Irish question on which all else hinges.[11]

The policy decision to introduce the Compensation for Disturbances Bill came from Forster, as his letter to Gladstone of 6 June reveals:

> . . . I may say that Law and I incline (1) to bring in a bill of our own (to counter O'Connor Power's) in the direction of Harcourt's words. (2) To make it temporary both on account of the present special distress and because we *shall probably have to amend the Irish Land Act generally.* (3) To state at the same time that we would appoint a small Commission to report on the working of the Land Act. The Commission might in time be of real service but if not should have a good reason for delay, especially as we shall by our temporary bill have *removed* the great cause of irritation.[12] [my emphasis]

Forster anticipated a Whig resistance and suggested that the Duke of Devonshire be compromised by having him chair the Commission to investigate the working of the Land Act:

> I feel sure our best chance of getting him is to ask him at once before he makes up his mind to refuse.[13]

Gladstone was less sanguine, as his reply of 25 June reveals:

> I must, I fear, say a few words to you about the Duke of Devonshire before I can see my way – to write to him with no chance of him accepting would hardly be advantageous.
> I hope you will be large and free today in showing the necessity of *doing something* and this you can effect far better than any other man. The other great question which I hope we may make clear in debate – for otherwise great misfortune may impend – is the strictly *bounded* character of what we do. We have only kept Argyll by showing how carefully our measure is framed to bar all inferences, all prejudices touching anything that lies beyond its four corners. The Irish Land Act is a sort of Land Charter, and I think it is vital to our chances of steerage through the rough waters to show that every question arising under it will be held over until the Commission shall have reported.[14] [my emphases]

In other words, the price of Liberal landed or, to be crude, Whig support was the assurance that the infringement on the rights of property implicit in the Compensation of Disturbances Bill was strictly confined to Ireland, was devoid of status as precedent and was temporary.

The Earl of Leitrim, defending the landlord interest, announced in the Lords that such monies as he had borrowed had been used to employ local men. He disputed the report of the Mansion House Relief Committee which alleged that a mere 15,000 men were employed in such works, out of a pauperised population of 358,000:

> He had only just received a telegram from a well-known gentleman in Ireland who was only doing what many others of his class were doing, to say that he was this week employing 1,200 men, and last week 1,000. These works had been going on since last October, before the government offered any loans at all. He knew that the noble marquess opposite [the Marquess of Lansdowne] and the noble Earl [the Earl of Kenmare] and many others had been employing workmen by hundreds during this distress. He himself had employed 845 men in Donegal as well as some on a smaller estate in Leitrim. He had had to borrow money and go into debt to carry out those works; and in one case where 241 men were employed he was assured beforehand that the work could never repay the outlay. Nevertheless, he had felt bound to carry it out, because the place *swarmed with people like a beehive or a rabbit warren.* [my emphasis]

He reminded the government of the assurances in the Queen's speech that they would take precautions to ensure that life and property would be secure, and asked for a reiteration of that pledge:

> And that this persecution of the landlords – he would call it by no other name – was not to be continued and that they were not to be stoned like the apostles of old in that cruel and ungrateful manner. He warned the government that if by weakness they alienated the sympathies of the respectable, the good, the true on the other side of the water, they would have so much fat in the fire that they would never again know what was a peaceable and loyal Ireland.[15]

Gladstone had told Forster that his most important task in speaking on the Compensation of Disturbances Bill was of impressing on the House '*the necessity of doing something*'.[16] Writing to Argyll on 15 June, Gladstone attempted to underline the *exceptionalism* that was to lie at the base of Forster's presentation of the case in the Commons:

> That in the state of things which required the legitimate interference of parliament to keep the people from starvation (which was just and only just been effected) it is impossible to apply, without qualifications of any kind, the ordinary rules of property.[17]

In introducing the Bill then Forster was careful to emphasise that it represented no radical departure:

> That it is brought in to carry out the spirit of the Land Act [of 1870], and that it is required as a temporary modification of that Act, under the special circumstances of the case. Now let me explain its principles. There is a limitation of time and there is a limitation of area – it is limited to the end of next year and to the area of those districts which are scheduled as distressed. We introduce these limitations first because we do not think the House is ready – and, in fact, we ourselves are not ready – for the introduction of any permanent Bill with regard to the Land Question; and next, because in the special circumstances of these districts, we think that a Bill with regard to evictions – why I shall explain hereafter – is especially urgent, and, in fact, to our minds, necessary.[18]

He was careful to point out that these districts had been scheduled, that is marked out as manifestly in crisis, under the Tory administration of Marlborough. All such scheduling had taken place before 29 February. Hence the Conservative administration, Liberals wished to emphasise, had acknowledged the existence of widespread and intense distress. In so recognising exceptional distress, Marlborough had implicitly conceded the need for exceptional legislation:

> Loans of very large sums have been granted to meet the distress of these districts on terms, I believe, never offered before. It was because we wanted to fasten this Bill on the attention of the House and the country, that when we thought it necessary to propose this measure, we first tried to introduce it as an amendment to the Relief of Distress Bill.[19]

In other words, they had failed to slip the measure through unobtrusively, as intended.

Under the terms of the 1870 Act a tenant evicted for capricious reasons, for any cause other than non-payment of rent, had the right to go to the County Court and claim compensation (i.e. a sum deemed to be commensurate with his capital investment or 'interest' in the property). This sum was assessed by County Court judges on the basis of the condition of the farm on departure as compared with on arrival, the number of years of occupation and the rent that had been paid. Crucially Forster now wished such an arbitration to be made in the case of tenants ejected for non-payment of rent. The settlement proposed that any sum so awarded would have deducted from it any arrears of rent then standing:

> If it shall appear to this court, firstly, that one of the tenants is unable to pay his rent; secondly, that he is unable to do so on account of the distress arising from the bad harvests of this and the two previous years; thirdly, that he is willing to continue in his tenancy on just and

reasonable terms as to rent and arrears of rent and otherwise; and fourthly, if those terms are unreasonably refused by the landlord – then, and then only, can he obtain such compensation as the court may see fit under the third section of the Land Act.[20]

Forster was frantically trying to emphasise that the Bill represented no fundamental departure in principle from the status of property embodied in the Act of 1870, that it was not a further tampering with the orthodoxy of contract, and that it was merely a mild mechanical adaption of the 1870 Act to deal with wholly exceptional circumstances for a limited period of time. He acknowledged that many members of the House remained opposed to the concessions of 1870, but expressed his view that:

> Looking back on the history of the relations of landlord and tenant in Ireland we must regard this clause [of 1870] as a just and wise one. And I will go further and say that my belief is that without some such clause as that Ireland would have had by this time to be governed by martial law . . . it had had the effect of putting an end to capricious evictions – and we know that, though Irish landlords will, as I believe, compare favourably with any others as regards justice and kindness, yet still capricious evictions did occur.[21]

This was a standard Liberal/Radical line on Gladstone's 1870 Land Act, containing standard Liberal ambiguity. If Irish landlords were no worse than landlords elsewhere in the United Kingdom, where the capacity for capricious eviction continued to exist, why did they require legislative restraint? The neo-Gladstonian reply would be that it was not their capacity arbitrarily to evict that was being challenged, but the necessity legislatively to compel them to compensate tenants for improvements made by tenants on the holding, given that almost all improvements were tenant-made, thus rendering the nature of the relationship fundamentally different to that obtaining in England, Scotland and Wales.

In cases of arbitrarily increased rent, under the 1870 Act the tenant had the right, if unprepared or unable to pay the new rent, to be served with a notice to quit, which enabled an assessment for compensation to be made in the County Court. Bearing this in mind, Forster said:

> I ask the Honourable Gentlemen whether I am not right in saying there is very good ground to suppose that in a good many cases the keeping up in 1880 of the same rent, or anything near the same rent as was paid in the good years before 1877, is really very much the same thing as if in good or average years that rent had been raised . . .[22]

Again, a reference to the spirit of the 1870 Act. His Conservative and Liberal opponents displayed minimal interest in the notion of the 'spirit' of laws and made it patently clear that they believed the law to be a rigid absolute, the matrix of civilised society, whose potency resided not in the spirit but in the letter:

> Then it may be said: 'If you did not bring it in then, why have you brought it in now?' Well, for this reason – that we found we could wait no longer. *Facts are accumulating upon us. Evictions have increased and are increasing. I have here the figures as to the evictions the Constabulary have had to conduct.* They are not all that have been affected, only those in which the aid of the Constabulary has been required – and I deduct from them all the cases where the evicted tenant has been readmitted. This list, moreover has nothing to do with process serving. The average evictions for the five years [ending in 1877] was 503 for each year; in 1878 the number of evictions was 743; in 1879 it was 1,098 and up to 20 June in the present year it has been 1,073 . . .
>
> Now I take merely the West Riding of Galway. Since 1 January of this year the number employed in protecting process servers has been 107 officers of Constabulary and 3,300 men and sixteen officers and 627 men in carrying out actual evictions; there have been from forty to fifty cases of process serving and twelve of actual evictions. *I have read these figures because I want the House to sympathise with the government in this matter.* [my emphases][23]

Effectively he was asking the House to 'sympathise' with the Irish executive in their near-incapacity to enforce the law. And from a *Liberal* point of view there were further considerations, considerations of what Forster was to call 'conscience', but could be more accurately described as the difficulty of administering what was declared to be a part of the United Kingdom in the following manner:

> Three or four Sundays ago I was informed that eighty-seven processes would have to be served upon a village in the wildest part of Galway, where there was a very poor tenantry and very poor roads and in which village [Carraroe] there had been an effectual resistance in the spring of this year. I was told that 150 men were told off for the duty and that the probability was that they would be resisted and would have to fire their way through the mob. Of course, I did what any man in my position would do. I gave instructions at once that the process server must be protected in the discharge of his duties, but that every possible care must be taken to avoid collision between the people and the Constabulary and that, therefore, a force must be sent out which would make resistance hopeless; and if the Constabulary was considered insufficient the aid of the military must be called in. The result was that a large force of Constabulary were sent down – a force of 200 men well led – and proceedings were conducted with the greatest success. If there had not been enough of men there might have been something approaching a battle. What happened, however, on that same day in another village in Galway not far off? A force of fifty men went with another process server – I was not previously informed – but the force was not strong enough to prevent resistance, and the consequence was that the Constabulary had to charge the mob with their swords drawn. I am glad

to hear that no one was killed, though several were wounded; but I trust none of the wounds were serious. Two days before that 100 men were engaged at no great distance in seeing an ejectment carried out. I am not going to condemn the landlords upon any one of these occasions, *and I am perfectly aware that the law must be enforced*; but what I want the House to consider is whether with facts such as these before them, they will not make such modification in the present law as will carry out the *spirit of the Land Act*, so that we may be enabled to *carry out the law with a clear conscience*.[24] [my emphases]

Forster had here articulated the central embarrassment which by 1880 made Liberal rule in Ireland difficult, if not impossible. For in Ireland the administration was asked to enforce laws that were popularly resisted in circumstances that were seen to be publicly repugnant. Moreover, Forster felt little sympathy with landlords who expected him to enforce the letter of a law which he deemed, in the particular circumstances of 1880, to be unjust and indefensible. His own private objection seems to have been less to the substance of the law than to the intent of the landlords in choosing so rigorously to enforce it. His Compensation for Disturbances Bill was then, despite his proclamations to the contrary, an attempt to restrain the landlords, remove the cause of the more dramatic confrontations on which the Land League fed, provide a hiatus period during which the land 'question' could be considered by the Commission and permit a clear consideration of the law and order problem of 'unjust' violence as opposed to legitimately provoked resistance.

The concessions implicit in his speech were more than manifest to his opponents in both Houses. He was conceding that the law was not a rigid and manifest absolute, that it was a relative reality that could shift and change in the light of circumstance. In this he was merely further developing Gladstone's concessions of 1870 which permitted a fundamental revision of the notion of property as commodity implicit in and inherent to the common law of England. He appeared to be further acknowledging that the violent resistance to law enforcement had a certain moral sanction. More damningly, he was conceding publicly what his correspondence with Gladstone and his consultation with his Law Officers made privately clear – that he doubted the capacity of the Irish administration to enforce the law. His daughter Florence reported accurately on the response:

The landlords are in a simple panic, and the *Times* is filled day after day with letters from peers and commoners, pointing out the evil consequences which the Bill, if carried, will entail, not only upon the landlords, whom it will ruin, but upon the tenants, whom it will demoralise. From strong and calmly reasoned and, from some points of view, irrefutable arguments, down to frantic shrieks of denunciation, such as have greeted every reform touching 'the rights of property' since the world began, Mr Forster has to meet every form and kind of opposition. Not only the *St James Gazette* and *Standard*, but also the

Times are dead against the government on this question, and when the Bill was first produced even such Liberal papers as the *Spectator* and *Daily Chronicle* were guarded in their approval and far from encouraging to the Chief Secretary's prospects of success. His most thorough-going and intelligent supporter in the press is the *Pall Mall Gazette* (now under Mr John Morley). Amongst Irish peers and landowners he has *one* ally – Lord Bessborough. As for the remainder, all alike, Liberals and Conservatives, are aggrieved and alarmed, even Lord Emly.[25]

Henry Chaplin claimed that it was no kindness that the Chief Secretary did to the people of Ireland when 'by propositions of this kind you fire their quick and sensitive imaginations and excite in their minds feelings, hopes and delusive expectations'. The measure proposed 'assails the rights of property in Ireland directly and indirectly the rights of property throughout the whole of the United Kingdom'. He quoted Forster back at himself:

> The Right Honourable Gentleman further said that the Irish land question was one of those questions with which it was impossible to deal without a general knowledge of principles and a full knowledge of details, and that if any mistake were made as to the actual condition of the country, the whole matter might be thrown into a state of confusion that would probably do infinitely more harm than good; and he [Forster] showed conclusively to the House that the government *did not possess this information* for almost immediately afterward he intimated to the House the intention of the government to appoint a Royal Commission for the express purpose of *obtaining that information in which he acknowledged that the government were deficient.*[26] [my emphases]

Forster's own language of research and information was deflected back to demonstrate that *any* 'precipitate' action could prove fatal in its consequences. It was, Chaplin alleged, *partial* information on eviction statistics that had led to this panic measure, but, he goes on to say, 'it is the anticipation of these revolutionary proposals on your part that is driving the landlords of Ireland, in self-defence, to make these evictions and to rescue their property from what they believe will be complete annihilation'.[27]

Conflicting belief was then the essence of the issue. Forster said that it was the *belief* in imminent and incipient eviction on the part of a starving peasantry that led to their uncontrollable clashes with the law. The contrary landlord belief, as articulated by Chaplin, was that they were driven to evict summarily out of fear of potential Liberal legislation which would render their property an unrealisable asset. Clearly both beliefs were less manifest logical deductions than political choices and constructions. Respective groups believed what it suited their political and economic self-interest to choose to believe. They further believed that any intensification of the power of their opposites in interest clearly involved a diminution of their own power. Hence the Compensation for Disturbances Bill was a move in the see-saw that placed the interests of the tenants nearer to the ground.

Forster stated that if the Bill failed to pass there was no alternative but to introduce martial law. This, according to Chaplin, was a clear indictment of the Land Act of 1870. As a Liberal 'solution' it had clearly failed. The habit of perceiving Ireland as a single issue in English political culture was not exclusively a Liberal propensity. 'Ireland' was constructed as a problem or a conundrum, in which time had no meaning. A proclaimed Liberal need to introduce martial law in certain circumstances in 1880 was demonstrable 'proof' to the Tory opposition that the Liberal Act of 1870 had 'failed'.

Colonel A. L. Tottenham rose before the House to inform them of the hurt and suffering of the landlords of Ireland:

> I rise, Sir, to enter an earnest protest on behalf of the landlords of Ireland and, indeed, I think I may say the United Kingdom, against the further measures of confiscation and interference with the rights of property which Her Majesty's government have thought fit to put before the House and the country.

In England he reminded the House 'if the tenant is unable to pay the rent he gives up his farm and there is the end of the matter, and the landlord is not driven to evict him'. In Ireland, though the eviction figures for the first half of 1880 were 1,073, that nonetheless represented merely one eviction per 600 holdings, a figure which he claimed compared favourably with the number of farms vacated in England, due to incapacity to pay. And where in Ireland, he asked, had the greatest increase in evictions taken place?

> Why, in the very counties where the agitation against payment of rent is all at its height – namely Galway, Mayo and Sligo, where process servers and bailiffs have been beaten in the execution of their duty. Where parties of men disguised have entered the houses of tenants, who were supposed to be inclined to pay, at night and sworn them not to pay; and where notices have been posted on farms and in the district warning no person to have anything to do with evicted farms on pain of death. Where threatening letters have been sown and broadcast; and where meetings have been held, attended by honourable members of this House, *where the rankest disloyalty and sedition have been unblushingly preached and no efforts have been spared to stir up the feelings of the people against the law, against the payment of rent and against their landlords who are their natural friends and protectors.*[28] [my emphasis]

Tottenham then proceeded to remind the House that he was foreman of the Grand Jury at the Winter Assizes for the Connaught circuit. Bills of indictment were sent to the Grand Jury for all offences committed. He proceeded to give the House the kind of 'information' that *he* believed was relevant for an understanding of what was going on in Ireland; an abstract of the crimes for which prisoners were arraigned and also of those for which nobody was made answerable. Agrarian crimes for the year ending 31 January 1880 numbered 977 for all of Ireland. No less than 480 occurred in the counties of Mayo, Sligo and Galway 'where the criminal agitation is now being carried out'.

The language of information retained priority, but in *this* analysis the primary information was not eviction figures or numbers of police involved in facing a civilian population, but statistics of crime. Respect for one form of quantification as opposed to another revealed an ideological bias. In emphasising crime figures, Tottenham was rejecting that perspective which viewed 'crime' as consequential, a result of near starvation, fear of eviction. Instead he propounded a view of the reality of the 'Irish problem' as being deliberately orchestrated crime for the purposes of undermining the nature of ownership and authority. More particularly, the problem was, at a wider focus, one of deference.

The nature of Irish crime statistics facilitated the 'restoration of order' position. Its categories for agrarian crime carried the century's history of rural unrest: firing at the person; wounding; assaults on process servers; killing and maiming of cattle; malicious injuries to property; assembling armed, or disguised, or unlawfully tendering oaths; seizing arms; sending threatening letters; sedition. According to Tottenham, in a phrase that was to resonate through Tory and Unionist political correspondence for the next decade, the individuals who committed the crimes that filled the categories were the 'ignorant dupes' of Nationalist control. Some of these dupes were interested in reaching America after eviction in a comfortable position, he claimed. Forster had drawn:

> a vivid picture of the horrors which might occur if this Bill were not to become law, and he appealed to the feelings of the House as to the difference between a man emigrating without means and finding himself helpless when he got to New York, *and the man who went out comfortably with the Suspension of Rent Bill in his pocket.*[29] [my emphasis]

As an expert on the 'Irish character', in the style of Maria Edgeworth, he informed the House:

> *The more they [the Liberals] concede to Irish demands for exceptional legislation, the more and the greater are the demands which will be made* and as the silence and avowed intention of the Irish members below the gangway not to oppose this measure might show him that they accept it as an instalment and *a peace offering to the agitation for which they are responsible, and that he is simply playing their game while they are laughing in their sleeves.*[30] [my emphases]

Tottenham concluded with a standard tale of the 'recognisable Irishmen':

> I should like to tell the House a little incident which was related to me by

an agent living in one of the districts scheduled to this Bill, as having come under his own notice. A tenant came in to the office and begged him, for charity's sake, not to press him for the rent, swearing by every saint in the calendar that he had done his best to make it up, but had only succeeded in making a part of it, and begged him to accept it for the present on account, putting down a roll of notes on the table. The rent was £8 and on the agent opening the roll, he saw that there were two £5 and two £1 notes. 'Why Pat', said he, 'I only want £8 and here are £12.' Pat's face immediately fell, and feeling in the pocket he replied 'Begorra, Your Honour, I gave you the wrong roll', and it then turned out that, notwithstanding his protestations of poverty, he had a second roll of four £1 notes, which he was trying it on with the agent to get him to accept and which he probably would have done had not the tenant over-reached himself.[31]

As 'the sole representative on this side of the House of the landed interest in the scheduled districts' Tottenham felt it to be incumbent upon him to remind the House of the stereotype of the duplicitous Irishman. His story combines the necessary stock image of duplicity and stupidity, while retaining the essential 'begorra' for local flavour.

He pointed out that the Land League had held, on the estate of Sir Arthur Guinness, Lord Ardilaun at Cong in Galway, a monster meeting couched in the public language of Daniel O'Connell. Significantly, while displaying 'that vituperation and abuse which is systematically showered upon the Irish landlords', the meeting's banner quoted from that arch-Liberal John Stuart Mill 'The land of Ireland – the land of every country belongs to the people of that country'. The Liberal base of the agitation then was being stimulated by Liberal governmental interference. Tottenham said:

I warn Her Majesty's government that if they persist in this hastily considered and ill-advised interference with the rights of property, they are simply pandering to that agitation which is the curse of that unfortunate country; they are letting in the thin end of the agitator's wedge; they will dangerously increase the tension of the relations, which, unfortunately, exists in some districts, between landlord and tenant; they will embitter the feelings which already exist; they will raise a frightful crop of litigation and discontent; they will render it impossible to collect rents justly due; and they will stop the flow of private expenditure on the part of the landlords who will no longer have resources to draw upon, and on many of these who are now heavily burdened they will bring ruin.[32]

As W. H. Smith said, the issue was essentially one of economic dependence and consequent unwillingness to follow the economic logic of the market-place:

Nothing was more sad than to see people who had been educated in dependence on the state suffering as they were at present, but it was clear that the revolutionary tendency of the Bill would aggravate rather than remedy their unhappy state.

The real cause of the distress was not a temporary seasonal set-back, but was due to:

> unobserved economical changes going on in certain parts of the country. It was well known that formerly many Irish labourers used to come over to England at harvest time, for whom, owing to various causes, employment could not now be found; the cause therefore of the depression being permanent – indeed, that employment would, without the fault of anybody, gradually grow less – could not be met by the Bill. Those labourers would simply be kept on small farms on which they could hardly live and their condition would soon be a problem of the greatest difficulty. Then in many cases the land became exhausted. These questions would have to be met in some other way than by the suspension of the law.[33]

Law, the Irish Attorney-General, disputed this analysis.[34] The events of 1879 and 1880 were, he claimed, a natural calamity. Even Roman Law had, he said, recognised the necessity of tempering the law in the face of natural disaster. While the structural causes of agricultural depression might have deep roots, it was undeniable that in Ireland depression had been aggravated by the failure of the last season's crop and by the failure of the landlords to grant voluntary abatements of rent in response to the calamity. The agricultural statistics clearly demonstrated the magnitude of the failure – a decline of £10 million in crop production in the year 1878–79; a decline in potato production from 50,500 cwt to 22,273 in the same period. Over a three-year period the loss on the potato crop was £10 million. Since the entire rateable valuation of Ireland was a mere £11 million, of which £5 million was in the now scheduled or distressed districts of the west, it was clear that the loss in potatoes alone over three years was a sum equal in value to the entire national rateable valuation.

Tottenham had admitted that in managing his own estate of four hundred tenants he had been obliged to evict only two tenants in decades. Surely, Law said, this was demonstrable proof that in general the tenants of Ireland were willing to pay rent when they could and that their present refusal in the distressed districts sprang directly from poverty and economic collapse. Therefore the government's proposed measure was merely an intelligent and compassionate response to avert mass evictions and social chaos. Eviction figures told their own tale for non-payment of rent: 1,269 were evicted in 1876; 1,323 in 1877; 1,749 in 1878; 2,667 in 1879. The projected figure for 1880 on the basis of figures for the first half of the year was 3,893. The lack of unrest in Donegal, a county with a social profile almost indistinguishable from Mayo, Law attributed to the existence of the Ulster custom in the former county, that is to say that tenants evicted generally for non-payment of rent were compensated on departure in a way that it was proposed to make temporarily general by the government's Bill. Randolph Churchill articulated again his firm view that the discrepancy in response was due *not* to tenurial differences, but to the existence of the Land League in Mayo and the other Connaught counties.

Churchill's father, the Duke of Marlborough, had stated in the Lords on the question of 'crime' that:

> There was a peculiar characteristic in the Irish people which was totally different to anything that existed in any other people, and therefore they had to cope with a state of things that was not like those prevailing in other parts. There was in Ireland an illegal combination for illegal purposes and there was a total absence of evidence with which to bring offenders to justice and it therefore became necessary to strengthen the ordinary administration of the law . . . In the province of Leinster in 1877 there were 48 cases of agrarian crime; in 1878 86 cases; in 1879 147 cases. In Munster over the same period the respective figures were 45, 74 and 136; in Ulster 52, 57 and 109; while in Connaught the figures were 94, 84 and 468. In all cases the majority of crimes were not brought to conviction – almost 90% were never actually solved.

This demonstrated to him that there was a 'total absence of evidence' on which the government could rely for the detection of crime:

> The only means which the government had hitherto had in their power was the taxation of a district by sending into it protection parties of Constabulary for which the district especially had to pay. That at all events was an inducement to the discovery of crime and it was a measure that was supported in 1875 by the noble Marquess, now at the head of the India Office [Spencer], who said that although under that law cases of hardship might occasionally occur, it appeared to him, on the whole, just and right that in the case of a district the great majority of the inhabitants of which knew something of the crime, or who might have taken steps for its prevention, the people ought to be made to feel in their pockets . . .[35]

Earl Cairns referred back to Cardwell's Act of 1860, which he saw as the true basis of contractual ownership of land in Ireland. This new Bill which the government proposed was, in his opinion, concerned with destroying contracts that were freely entered into.[36] Beaconsfield pointed out that the Bill 'contradicts all those principles of political and public economy of which you [Liberals] have hitherto been champions in the state'. And why, he asked, was such a measure proposed:

> . . . in consequence of the fear which the government has that if not passed we shall have, perhaps, to encounter civil war in Ireland . . . I was

the member of a government that had to encounter something like civil war in Ireland, and therefore have some acquaintance with the feelings of responsibility which, under such circumstances, an individual would be subject to. I am sure, had it not been for the firmness of the noble Duke [the Duke of Abercorn], who was then Viceroy of Ireland, the great resources and courage of the ever lamented Lord Mayo, and – though he is present, I cannot refrain from saying, because justice requires it – had it not been for the ceaseless vigilance of my Rt Hon Friend behind me, the noble Viscount [Cranbrook] who was then Secretary of State, it is possible very great evils might have occurred.[37]

For Beaconsfield there could be no justification for a major departure from the economic principles which had become canonical in mid-Victorian politics.[38] Were they suddenly to abrogate the rights of property by 'devising strange and fantastic schemes' to appease the forces which threatened the fabric of civilisation in Ireland? Here at least Beaconsfield lived up to his prophetic status by declaring the terms in which Tories were to respond to such a challenge:

> But, my Lord, if you ask me whether I could consent, for the sake of preventing disturbance of that kind in Ireland, to sacrifice the eternal principles of justice, I should, under these circumstances, be prepared to say 'I will not make that sacrifice'.[39]

War to the Knife

War to the knife, sir – war to the knife,
The next thing will be a state trial.
The Whigs always start with a state trial.
Something for the lawyers, you know. Whigs . . . rogues, sir.
Joseph Biggar to Hartington, House of Commons, August 1880[40]

Forster had never entertained strong hopes of success for his 'Compensation Bill', as he called it. His strategy in introducing it is made clear in a letter of 18 June to Cowper:

> I am very uneasy about the state of things in the West. There is disorganisation there which may quickly amount to anarchy. May I beg you to tell me for the information of the cabinet what steps Colonel Hillier [Head of the RIC] proposes to make the law obeyed. I am prepared to support any measures that may be really necessary, but we must exhaust the present law *before we return to exceptional law*, and we must also be sure that the police cannot do the work before we get the help of the military for patrols or otherwise, I have often greatly lamented that I had not the opportunity of talking matters over with you. Perhaps however it is as well that you are out of the responsibility of the ejectment clause, or rather bill which I propose. *My chief or rather overpowering reason for it is, that with it I can with a clear conscience enforce the law.*

> Of course the law as it stands must be enforced, but if I think that under the special circumstances of this year it needs special modification, I must throw upon others the responsibility of not permitting that modification.[41] [my emphasis]

That responsibility was in fact thrown upon the Lords, who threw the Bill out. In all subsequent accounts, most potently in the hagiographic representation of Gladstone by Morley,[42] and in Hammond's classic *Gladstone and the Irish Nation*,[43] this denial of the Lords' is represented as another 'lost opportunity'. Hammond's account[44] is based on Gladstone's *Nineteenth Century* (1888) review of T. Wemyss Reid's life of Forster.[45] The language of 'the problem', 'the solution', 'the lost opportunity' and the 'wrong turning' characterises all discussion of the policy of London in these accounts. Such language is the ineffable corollary to a perspective that views the complexity of the internal politics of the island of Ireland exclusively through the simplicities of an Ireland projected as a single question onto a London axis. Through that channel the complexity of the politics of the island of Ireland thins out to a siphon poured from Dublin to London and redefined there as the 'Irish problem'. It is a formulation colluded in by Nationalists at all times, since their desired vision and the administrative imperatives of the 'problem perceiving' administration are mutually reinforcing.

The position in which Forster found himself in August 1880 was hidebound. He could not suspend the 'ordinary law', because it was a base position of the Liberal administration that the ordinary law could be made to work. He did not feel morally justified in administering the 'ordinary law' since he believed that exceptional circumstances and landlord intransigence made it unjust. The adaptations that he had demanded to render the ordinary law 'just' had been denied by the House of Lords. No further initiative on the question of the agricultural crisis was possible until such time as one or both of the relevant parliamentary commissions reported. He was excoriated by the landlords for what they saw as his attempt to default them of their rents. To the mass of Land League activists he was 'Buckshot Forster' who had protected sheriffs and bailiffs with massive displays of military force. Moreover, he was seen by his Liberal colleagues to be failing in his job, which was to 'control violence'. His success or failure in this area was monitored exclusively by the graphs of the crime statistics which were totted up in the Castle for transmission to the cabinet. The political options open to him were minimal. Speaking on the 'State of Ireland' debate in the Commons on 23 August he:

> trusted that very speedily such measures as may be necessary to put the relation of landlords and tenant in Ireland on a better footing and tend to bring about a better state of things[46]

would be effected. The remaining option within the existing law was the possibility of controlling violence by the prosecution of Land League leaders for conspiracy. Evidence available in individual outrage cases was slight. Trials by jury tended to end in acquittals. The statistics of successful prosecutions, not to mention successful detection which was their precondition, were low. Conspiracy, as an option, could be made to hold under the ordinary law. This, however, required a perspective on violence utterly at variance with that advanced by Forster during the debate on the Compensation for Disturbances Bill. Then he represented violence as a consequence of unjust evictions or exactions. His new perspective involved the necessity of viewing violence as conspiracy: Land League conspiracy. It was not that the nature of the violence had altered, though it had intensified, but that there were few options available to him in his struggle to fulfil his primary brief to the satisfaction of his cabinet colleagues. That brief was to keep Ireland quiet, to 'get the crime statistics down' and to allow the 'Irish question' to recede from the forefront of politics. Moreover, he had to reassure his own party and the Tory opposition that the continuing flagrant rejection of the demands of property and social legality would not be countenanced.

The Attorney-General, Hugh Law, and the other Law Officers in Dublin Castle were put to work during the parliamentary recess in September to devise suitable legal lines of action. On 8 October Forster reported to Gladstone:

> A G slow . . . but without doubt his difficulties are great, both as regards the facts and the law. Parnell and Co have clever law advisers of their own. It is not easy even to find technical proof of the connection of any one of them with the Land League, and the Land League has hardly any written rules and publishes no list of officers. *The speeches are in fact almost the only evidence*, and these are framed as carefully to keep within the law . . . My expectation is that the opinion [i.e. of the Law Officers] will show (1) that we have *strongest moral grounds* for a prosecution, (2) that we have *doubtful legal grounds*, (3) that *we cannot expect* a conviction . . . Pros. (1) We shall be doing about the only thing we can do without fresh legislation. (2) We should be trying to *punish* [Forster's emphasis] men who without doubt are great criminals – most mischievous criminals. (3) We should prove to everyone that we do not fear the agitators. (4) We should make it clear that we are not in league with them. So great is the excitement that there are many who say and even some persons not ill-disposed who think that we are not sorry for the outrages as making a strong Land Bill necessary. (5) We should also make clear that *we did not mean to let Parnell's law be put in the place of 'the' law* – everyone – law-breakers included, would feel that having taken up the gauntlet he had thrown down we should have to ask for future power if present powers do not suffice.[47] [my emphases]

This letter of Forster's is revealing. The central revelation may be said to pivot around the question of confidence. Gone is his former preoccupation with the oppressed tenantry; there he has tried and failed. Their putative disengagement from outrage has been lost as an option in view of the Lords' decision. Therefore the problem is recast as a fundamental question of law and order, which represents the desired perspective of both Houses. And it has credibility. There *is* a Land League conspiracy. It is perhaps more governmentally expedient to concentrate on the orchestrated antics of the Land League. Also, Forster is conscious of having been compromised by his espousal of the tenants' position. He has been accused of being in league with the Irish Party. More dangerously, they have been permitted to see the Liberal government a potential 'soft touch'. Most damning of all is the sense that the proposed Liberal concessions were granted out of fear of the agitators. For the Chief Secretary of Ireland to be forced to announce that he desired to demonstrate that the Queen's law ran is indicative of how out of control he saw the situation as being. The image of picking up the gauntlet thrown by Parnell is even more revealing of that inherent lack of confidence. And the remedy proposed – a state trial of the Land League leaders on charges of conspiracy, a massive legal undertaking – was to be initiated without any reasonable hope of success. It was a charade designed as a necessary conscience-clearing Liberal step in what looked like being an inevitable movement towards the suspension of the ordinary law.

On the other side of the equation Forster presented to Gladstone 'the cons':

> (1) Great enthusiasm could be excited for Parnell, subscriptions would flow in from America, (2) the quarrel between the Land Leaguers and the Nationalists would be healed, but I do not think that question helps us now, (3) some of the more moderate Home Rulers would be driven to join him [i.e. Parnell], (4) he would probably obtain the triumph of no conviction [i.e. from a Dublin jury] . . .[48]

Despite all these factors, Forster felt that if the Law Officers came out in favour of prosecution, he should favour it. The prosecutions might at least have the merit of carrying 'reasonable public opinion' with the government. He added:

> I am, however, by no means sure that prosecution will stop or even materially check the outrages. No one can say but that Parnell has incited these outrages, but they may now be beyond his control. If within his control it is reasonable to hope he would for his own sake do his best to stop them pending his trial. The outrages continue and spread from one county to another. I believe that if we can not prosecute we shall be drawn to a special session for the suspension of the habeas corpus. And even if we do prosecute we may have also to do this, but at any rate, we should be able to tell parliament that we had done what we could with our present powers.[49]

A factor that influenced Forster was the deputation that he and Cowper received from a large and influential group of landlords on 7 October. Over sixty landlords called and in their verbal pressure made plain the position summarised in their spokesperson Donoughmore's letter of 8 October. Written on the notepaper of the Kildare Street Club, the urban resting-place of all significant landed society, it urbanely made the landlord position menacingly clear. Donoughmore began by reminding Forster that in the political atmosphere which he had permitted to prevail landlords could not publicly proclaim their views as a group 'owing to the great personal risk which many gentlemen would undergo should their names appear in connection with any public memorial'.[50] Succinctly, the landlords wished to remind Forster of the 'facts':

(1) That a system of lawless terrorism prevails . . . daily increasing and spreading wherever the meetings of the Land League take place.

(2) . . . not only are the lives of landlords, agents and bailiffs as well as those of people carrying out the ordinary processes of the law rendered insecure, but men of position and stake in the country are intimidated in their magisterial and county duties, while respectable and hitherto law-abiding farmers and tradesmen are forced to join in combinations against the rights of property and maintenance of order.

(3) That a state of things is hereby created and maintained which ought to be impossible in any civilised country enjoying the protection of responsible government – that *attempts to enforce the law have become a mockery* and that the only passport to safety in some parts of the country is obedience to the orders of persons whose avowed objects are the carrying out of a conspiracy against *the rights of property and the welfare of the Empire*. [my emphases]

As a remedy for these ills the landlords 'urged' the government:

who we know has the power and we hope it will have the will as guardians of the public order, irrespective of any suggestions on our part, to take steps, by the suspension of the Habeas Corpus Act, the re-enaction of the Peace Preservation Act and the introduction of measures preventative of meetings where conspiracy, sedition and communism flourish, to control the situation.[51]

Few of these landowners were Liberals. Since the disestablishment of the Irish Church by Gladstone in 1869 they had viewed Liberal governments under his control with suspicion and irritation. As far as they were concerned the Union was a necessary accommodation with London to ensure the maintenance of their power on the island of Ireland after the disaster of 1798. They could not, as they saw it, stand alone, and so they turned to London and their superior relative position within the United Kingdom to protect them. Their reward since 1800 had been consecutive governmental concessions to their hereditary enemies: by the granting of Catholic emancipation, the abolition of tithe payments to the established Church, the disestablishment of that Church, the Land Act of 1870. Thus, though their power was based upon a cleaving to the British connection and a sense of their Englishness, the fragility of the London government's commitment to the maintenance of their

interests was increasingly apparent. Their dependence grew in inverse proportion to their trust. The strengthening of Catholic and landless interests by
concessions of the London government weakened them as a force in Ireland,
while rendering them increasingly reliant on their governmental betrayers for
protection against seditious native forces. Westminster, particularly Liberal
Westminster, required scapegoats for the sustained nuisance value of Ireland,
and the Irish landlord class were the most easily located target. As a base
indictment of Irish landlords the Devon Commission was the official first
text.[52] The relationship was not as loaded against the landlords as a first
analysis might suggest. They retained considerable leverage through their
family connections with the chief Whig and Tory families and through the
dependence of county society and the law upon their persons.

Cowper and Forster responded quickly to their most immediate demands.
Most of the landlords who had visited were from the 'disturbed districts':

> We called a council yesterday and proclaimed Mayo and Galway as
> disturbed counties, thereby gaining power under the old Constabulary
> Act to send in police above the parliamentary quota, half of the expense
> to be paid by the county. I have asked the military authorities and they
> have agreed to fill the barracks in these counties and to send in infantry
> to four fresh places so that we shall have a large force in Mayo and
> Galway.[53]

On 10 October Forster and Cowper met the Law Officers at three. They
were in favour of prosecution. However, as Forster said: 'The step is a very
serious one and will cause an excitement quite equal to the O'Connell
prosecution.' It would be a few days before the Law Officers would be ready
to take the first public step, but 'if the blow is to do any good the sooner it is
struck the better'. Forster was not over-optimistic about the prosecutions
producing any lasting effect. The question of suspending the habeas corpus
was not set aside, although the efficacy of suspension, in effect the 'arrest and
detention of men on suspicion when the whole population sympathises with a
man who commits an outrage, knows that hardly any witness will give
evidence against him and that a jury in his own district will certainly acquit
him' was not by any means self-evident.[54]

In the archives of Dublin Castle there are cartons marked 'Queen vs Parnell
and Others'. The brief for the Crown was handled by the firm of William Lane
Joynt and the boxes contain the records prepared for the trial. They are in the
main police reports – the usual standard monthly reports from the extremities
to the core and reports specially solicited in pursuit of evidence against the
charged Land League activists. In effect the Crown brief was prepared to the
political agenda of Forster and the Law Officers, and the special police
responses to their detailed enquiries were 'printed up' for the trials. The bulk
of the evidence consists of the verbatim reports of police note-takers who

attended and recorded every Land League meeting. Ironically, apart from newspaper reports which are frequently inaccurate and concerned exclusively with 'resolutions passed', these police reports are the primary source for an understanding of the Land League phenomenon. For here in full are described not merely the substance of resolutions passed, but the style and imagery, tone and pageantry of the events.

In anticipation of a favourable decision to prosecute by the Law Officers the gathering of information had been initiated by the Castle:

> On the 1st of this month Burke sent to the County Inspectors of police queries to which we are now receiving answers . . . I have the answers for Connaught and Munster and I think them so important that I send them to you though in uncorrected proof. In looking over them now please bear in mind that the disorder which had existed for months in Connaught is taking hold in Kerry and Cork. The last two or three days there has been some diminution in outrages . . . Unless we see a real improvement then [1st week in November] I am most reluctantly driven to the conviction that we cannot face the winter, i.e. January and February, without special legislation . . . we cannot conceal from ourselves it must be special legislation of the most high-handed fashion . . . any Bill of real use, short of the suspension of the habeas corpus would have to be a much stronger Bill than the Westmeath Act because we could neither limit it to a confined area, nor to suspected members of any society. *It must in fact give power to the Irish Executive to shut up any person they consider dangerous.* Burke has also sent around queries to the RMs. We shall have their answer in a few days which I will send you. We shall also by that time [i.e. mid-November] have discovered how far the good priests can help us. Nothing can be better than Archbishop McCabe's charge and the declaration at Cork by Bishop Delaney and others – against that we have some Bishops doing very much harm – the Archbishop of Cashel, the Bishop of Ossory, old MacHale and some of the very worst agitators are priests, generally curates. They ought to be prosecuted but I am loath to include them. I do not wish to set the *esprit de corps* priesthood against us if it can be helped. Just now the Pope could do real good especially since this is the time when several of the bishops – Cashel amongst them – are going to Rome – could Lyons give a hint to the Nuncio at Paris?[55] [my emphasis]

Forster thought that the lull in ejectments was temporary:

> The landlords are behaving well; from fellows who dare not do otherwise, they are too busy taking care of their lives to look sharp after their rent. I do not believe many ejectment decrees are being obtained . . . but if the rent be not paid by January, and if the landlords are strengthened by a Coercion Bill, we shall probably have a flood of ejectments, many of them for rack rents . . . I fear we shall be drawn to a Land Bill. The Commission [Bessborough's] is working very hard and well and I think will report before February . . . I cannot deny that in many cases there is ground for panic.[56]

Gladstone approved of the policy of selective prosecutions of leaders and hoped that at the first cabinet of the new session on 10 or 11 November the effects of the prosecutions could be gauged:

> making much of the first stroke and making it as marked and pointed as possible. *I do not know whom you are to prosecute* but I hope not too few *if they are bad men* and at the same time *men of mark*. [my emphases]

On the secondary question of the suspension of the habeas corpus he was instinctively opposed both on the grounds of perceived morality and on the grounds of expediency:

> I look on it with feelings not only of aversion on general grounds but of doubt and much misgiving as to the likelihood of its proving efficacious in the particular case. The crimes which at present threaten to give a case for interference *grow out of certain incitements made by speech. What we want is to enforce silence.* I do not see how this is to be done by habeas corpus [i.e. the suspension of] *if* it cannot be done by prosecution. Legal prosecutions can be multiplied if necessary far more easily than apprehensions, necessarily arbitrary, under the suspension of the H.C. Act . . . the Westmeath Act we know beforehand pretty exactly who were the handful of people it would be necessary to apprehend as ringleaders in crime . . . but quite another matter to apprehend Parnell, Biggar and Co who not only are not suspected of intending to commit crime, *but who we know have no idea of committing it* and who only think of intimidating landlords with a possible crime now and then to back the intimidation. [my emphases]

Again on the habeas corpus question he said:

> I have not yet heard how it is to be effectual and there arises the odious question whether we are to impound a lot of obscure tools, while the real instigants go free. *It will be a very great misfortune if, departing from the precedents of 1833 and 1870, we have to propose any measure of coercion without at the same time declaring our intention in the matter of remedial legislation.*[57] [my emphasis]

Gladstone further stated that it was impossible to know before the Land Commission reported after Christmas quite what should be proposed about land. He agreed that the rejection of the Compensation for Disturbances Bill had brought matters to a head:

> But I do not abandon the double hope as to our stroke on 2 November.
> (1) That it may do much to paralyse the Land League and arrest its mischief and (2) that the landlords will not tempt fortune by a sudden recourse to wholesale evictions . . . do not suppose I dream of reviving the Irish parliament but I have been reading Union speeches and debates and I am surprised at the narrowness upon which that parliament was condemned. I think the unavowed motives must have been the main ones.

The reconsideration of the Union, the quest for origins derived from Mill, was characteristic of Gladstone's thinking at this time. Also characteristic was the respect for precedent in relation to policy. The suppression of agitation in 1833 and 1870 had been accompanied by tithe abolition in the former and the 1870 Land Bill in the latter. Therefore any repression in 1880-81 was, as he saw it, to be accompanied by concessions:

> I was surprised by the number of police in 1878 . . . Forty or fifty years ago when the people were eight million and far less *legal* than now there were 8,000 police – there are now I believe near 12,000 for two thirds of that population. It was a great, nay a gross mistake of Sir Robert Peel to take the whole charge on the Consolidated Fund.[58]

Announcement of Land League prosecutions was made in the Dublin newspapers on 3 November. The MPs declared to be prosecuted were Parnell, Biggar, Dillon, Sexton and Sullivan. The League Officials prosecuted were the League Secretary and local paid organisers: Thomas Brennan, Patrick Egan, Malachi O'Sullivan, Michael Boyton, Patrick Sheridan, Patrick Gordon, Matthew Harris, John Walsh and John Nally. Two days later Forster, who was attempting to accommodate the fact that the Queen was 'specially interested in the prosecutions', was writing to Gladstone in renewed dejection:

> I send you my present impressions for what they are worth. [Gladstone had to speak in the Commons on the following Tuesday.] The outrages continue very numerous. October is almost the worst month since the famine, and for numbers the last is the worst week of October. I asked Colonel Nelligan his impression . . . His reply confirmed my own estimate from the perusal of the outrage papers. They are increasing in number and area but somewhat diminished in atrocity. On the other hand we have very large numbers of persons under personal protection . . . and we might have one or two murders any day. . . . We must have power to proclaim any part of Ireland – and to arrest anyone we suspect to be principal or accessory to any felony or principal in any misdemeanour but we must not be obliged to say that we believe such a person to be a member of any secret society.[59]

Forster also believed that the concession of a new Land Bill was essential. There is no analysis of why this should be so, merely a tacit acceptance that the 'three Fs' are the crux of the matter:

> I find moderate opinion working up to this about the country. No Ulster Liberal has a chance of return who does not pledge himself to it and even the Orangemen cry out . . . If by any means we could get the country quiet I think the proposal of such a Land Bill would make us absolute masters of the situation and what is of far more importance would give Ireland *a new start* . . . get the country quiet first, or our reform would be seen as a concession to threats and would probably lead to further demands.[59] [my emphasis]

In Forster's view the best way of:

> getting through the winter without suspending habeas corpus would be
> to back up the prosecutions by your announcing a strong Land Bill
> would be proposed if the country was quiet. But such a Bill could not be
> carried and would not be proposed while outrages prevail. The shrewd
> farmers who at present believe in Parnell's statement that the agitation
> will be the measure of Land Bill would then feel that, on the contrary,
> the Bill depends on their good behaviour.[60]

Dublin diverged from London in advocating the suspension of habeas
corpus. The story of Gladstone's resistance to its suspension has been
repeatedly invoked, together with egregious statements about the moral
abhorrence of Chamberlain and Dilke for such a course of action. Gladstone
was also toying with schemes for a Grand Committee, or a form of devolved
local government in Ireland, a scheme rejected utterly by his cabinet
colleagues. The debates of November and December in cabinet are of no
public consequence, except in their conclusion. Importantly, the minute
charting of individual views is relevant only in terms of the desires of
Gladstone and Chamberlain to emerge from the cabinet's pro-coercion and
anti-suspension of habeas corpus decisions with their Liberal reputations
unscathed. The requirement is therefore for a scapegoat, or rather two
scapegoats: Forster and Cowper. Forster's actions in the autumn of 1880 are
now read through the prism of his divergence from government policy in
early 1882, and Cowper is represented as an inconsequential halfwit.
Hammond represents Cowper as alarmist. His memo of 8 November to the
cabinet is dismissed by Hammond in the following terms:

> Cowper's argument was a little lacking in coherence, as Gladstone saw,
> and it showed that his nerves were suffering under the strain.[61]

Cowper and Forster were declared to be unreliable when they voiced unpalat-
able truths. Cowper's memo is far from incoherent. In fact, it is reasonably
accurate when read *in toto*. The highly selective and deliberately distorting
quotations from it in Hammond certainly read incoherently, but in its full form
it is a reasonably accurate account of the position of the Irish government:

> The state of the country is undoubtedly most serious. I am quite willing
> to admit that it is in the interests of the landowners to exaggerate, and
> that they have many friends in England and many means of influencing
> a large portion of the press. But the Cabinet will be more likely to judge
> the state of things by the facts and figures which they have before them.
> I will not largely allude to these. I will only point out that the number of
> outrages does not by any means represent the serious state of the
> country. The reason that in many places the list of crime is not much
> longer is that those who would profit from it are complete masters of the

situation, and that their temptation is therefore removed. Nobody dares to evict. Tenants of evicted farms, even those who have been in possession for more than a year, are daily giving them up. Eighty persons are under police protection . . . We cannot yet say for certain how far the autumn rents will be paid, but it appears already that in many places tenants have refused to pay more than government valuation. Landlords will not agree to this. They will evict and then a great increase in outrages may be expected. *It will then be too late to give us extra powers.* If these are to be the decision must come at once. Her Majesty's government may well be reluctant to repeat once more the dreary old story of special restrictive legislation for Ireland, the evil of which has so often been exposed. I cannot regard it as an error to have trusted even for a short period to the common law for the maintenance of order in this country. And if we could be sure of going through the coming winter with no greater amount of outrage than we have now, large as that amount is, so great is my detestation of coercive measures that I should hesitate to recommend them. But I feel strongly that there is nothing to prevent outrages from largely increasing in any moment, both in number and atrocity; and if this should be the case, I should reproach myself for the rest of my life with not having put my opinion on record that in the present state of feeling *the law is not strong enough as it stands. For the ordinary law to be sufficient to repress crime it is necessary that the majority of the population should be on the side of the injured person; and in the disturbed parts of Ireland the vast majority are, in cases of an agrarian nature, invariably on the side of the criminal.* In spite then of all my wish being that we could trust to the ordinary law, I must repeat my conviction that to make up our minds to face the winter without stronger powers would be very dangerous.[62] [My emphases]

This was precisely the kind of analysis that Gladstone did not want to hear. It was a point of Liberal principle that Ireland was to be administered under the ordinary law. It was a part of the United Kingdom, not some conquered colony and it was more than ideologically embarrassing to admit that it *could not* be ruled under the ordinary law. The fundamental premise of respect for individual liberty was contingent upon the consent of the governed. For Cowper to admit that there was no such consent to the legal system was a severe blow. The fact that both he and Forster were placed in an impossible position from a practical point of view was irrelevant to Chamberlain, Dilke and Gladstone himself. No member of the cabinet, except for Spencer, had seen anything of the daily chaos. They found their principles more exacting than the demands of practical politics. There was, however, *some* practical ground for rejecting rights to summary detentions of suspects. That ground was most clearly delineated by Chamberlain:

It is really impossible to believe that the arrest of thirty subordinate agents as proposed by Mr Forster would immediately stop threatening letters and assaults on life and property which are rife all over the country. It would be like firing with a rifle at a swarm of gnats. The tenants of Ireland are universally in a state of excitement under which any one of them, in face of provocation, may take the law into his own hands. The remedy must be one which affects all – not the arrest of individuals when a whole nation has more or less escaped from the ordinary respect of the law. The condition has been brought about by an unjust law – or by a law which under the exceptional circumstances of the country has practically worked injustice . . .[63]

The chief ally of both Forster and Cowper within the cabinet was Spencer who had been Lord Lieutenant for Ireland during the so-called Westmeath crisis. However, Cowper derived from correspondence with Spencer the sense that the most stringent coercive measures would not be instantly successful, as he revealed in his cabinet memo:

In considering the returns of crime over the last forty years in connection with the passing of various Acts for the Preservation of Peace, we see that every measure, great or small, which increases the power of the government is immediately followed by a decrease of crime. It might be inferred that the mere expression of determination implied by special legislation of any sort had a deterrent effect. We must however remember that the people of Ireland are wiser than they were; or if not wiser at all events more cunning and better informed by experience of the real power conferred by each coercive Act. The old idea that the smallest action is sufficient to cow them may not be so true as it once was.[64]

If the analysis of Gladstone and Chamberlain was correct, and if the prosecution of Parnell and friends was also admitted to be unlikely to be effective in ending disorder, it is difficult to see how the façade of governmental control, which was generally admitted to have broken down, was to be restored. The classic Liberal analysis was based on the notion of entering, albeit in a very particular way, into the minds of their opponents – in this case the 'Irish people'. Gladstone had resolved to his own satisfaction in 1869–70 precisely what lay in the minds of those people. Gladstone had developed his sense of that mentality through the rather rarified analysis of John Stuart Mill. Mill's analysis in turn derived from mid-century scholarly works on early Celtic or Brehon Law. The existing system of land tenure, according to this analysis, went against the atavistic survival of a rural communality of land as the Irish ideal. While land resentment undoubtedly had its origin in an unclear folk tradition of dispossession, and was undoubtedly aggravated by the experience of the famine a mere thirty years before the start of the so-called Land War, it seems unlikely that the Brehon basis was anything other than a Liberal romanticisation of a 'backward people', a romanticisation fuelled by Irish Nationalist endorsement. It was, however, to be a legislatively potent romanticisation that altered the structure of Irish rural society in two decades. Land agitation in 1880 simply sent Gladstone and those few true Liberals back to their analysis of 1870. The 'answer' to the 'question' was therefore tenurial. This 'answer' did not seem most apparent to those on the ground. As Cowper wrote to the cabinet:

> The only remedy suggested by every landlord and every agent is suspension of the Habeas Corpus Act . . . The same remedy as to the whole of Connaught, except Sligo, is recommended by the Police Inspectors in their answers to a recent circular. The opinion of the Resident Magistrates will be seen from the return which has been printed. Authority would therefore point to the suspension of the Habeas Corpus Act as the proper remedy and Common Sense would appear to make the same suggestion. The sudden imprisonment of those who are known to instigate or commit these crimes would strike a general terror in a way that nothing else would, for no man would know how far he was suspected or whether his own turn might not come next. The police in many districts have a list ready of those who are at the bottom of the mischief; and in all places could probably pick out somebody to make an example of. This would no doubt be a very high-handed proceeding, but what is really objectionable is going *at all* beyond the limits of the law as it now stands. If we are to have such a hateful thing as a coercive bill let it be effective. Speaking in the cause of Liberty, it seems to me that to be constantly giving a little more power to the government than is given by the Common Law is more demoralizing than to pass a really stringent measure for a short period and on a great emergency.[65]

The cabinet of 17 November was the one at which Forster had hoped to force the issue but, as he wrote to Cowper, decision was postponed once again. Gladstone came up with some scheme of his own on which he instructed Forster to consult Burke. Burke 'merely telegraphed to say "No" as to Gladstone's proposal'. Forster was pursuing a battle with Gladstone that swung on the issue of whether outrages were *caused by* evictions. Again he proceeded to do battle with statistics. On 17 November Forster wrote to Burke:

> Only time for one line. No decision, adjourned till Friday. We must decide then. Send me tomorrow any fresh facts you have concerning necessity of suspension. Tell me what you think will be the position of affairs if we do nothing till a January session and what if we wait till February. Also tell me this. If we can have no suspension of HC, if we are forced to this, what would you do? Mr Gladstone very much wants the eviction returns for which I telegraphed. I hope you will have sent me for the four provinces October evictions if possible, first fortnight in November, and can you separate the last quarterly return into each of the three months? He persists in thinking the evictions may have caused the outrages.[66]

Decision was postponed again at the cabinet of 19 November. Cowper was by this time contemplating resignation. Parliament had been prorogued until 2 December and this did not augur well for a swift move on the matter. Gladstone replied to Cowper's threats by stating his own position:

> The paralysis of very important rights affecting the tenure of land is the

special characteristic of the present mischief in Ireland and it may be right to apply a thorough remedy a little later rather than a partial (indeed as I think very doubtful) remedy a little, and only a little, sooner. What I personally think a very doubtful remedy is a suspension of the Habeas Corpus Act proposed alone, carried after much delay, in the teeth of two thirds of the representatives of Ireland (without taking British allies into account) and used in order to cope with a wide spreading conspiracy embracing in certain districts large fractions of the population, and largely armed with means other than material for action. You may rely upon it that, when the time you indicate [January] arrives, the Cabinet will look at the question of defending proprietary rights without any mawkish sensitivities; and the suspension should you and Forster then still see cause to desire it will be most impartially entertained. For my own part what I lean to expecting is, that *if requisite it will not be sufficient*, and that *we may have to legislate directly against the Land League*, not only against its name only, but *against the purpose of all combinations aiming at the non-payment of debts and the non-fulfilment of contracts the very least, when these aims are so pursued as to endanger the public security.*[67] [my emphases]

Cowper decided not to resign, not because he was persuaded by the line Gladstone advocated, but for vague notions of duty. As he wrote to Argyll:

> . . . I felt that my resignation would have forced Forster to resign too; which would have involved Hartington and others including, as I now see, yourself. This would, I suppose, have compelled Gladstone to give way, but a Coercion Bill with Bright, Chamberlain and Dilke against it and the Premier himself an unwilling advocate would have been a long time in getting through; and if there is a chance of its being brought forward in January by a United Cabinet it will have been worth waiting for.[68]

Spencer wrote and said that the radicals would have 'swung' after a token resistance, provided that they were assured of 'remedial measures' as well:

> With Bright and Chamberlain in the Government there is no doubt that the passing of any measure in January will be nearly as quick if not quicker than passing the same measure in December with them in opposition. All this however is but poor consolation, for I do not see that such an argument can be made in public, and how we are to defend taking only in January steps which ought to have been taken in November I do not know. The only possible answer to the argument seems to me to be that we were waiting for the Result of the Trial . . .
>
> I feel now as if we had been outmanoeuvred, and if we do not look out we may be altogether defeated; for the next move will be to say we must try and see what the promise of a Measure of Land Reform will do without coercion . . . The question of Remedial measures is a very difficult one. We are very likely to split on that; I do not think it possible that Argyll will swallow anything approaching the three Fs or Valuation of Rents, and Hartington and Granville feel nearly as strongly on both

these points. I am very little behind them in dislike to these principles. I don't think Gladstone likes them, he abhors Fixity of Tenure . . . but of course necessity may drive us to anything. I mean not the necessity of keeping Office but of solving the Irish question.[69]

3 A LIBERAL DILEMMA

The old fenianism was politically of little account . . . Matters were very different after Mr Gladstone, by successive acts of what I maintain were criminal legislation, deliberately fostered treason and encouraged outrage in Ireland. Irish agitation would never have reached genuine importance unless it had been steadily assisted in its noisome growth by the so called GOM, at whose grave may be laid every calamity which has affected Ireland since it had the misfortune to arouse his interest, and the ill effects of whose demoralising interference will bear fruit for many years to come.

S. M. Hussey, *The Reminiscences of an Irish Land Agent, Being those of S. M. Hussey*, compiled by Home Gordon, London, 1904

What I personally think a very doubtful remedy is a suspension of Habeas Corpus Act proposed alone, carried after much delay in the teeth of two thirds of the representatives of Ireland (without taking British allies into account) and used in order to cope with a widespreading conspiracy embracing in certain districts large fractions of the population, and largely armed with means rather than material for action.

Gladstone to Cowper, 24 November 1880, Earl Cowper, *KG: A Memoir by his Wife*, London, 1913, p. 435.

We are not in face of secret societies or of small knots of conspirators . . . You might arrest half a county and still Captain Boycott's position would be as intolerable as ever, and Lord Leitrim's and Lord Mountmorres' murderers would go unpunished . . .

Chamberlain to Gladstone, November 1880, J. L. Garvin, *The Life of Joseph Chamberlain*, i, 1836–1885, London, 1932, pp 328–9.

The tenants of Ireland are universally in a condition of excitement under which any one of them, in face of provocation, may take the law into his own hands. The remedy must be one which affects all – not the arrest of individuals when a whole nation has more or less escaped from the ordinary respect for the law.

Chamberlain to Gladstone, November 1880, J. L. Garvin, *The Life of Joseph Chamberlain*, 1, 1836–1885, London, 1932, p. 338.

In conclusion I must say, from all accounts and from my own observation, that the state of our fellow countrymen in these parts I have named is worse than that of any people in the world, let alone Europe. I believe that these people are made as we are, that they are patient beyond belief, loyal, but, at the same time broken-spirited and desperate, living on the verge of starvation in places in which we would not keep our cattle.

Letter to *The Times* from General Gordon, 3 December 1880.

Under the Act of 1881, 44 Vict., C 4, the Irish executive obtained the absolute power of arbitrary and preventive arrest, and could without breach of law detain in prison any person arrested on suspicion for the whole period for which the Act continued in force . . . The government could in the case of certain crimes, abolish the right to trial by jury, could arrest strangers found out of doors at night under suspicious circumstances, could seize any newspaper inciting to treason or violence, and could prohibit any public meeting which the Lord Lieutenant believed to be contrary to the public peace or safety,

Albert Venn Dicey, *Introduction to the Study of the Law of the Constitution*, London, 1885, p. 243.

A State Trial

On 1 November 1880 the Crown filed 'informations' in the Crown Office of the Queen's Bench Division of the High Court of Justice in Dublin. The 'certain persons' named in the charges made by the Crown were fourteen in number: Mr Parnell MP, Mr John Dillon MP, Mr Biggar MP, Mr T. D. Sullivan MP, Mr Sexton MP, Mr Patrick Egan, treasurer of the Land League, Mr Thomas Brennan, secretary of the Land League, Mr Michael O'Sullivan, assistant-secretary of the Land League, Mr Patrick Boyton, Mr Matthew Harris of Ballinasloe, Mr J. Nally of Balla, Mr P. J. Gorman of Claremorris, Mr John W. Walsh of Balla and Mr P. Sheridan of Tobercurry. The charges against these individuals, listed in the complex and lengthy informations, were centred around a cluster of key accusations. In essence the charges were: conspiracy to prevent the payment of rent; conspiracy to resist the process of ejectment; conspiracy to prevent the taking of farms from which tenants had been evicted and conspiracy to create ill-will among Her Majesty's subjects.[1]

The practice of prosecution by ex-official information, more succinctly described as a State Trial, had notable precedents. The press and public commentators were, however, driven back on the most dramatic State Trial of living political memory, that of Daniel O'Connell at the Court of Queen's Bench, initiated in Dublin in October 1843. The preliminaries at that time occupied almost three months, and the trial proper did not begin until January 1844.[2] The trial of 1880 was to be held 'at bar', that is before the full court of Queen's Bench, and trial was to be by jury of the city of Dublin. The judges of Queen's Bench were the Chief Justice May, Mr Justice O'Brien, Mr Justice J. D. Fitzgerald and Mr Justice Barry. On the day following the filing of information summonses were served upon the defendants. This task was placed in the hands of Detective Officers of the G Division of the Dublin Metropolitan Police. At 11 a.m. two detectives proceeded to Morrison's Hotel where they expected to find Parnell. Finding no trace of him there, they proceeded to his other Dublin haunt, the Imperial Hotel in Sackville Street. He was in the coffee room with J. J. O'Kelly MP, James Redpath and Timothy Harrington. Mr Parnell 'accepted service with a smile, and resumed luncheon while his friends scanned the indictment – a formidable document containing not less than nineteen counts'.[3] Thomas Brennan was next presented with his indictment, which was immediately published in the evening papers. The offices of the Land League in Abbey Street were visited by detectives in pursuit of Sexton and Egan. T. D. Sullivan was found penning an editorial for *The Nation* in offices across the road. As an indication of the confused nature of Dublin Castle information, the indictment did not carry Sullivan's correct Christian name, thus enabling him to refuse to accept it. Gorman, Biggar and Dillon were 'out of town', in Claremorris, Belfast and Tipperary respectively. Walsh and Boyton were expected back in the evening. An Executive Committee Meeting of the Land League was held in the Middle Abbey Street office on the afternoon of 2 November, and a sub-committee of Parnell, Dillon, Sullivan, Egan and Brennan was formed to make arrangements for a legal defence.[4] The solicitor for the defendants was V. B. Dillon. The Crown and Treasury Solicitor was William Lane Joynt.[5]

The Crown was represented at the official preliminary of the trial on 10 November by the Attorney-General Law, the Solicitor-General Johnson, Sergeant Heron, Naish QC Law Adviser, James Murphy QC, A. M. Porter QC, C. Molloy and D. Ross instructed by William Joynt. The defendants were represented by Francis Macdonagh QC, William McLoughlin QC, Peter O'Brien QC, Mr F. Nolan QC, and Luke Dillon. The defence counsel, lead by Macdonagh, protested at the vague and non-specific nature of the case made against them.[6] The Attorney-General had filed his *ex-officio* informations without any prior investigations. There had been no prior investigations before magistrates 'so that the parties might know to some extent what were the overt acts which were sought to be brought in evidence against them, and no previous finding of the Grand Jury'. In the case of the Queen vs O'Connell, where there were overt acts charged, a bill of particulars was given. In that instance the Bill of particulars set out the indictable speeches made, the resolutions moved and adopted, the acts done, the letters and other documents read and the details of what was said and done at the indictable meetings.[7]

Macdonagh's case essentially was that since the Crown brief was to be backed by all State records, in particular the reports of the Royal Irish Constabulary in conjunction with the information of informants, the defence was rendered almost impossible since they had no prior knowledge of the specific instances to be pressed against them. The clerk of the Crown, Goodman, agreed that the defendants or their barristers should be furnished with a published order of particulars of the case against them, though the question of 'full' particulars was not one upon which the judges were prepared to be drawn.

While Foster was less than optimistic about the chances of a Dublin jury convicting Parnell and Others, the defendants' barristers claimed to be alarmed by the nature of items published in the Unionist press, which they argued, prejudged the trial.[8] Specifically indicted was the *Dublin Evening Mail*. They brought a motion for attachment for contempt of court against the paper on 24 November, citing in particular the copies of the *Mail* published on 3rd, 4th, 6th, 15th and 18th of November respectively. They named the publisher, James Develing, and the printer, Richard C. Mates, for contempt of court in publishing these copies, and further cited the proprietors George Tickell and James C. Maunsell for articles and letters calculated to prejudice, prevent and interfere with the fair trial of this information regarding the Queen vs Parnell and Others. The tone of the *Evening Mail* is perhaps captured by an article of 3 November, in which the legal status of Ireland is discussed:

> The trials may end in disagreement of the jury or a verdict contrary to the evidence may be given due to intimidation; but the ample discussion which the case may receive at the hands of both counsel and judges can hardly fail to clear the public mind of a good deal of the nebulosity and confusion in which the subject is at present involved. Another question on which needful light will be thrown is how far Ireland is fit for Constitutional Government . . . Liberal orators are never tired of insisting on the differences which exist between Celt and Saxon, between Irishmen and their English and Scotch fellow subjects, and using these differences as reasons for the application of special legislation to this country. Mr Joseph Cowen MP, went so far the other day as to hint on these grounds that a tribal tenure of land would be more appropriate to Ireland than the system of free contract which has been imported from England. If this be really so, it is evidence that our claim for such an English institution as the Habeas Corpus Act is seriously impaired. The same differences that invalidate the British tenure of land, serves also to invalidate our right to the Englishman's best security for his personal freedom.[9]

In late November Parnell was away[10] and in his absence Patrick Egan made an affidavit detailing the extent of influence that the article would, in his opinion, have on jurors:

> I do not belong to any such gang as mentioned and characterised in the *Dublin Evening Mail* of the 15 inst as 'Mr Parnell and his murder gang'; and I humbly submit to this honourable court that it is contrary to the first principles of justice that parties who are put upon their trial for a criminal offence should be stigmatised by an influential newspaper circulating in the very place where the Crown have selected the locality for the trial. I say that unless the continuance of such unjust expressions and articles shall be repressed I cannot, nor do I believe any of the traversers can, have any hope of a fair trial. I believe that the intent of the writer of those letters and articles was to influence against the traversers the hostility of the jurers, the people of Dublin. I say that my

motive all through and since the period of my joining the Irish National Land League, was for the benefit of my country and the advancement of its welfare. I never approved of and do not approve of, any violation of the law, and when put on my trial in the face of the law I now claim its protection.[11]

The Land League manifesto of 6 November delineated the approach that the defendants intended to pursue throughout the hearing of the case, and clearly underlined their propaganda base in relation to government recourse to the courts.

Fellow countrymen and friends – at a crisis of tremendous importance to our country, we confidently address ourselves to you. The British government of Ireland obeying the dictation of a privileged order of persons, a cruel and selfish class for centuries past the burden and curse of our land and people have cast to the wind the traditions and principles of that Liberalism to which they profess to be devoted, and have set in motion the legal power of the state, and availed themselves of the resources at their command in the public revenue to arraign at a criminal bar the chief man of the Irish race, and with him others of the most active and distinguished labourers in the cause of Ireland's social regeneration . . . although our movement is directed against a code of laws so oppressive as to paralyse the one national industry of Ireland, and although we have been assailed with the most venomous malignity, and pursued with the most unscrupulous falsehoods, yet can we solemnly declare, in the face of the civilised world that all our objects are in keeping with perfect justice to all men, and that all the means we have recommended for the attainment of these objects are reasonable, peaceful and thoroughly legal, offending in no degree against natural right, moral obligation or intelligent human law.[12]

The process of selecting a jury panel was controversial and tortuous, with each side disputing jurors they viewed as unsympathetic. The base 'jury book' in which names of potential jurors in the city of Dublin were listed by the Sheriff was deemed dubious by Macdonagh. He demanded access to the books of 1878 and 1879 to check that the transfer of names had been successfully accomplished. He was in effect impugning the integrity rather than the efficiency of the Sheriff. The municipal politics of Dublin lay close to the surface of the discussion.[13]

Most remarkable in reading the court exchanges is the urbanity and collusiveness of the parties involved. The balconies were packed with journalists from the *Freeman's Journal*, the Unionist press and the fringe Nationalist press, including the rather shifting press controlled by Richard Pigott. Urban, metropolitan Dublin – where the Land League central offices were located, where Irish parliamentary party members met and socialised, schemed and planned when not in London – was the political core of the Land League movement. Yet Dublin presented so stark a contrast to the rural Ireland that was delineated in police and Crown reports that it was difficult to reconcile both to the world of League Irishness. Jostling crowds on the quays, packed and much sought-after seats for society ladies, faced paid organisers and Westminster MPs in the dock. All heard stories of poverty and brutality, of intimidation and starvation in one-roomed mud cabins.[14]

On 13 December the jury panel selection was made, before John Fox Goodman, Clerk of the Crown. The attendance was confined to three of the defendants, the respective counsel, the Lord Mayor of Dublin, the High Sheriff Sir J. W. Mackey and the Sub-Sheriff Mr Campbell. The forty-eight selected to compose the panel of jurors read like a map of the varied professional and commercial interests of the city of Dublin.

The list is worth noting since it clearly reveals a selection of individuals who do not seem to conform in any way to the Dublin Castle stereotype of Irish juries as wretched propertyless dupes. It also serves as a reminder of the complexity of the society of Dublin, in marked contrast to the one-dimensional Ireland of half-starved tenants that the Land League so persistently projected:

1. James Sloane, 3 Stephens Green North, ironmonger
2. Robert Dolling, 34 Mountjoy Square South, land agent
3. Patrick Dolan, 51 South George's Street, grocer
4. Henry Dockrell, 41 South Great George's Street, merchant
5. James D. Power, 2 College Street, stockbroker
6. Michael Doyle, 29 North Earl Street, clothier
7. Henry Dudgeon, 113 Grafton Street, stockbroker
8. Edward Kennedy, 88 Amiens Street, tobacco manufacturer
9. Thomas Hayden, 21 and 24 Duke Street, publican
10. William Moloney, 45 Henry Street, costume maker
11. William J. Moloney, 43 Mountjoy Square South, merchant
12. William Burke, 5 Lower Baggot Street, grocer
13. William Dowse, 16 Lower Mount Street, gentleman
14. Joseph E. Mills, 8 Merrion Row, confectioner
15. John Regan, 8 Bride Street, glass merchant
16. Richard S. Clifford, 38 Thomas Street, wholesale grocer
17. Joseph B. Culverwell, 1 North Great George's Street, secretary Northern Railway Company
18. James Murphy, 5 Queen Street, grocer
19. James Tyrrell, Grand Canal Place, corn merchant
20. Richard Hunting, 1 St Stephens Green North, sewing machine manufacturer
21. Lawrence Hefferman, 116 Upper Abbey Street, cooper
22. Arthur Webb, 34 Upper Sackville Street, clothier
23. Stephen Mallin, Dawson Street, merchant tailor
24. Hugh Lloyd, 9 Eden Quay, hotel keeper

25. John R. Wigham, 35 Capel Street, ironmonger
26. James R. Corcoran, 29 and 30 Sir John Rogerson's Quay, corn merchant
27. James Bennett, 6 Upper Ormond Quay, auctioneer
28. William Hopkins, 1 Lower Sackville Street, jeweller
29. Joseph Madders, 17 Leinster Street, fruitier
30. Thomas Dunne, 95 North Sea Wall, grocer
31. Joseph Connolly, 49 Great Britain Street, grocer
32. Edward Hurse, 152 Capel Street, grocer
33. Nicholas Hopkins, 80 Grattan Street, grocer
34. Henry Standind, 4 Grattan Street, ironmonger
35. Thomas T. Smith, 3 Salem Place, gentleman
36. Robert B. Smith, 31 Fitzwilliam Square, Lieutenant Colonel
37. Patrick Macken, 54 North King Street, vintner
38. John Ormsby, 8 Rutland Square East, gentleman
39. Patrick Biggins, 34 Upper Abbey Street, gentleman
40. Robert Murphy, 10 Upper Mount Street, gentleman
41. Joseph Mitchell, 18 and 19 Grenville Street, vintner
42. James Hughes, 11 Andrew Street, merchant
43. Patrick Fitzpatrick, 66 Great Britain Street, butcher
44. Richard H. Kirwin, 42 Upper Mount Street
45. Luke Doyle, 2 and 3 Pill Lane, ironmonger
46. Robert Woods, 205 and 206 Great Britain Street, sugar boiler
47. Thomas Crosby, 1 and 2 Eden Quay, rope manufacturer
48. John Bicury, 11 Grantham Street, brush maker

Though many of the selected jurors were nationalist sympathisers, they in no way subscribe to the caricature of the Irish jury as duplicitous, propertyless, rural illiterates. The names of the panel are a litany of members of the business community of Dublin. Names like Dockrell and Lloyd were to survive as owners of large businesses into the next century. All of the businesses listed were located within an area of one square mile at the heart of the city of Dublin, stretching from St Stephen's Green to Baggot Street, Mount Street, behind Trinity College to Nassau Street, along by the quays and over to the northside streets and squares: Henry Street, Abbey Street, Sackville Street and Mountjoy. In a city of Dublin's size most of the jurors would have known of one another, even if they did not know one another personally. It was clear from the discussion of disputed jurors between Goodman and Macdonagh that most of the names drawn were known personally to at least one or two members of the court.[15]

The trial officially opened on 28 December 1880. The Lord Chief Justice retired from the case due to prejudicial comments that he had made previously,[16] and Mr Justice O'Brien had resigned due to ill health. The case was to be heard therefore before Fitzgerald and Barry. The Parnellites

dramatically played the opening of the case for full effect. Assembling at
V. B. Dillon's house in Rutland Square the accused were accompanied to the
gate of the Four Courts on the quays by a large party of MPs. The O'Gorman
Mahon MP walked first accompanied by W. H. O'Sullivan. Next came
Charles Stewart Parnell, arm in arm with the Lord Mayor of Dublin. They
were followed by John Daly MP, B. C. Molloy MP, R. Power MP, J. H. Gill
MP, John Dillon MP, R. Lalor MP, J. J. O'Kelly MP, John Barry MP, Justin
McCarthy MP, J. G. Biggar MP, G. M. Byrne MP, Mulhallen Marum MP,
J. F. Smithwick MP, T. M. Healy MP, T. Sexton MP, R. H. Metge MP, A. J.
Commins MP, J. C. McCoan MP, T. P. O'Connor MP, W. J. Corbet MP,
E. Leahy MP and C. Dawson MP. Egan, Brennan, Boyton, Harris, Walsh,
Sheridan and Davitt marched ahead.[17] A huge crowd gave the procession an
ovation at the gates of the Four Courts. The gates of the Courts were barred
by police, the adjoining quays were covered by police patrols on horse and
foot. The court of Queen's Bench was tiny, built in the days of the Irish
parliament, and did little to dispel the tension of the confrontation. The press
were in the grand jury gallery, some nine feet above the court. There were few
members of the Landlords' Committee present, though Lord Randolph
Churchill was clearly in evidence. Twenty four names from the jury panel
were called; eighteen answered, then pleadings to be excused began. One was
deaf – he was excused. Another had undergone an operation, he too was
excused. Others produced doctors' certificates which were then challenged by
the accused. Exercising their full rights of challenge, the traversers could have
forced the postponement of the trial. They did not – though the composition
of the final jury could scarcely have displeased them: eight Catholics, three
Protestants and one Quaker – Webb. The final list was James Corcoran,
William Hopkins, Edward Hurse, Thomas Dunne, John Bicury, James
Tyrrell, Thomas Crosby, Joseph Mitchell, Arthur Webb, Nicholas Hopkins,
Patrick Macken and Patrick Biggins.

The essence of the case was conspiracy.[18] Ross, for the prosecution, made
the nineteen counts reasonably succinct.[19] The defendants, it was alleged, did

> conspire and solicit and procure large numbers of tenants holding farms
> at a rent, in breach of their contracts, to refuse and not to pay the owner
> of farms the rents which the said tenants were bound to pay and which
> the said owners of lands were entitled to be paid under the said contract.

The charges reiterated the line that they did 'unlawfully conspire and
agitate by unlawful means' to fulfil their intent of impoverishing the landlords. As the charge put it:

> . . . by threatening to cut off and utterly exclude from all social inter-
> course and communion whatsoever and from all intercourse and
> dealings in the way of buying, selling, and other business, and to shun at

all times and all places as if affected by a loathsome disease, and to hold up to public hatred and contempt and to subject to annoyance and injury in the pursuit of his occupation and industry, any and every tenant of such farms aforesaid who shall pay the owner thereof the rent which he, the said tenant, shall and might become lawfully bound to pay under his contract of tenancy.

Furthermore, the defendants were charged with intending to impede, frustrate and bring to nought the administration of justice. The intent was

to excite and promote feelings of ill-will and hostility between landlords and tenants, and to excite and promote feelings of ill-will and hostility towards the landlords of Ireland, amongst the rest of her Majesty's subjects in Ireland.

The language of the nineteen counts hammered relentlessly at the accusation: unlawfully combining and conspiring, threatening and menacing; conspiring and soliciting by unlawful means; impeding and frustrating; bringing justice into contempt; and, with ineluctable repetition, unlawfully conspiring to fulfil an unlawful intent. Such was the nature of the State Trial to which the putative political leaders of the Nationalist movement were now exposed. In implicating them in this level of argument, however, the government was also implicating itself. The trial dragged on for twenty days during which a litany of police reports, journalistic reports and casual accounts of Land League meetings were produced that sought to demonstrate the guilt of the traversers. On 25 January 1881, after an uneasy day of waiting, the jury announced that they were unable to agree. Privately it was revealed that they had split ten to two in favour of an acquittal. Parnell left the court after the verdict and went to the North Wall to proceed to the House of Commons. The Land League called a celebration meeting. But the State Trial, dramatically important as a stage of policy, was politically redundant before its conclusion.

The debate had moved to London. The policy of the Forster administration and the London government had been, up to August 1880, one of viewing agrarian violence as legitimate protest against an economic squeeze, albeit a protest that threatened to subvert governmental authority. On deciding that there was no method of controlling rural disorder, and no prospect of instantly compelling landlords to react more favourably, the imperative of control demanded a perspective of conspiracy. All members of the cabinet were dubious about such a strategy. The prosecution of Members of Parliament, even Irish Members of Parliament, was an odd course to take. Quite what a successful prosecution would or could result in was difficult to see.

Why such a course of action would result in a cessation of violence, even Forster could not suggest, though he had some vague notion that Parnell would order a halt to all action to 'try for a favourable trial result'. Presumably this shock to the nationalist system would prepare the way for a calm reception of ameliorative measures. But the decision had less to do with the needs of the situation in Ireland than it had to do with demonstrating to other English politicians, to the English public and lastly to the landlord class in Ireland, that 'something would be done'.

The idea of conspiracy was a complex one. Clearly the directive, the strategy and the dynamic of the Land League was central. But the central organisation had merely been grafted on to an existing local protest. What the prosecution needed to demonstrate was that crime and violence were directly linked to Land League organisation, i.e. the setting up of a Land League branch in an area. If the statistics of crime could be produced to demonstrate such a connection then the case was, in the government's eyes, if not in the eyes of the Dublin jurors, proven. For if this were the case then clearly the situation was not one in which the normal Liberal rules could apply. Joseph Lee has spoken of an 'agitation calendar',[20] the timing at which violence manifested itself intensively in certain areas. In this so-called 'agitation calendar' Kerry lagged eighteen months behind Mayo, where the worst agitation was located in 1879. North Kerry was more prosperous than Mayo. The squeeze did not hit there at the first subsistence pinch. The fifty per cent fall in butter prices in 1879-80 affected this dairying area, as did the thirty per cent fall in pig numbers consequent on it. Evictions in Kerry rose rapidly. For the first nine months of 1880 it had the highest rate in the country. The Land League was not formed in Kerry until September 1880 and was, as Lee points out, a response to Samuel Hussey's burning of evictees' houses to prevent repossession.[21] Whatever the causal train was, the Liberal government was committed to an idea of orchestrated Land League violence from the date of their decision to prosecute the Land League leaders. It was a commitment to the notion of criminal conspiracy.

The Protection of Persons and Property (Ireland) Act, 1881

The effective failure of the Land League prosecutions was not a surprise. At the cabinets of 30 and 31 December, when the outcome of the trial was known, it was agreed in principle to suspend the habeas corpus.[22] Gladstone undertook to take responsibility for a 'measure of land reform'. Gladstone's preference would have been for a tightening of the laws against the Land League, permitting the fight against the League to proceed under the ordinary law, but he went along with Forster's preference for a more drastic solution.

All sections of the Liberal party had viewed the Land League prosecutions as a gamble, the primary aim of which was to buy time. In advance of the jury decision, however, Gladstone had reached his crucial and revolutionary decision on land. The outcome of the State Trial therefore became redundant in advance. Concession on land was deemed to permit a stringency of coercion –

hence stronger measures than the trial became possible. As Colin Matthew has emphasised, Gladstone's movement towards acceptance of the idea of a new Land Act was not a simple or an easy one.[23] He tried to lean on Bessborough, chairman of the Liberal Commission of enquiry on land tenure not to recommend radically, as his letter of 9 December to Forster reveals.[24] He moved towards the introduction of a radical Land Bill only when he had considered the available alternatives. Then he became utterly committed. Coercion by suspension of the habeas corpus detention without trial of suspects, was a price that he was willing to pay to sell the Land Act to his more reluctant cabinet colleagues.[25] Chamberlain and friends were prepared to accept coercion, only because of the extreme nature of the proposed Land Act.[26] And Forster got what he had demanded. It was a delicate balancing of interests.

Gladstone was 'very desirous to keep if possible on the lines and basis of 1870 Act'.[27] He wrote to the difficult Argyll on 29 November and prepared a memo on 9 December detailing his view of the intent of the 1870 Act. Yet on 3 December he had confided to Forster that

> the three F's in their popular meaning . . . will I fear break the cabinet without reconciling the leaguers.[28]

The terms of the 31 December cabinet decision on land were:

1. to stand on the principle of the Land Act of 1870;
2. to propose measures of self-government.[29]

Forster pushed him a note across the table: 'To what does this conviction pledge us?' Gladstone's scribbled response was:

> We are pledged to take LA [Land Act] for starting point.
> Each man has his own interpretation.[30]

Apart from reading Gavan Duffy's *Young Ireland*, Gladstone had been tentatively in touch with Captain William O'Shea. In formulating his decision on coercion Gladstone drew on historical precedent. To Forster on 4 November he wrote:

> Could you direct a short memo on the tithe agitation of 1831–2 (I think) to be prepared for the cabinet? It would be important to know its relation to crime and the Coercion Act of 1833.[31]

John Morley expressed Gladstone's own private misgivings on the suspension of habeas corpus in a leader in the *Pall Mall Gazette*. Gladstone had written to him on 27 October:

> I have not as yet obtained any sufficient answer to the question I have sometimes put 'how is the suspension of habeas corpus to frustrate a

conspiracy against property and bring about payment of rents'? Even if it became necessary hereafter, which God forbid, for the protection of life and the repression of violence, this, taken alone will not meet the specific form of social disease which is now afflicting Ireland.[32]

Forster's justification for his view was presented in the form of a question and answer memo:

Tenants refuse to pay rent, because they know that they will not be evicted.
Why?
Because the landlord does not take back his land.
Why?
Because no fresh tenant dares to take the farm and no labourer dares to work for him, if he farms for himself.
Why?
Because outrage is feared. Sympathy would not keep back fresh tenants and labourers, nor would it prevent a shopkeeper selling to a man who is boycotted, but fear is powerful.
Why then these outrages?
Because the men who plan and perpetrate them know that they can do so with impunity: no witnesses will give evidence against them; no jury will convict them.
If they knew we could arrest and imprison them they would at once fear us, but not before. Parnell and company will rule the country until we can lock up these outragers who are his policemen.[33]

Forster continued, in a cabinet memo of 15 December:

I believe that the only means that will be effective will be one that these criminals fear, and the only measure which they have reason to fear is the power of discretionary punishment – that is the suspension of the Habeas Corpus Act. It is impossible to overrate the objection both in principle and in administration to such a measure and the difficulty in passing it in both parliament and party, and nothing would justify such a course except the fulfilment of three conditions. 1.That with its present constitutional powers the government is unable to fulfil its first duty of protection to the person. 2. A reasonable belief that no less arbitrary exceptional powers would be effectual; but that this measure would be effectual. Would the employment of a stronger law against the Land League be of use? It would, I think be even more difficult to pass than the suspension because it would be less exceptional, and English and Scottish members would fear that the right of meeting was being invaded. Nor must we forget the, to my mind, most important consideration. It is true that the Land League has stimulated men to commit these outrages, but its principal leaders have not planned or perpetrated them themselves. The actual criminals are old ribbon men and old fenian *mauvais sujets*, and, though they are also generally members and local leaders of the League I do not believe that they are now under the control of Parnell and his parliamentary friends. If we had the habeas corpus suspended at this moment we could not arrest Parnell and Dillon under such suspicion. We should have no excuse for doing so. The excuse for the suspension is the inability to obtain legal evidence by reason of terror or sympathy combined with the moral certainty of guilt . . . I believe that upon the proclamation of the worst districts, say the two counties of Mayo and Galway, a few arrests would at once check outrages; as before some of the worst perpetrators and planners would decamp, and the others would be seized by a most wholesome fear.[34]

A policy of obstruction and delay had been agreed upon by those of the Irish party who were under Parnell's control. On 4 January 1881 the Bessborough Commission reported and recommended fundamental changes in the tenure of land. Parnell had earlier decided that the policy of the League was to keep up the momentum of dissatisfaction with landlordism, while remaining non-specific about measures to be taken. The imminent passage of a coercion bill was not in doubt from the beginning of 1881, and the Parnellite tactic was one of 'wait and see'. The League executive moved funds to Paris in January, in anticipation of direct action against the organisation. At the Paris meeting of the League in February 1881 (the celebrated 'barmaid' meeting which led to the resignation of Tim Healy as Parnell's secretary) it was decided *not* to withdraw the parliamentary party from Westminster after the passing of the Coercion Bill, as had previously been suggested.

Davitt said that the suspension of the habeas corpus could crush the entire movement. Had the Irish party decided to withdraw from Westminster and remove to Ireland after its passage they would have put themselves in the position of local suspects, individuals who could be silenced. Parnell's focus was always the Westminster stage. He saw that action in Ireland alone had significance only as statistical information on the floor of the House. Parliamentary democracy gave the Land League its strength through the forum of parliamentary action. To withdraw permanently to Ireland would be to opt for the status of rebels or conspirators. Moreover, the Bessborough Report held out the possibility of legislative changes on land. Gladstone, with limited assistance from the parliamentary draftsman Thring, in fact drew up the first of fourteen drafts of the Land Bill on 10 and 11 January.

On 11 January, during the debate on the Queen's speech, the Irish Solicitor-General, W. J. Johnson, detailed in the Commons the nature of Land League conspiracy and crime, as a preliminary justification for the need to introduce coercion. T. D. Sullivan asked

whether it was in order to repeat here the speeches which had been made at the prosecution of traversers in the Four Courts at Dublin? Listening to the honourable and learned gentleman he could hardly believe he was sitting in parliament at all. It was merely a repetition of the accusations brought forward by the Attorney-General at the trial, and the case ought not to be tried twice over.[35]

Johnson's speech was derived from the files that had constituted the Crown briefs in Dublin, though a very abbreviated version of that material. He quoted at length from the *Lays of the Land League*:

> No! we shall leave untilled, unsown,
> The lands however fair,
> From which an honest man was thrown,
> Upon the roadside bare.
>
> As if a curse was on the spot
> That fields to choke with weeds.
> These are the things that shall be done,
> So swears our banded host,
>
> In the name of the Father,
> And of the Son,
> And of the Holy Ghost.[36]

The 'briefs on behalf of the Crown' prepared for the Dublin State Trial and signed by William Lane Joynt, dated 16 December 1880, were quoted by Johnson in the House while having previously constituted the Crown case in Dublin. In evoking the language of Land League meetings the police reports that constituted the brief alarmed even Gladstone.

Parnell in his speech of 7 January in the Commons insisted that the Land League was a legitimate, legal and open organisation; that attempts to associate the League with criminal activity were suspect. He admitted that there had been some 'unfortunate language' used, but insisted that the League had attempted to check violence. Also he took issue with government statistics on agrarian crime, claiming that if Forster wished to extend his propensity for comparison with the dim and distant past, he might recognise that in relative terms the state of Ireland had often been worse. He claimed that there was a conspiracy in the British press to exaggerate the extent of Irish rural crime, and that this desire to exaggerate sprang from a fear for the long-term interests of the landed class. He went so far as to defend what he described as the unwritten alternative law of the people, claiming that their

> combination to achieve their desired goals of reduced rents and security
> of tenure was perfectly legitimate and in no way contrary to the law of
> the land . . .

and further added that the nature of the difficulties of the Dublin Castle administration lay in their lack of understanding or sympathy with the people.[37] The first part of Parnell's accusation was at best disingenuous; lack of knowledge on the ground was scarcely a Castle fault. Parnell's speeches, those of T. P. O'Connor and other members of the Home Rule party all represent the permanent officials as invidious, and the Liberal leadership as misguided and ignorant.

Extreme language did not originate in the mouths of local 'hooters' and 'groaners'. It emanated principally from paid League officials, but found its most parodic apotheoses in the mouths of rural characters like 'Scrab' Nally, upon whom William Lane Joynt had been particularly eager to concentrate. The substance of the indictment of the Parnellites in the trial and in the House of Commons was not, however, confined to their language (though in the incitement charges language was relevant to the concept of conspiracy), but to allegations of direct control of violence. Though such allegations were put forward by a Liberal government, this was difficult and embarrassing for prominent Liberal politicians who, however much they disliked the Parnellites, did not believe that they actively controlled violence or indeed had the capacity to contain it, if they did.

Parnell's frequent disappearances during January and February did not enhance the esteem in which he was held in the Commons; and the oppressive increase in obstruction did little to improve the Nationalists' popularity. It is clear from the diary of Florence Arnold-Forster that most of London society viewed the Irish members with complete derision: though it is perhaps more surprising to recognise how fully Chamberlain shared that sentiment. Her line that she 'liked the Irish' as a result of her Dublin experiences was greeted by him with unadorned amazement. When, however, the contents of the detailed Land League trial reports are read it seems clear that the image of Ireland available in the London press was not pleasant.[38]

There was detailed description at the trial of the chief Land League meeting in the Phoenix Park when Davitt's charter was first revealed.[39] There were litanies of meetings and reports of what was said; at Beaufort in the parish of Touagh on 16 May, at Ballyglass in Mayo on 13 June, on the same date a meeting in Killasser, in Ballinlough on 27 June, at Ballinamore in Leitrim on 29 June, at Rainsboro near Knocnarea on 4 July, at Finea on the borders of Cavan, Meath, Westmeath and Longford on Corpus Christi Thursday. Every meeting was to initiate a Land League branch. Through such reports in London Ireland was represented as a hot-bed of sedition.[40]

Parnell insisted that the Land League was legal and orderly; but popularly in London it was seen to be the direct source of the 'appalling crime statistics'. He protested that at least half of the statistics of 'offences' were composed of threatening letters which, he claimed, occurred in all societies at certain times.[41] In preparing the Crown trial brief Joynt had been scrupulous in ascertaining details of language and style. A memo on the meeting at Ballyglass was annotated by the lawyers in the following way:

> Produce and identify placard. Print it. Prove it was widely posted. Ascertain and submit to the Attorney-General short account of these men. Prove circumstances (marching, scarfs, imitation pikes, banners, 'down with tyrants etc.') and was conducted – (Cries, exclamations etc. and observations).[42]

To both Gladstone and Forster the association of Land League meetings with outrages was dubious. They took a more complex view of the nature and origins of disorder in private correspondence.[43] Forster had, however, believed for some time that only the capacity arbitrarily to detain suspects could root out the prevailing atmosphere of defiance and disorder. Even if Parnell and his friends did not direct and condone the actions taken at local level to resist landlord sanction or exclude individuals who failed to participate, they were in the eyes of both Gladstone and Forster at least morally responsible. The failure of the Crown prosecutions in Dublin ensured that the traversers' 'moral role' in fostering conspiracy could not legally be made to stick; therefore the only remaining government expedient was the one remaining remedy of control – the suspension of habeas corpus and the detention of suspect individuals. Publicly, the government spoke in the language of controlled conspiracy, of the necessity of rooting out a *limited* number of troublemakers. Privately, it was governmentally believed that there was general public sympathy for those who resisted landlordism. The hope was that by making an example of a few individuals the rot could be halted.

In the Crown brief used by the Solicitor-General, Johnson, in the House of Commons, certain passages emphasised that there were different classes of tenant farmers involved in the agitation. Quotations illustrating the fact that many paid League organisers exhorted their audiences to pay those 'who kept you from starving', that is to say the local shopkeepers, before paying the landlord a 'fair rent', were noted and commented upon. In general, however, for policy purposes tenants were viewed as a solid monolithic block devoid of internal differentiation.

This is yet another example of an unconscious collusion between government and Nationalist representations. The fear of losing even further control panicked the Castle administration into a refusal to differentiate. The interests of the Land League demanded, particularly for American consumption, an image of an undifferentiated near-starving tenantry. Thus the economically squeezed farmer of the west and south-west became the prototype of the 'Irish tenant'. There was a self-consciousness in the representation of all of Ireland in terms of the condition of the western margin, but it was a politically potent absorption.

Davitt, locked in the bitter romance of his own history imaginatively remained wedded to the image of a family on the roadside near Straide thirty years before.[44] Rendered potent by exile, this emigrant rage and nostalgia is reflected in his political pronouncements. Many of the paid organisers of the League were Irish-American and this compounded the League's powerful imagery of desolation. There was a great ambiguity in the language and imagery of the League. 'Paudeen O'Rafferty on the Landlords' Ten Commandments'[45] is a puzzling manifesto. Dedicated to 'Exterminators and Rack-renters, as also to the people who work', it purports to be the creed of 'the Right Hon. Lord

Clan Rack-rent, Earl of Idleness, and Viscount Absentee'. It writes about social conditions more common to Maria Edgeworth's *Castle Rackrent* than to the 1880s. As a text, however, it is about deference rather than hunger.

> 1st. I am the Landlord, thy Master, who paternally condescends to take charge of thy earnings in the shape of rent.
> 2nd. Thou shalt have no other Master but me, and no other use for thy money than to be duly paid and delivered in my Rent Office upon every gale day, in order that I may live in a state befitting my rank, and be sumptuously fed and delicately cared for, without stooping to the ignominy of Labour or feeling the hardships of want.

The idea of parodying the Ten Commandments, the evocation of Paine's *Rights of Man*, the emphasis on gaming ('thou shalt not kill any rabbit, hare, fox or bird that may visit thy farms') is closer to a tradition of English radicalism, of 'Captain Swing' than to any earlier language of Irish rural protest.

> 3rd. Thou shalt not speak disrespectfully or with covered head to thy Master, his Agent, Bailiff, footman or dogman, or murmur or complain against the holy doctrine – 'Obey thy Masters'.

The ten commandments of Lord Clan Rack-rent are answered by 'Paudeen O'Rafferty's Opinions upon the Foregoing Creed':

> God, the Creator of this Universe as well as the Land of Ireland, is my only Landlord in Justice, for it was He who made all creatures and all things, whereon they should live, and stipulated the rent to be paid when He declared that mankind should earn its bread by the sweat of the brow.

This neo-biblical language lies uneasily beside an ostensible anti-clericalism that never subsequently surfaces:

> Religion is expected to preach doctrines to people which make slavery and poverty the chief ends of life, and cowardice and submission to every wrong a passport to everlasting happiness.

In this disjunctive language of Paudeen O'Rafferty, a stage-Irish self-representation of Boucicault farce,[46] this endearingly entitled gentleman is finally revealed to live at an address that would be found far-fetched even by *Punch*: Krucknaspulugndthawn, in the county of Mayo. The Clan Rack-rent/O'Rafferty address was specific in intent. It was designed to appeal to the tradesmen and workers of the city of Dublin, but it is revealing of the curious blend of elements that contributed to the Land League public voice.

Local studies have revealed that League organisation at a local level was frequently initiated and controlled by townsmen.[47] Habeas corpus was suspended in March 1881 under the Protection of Person and Property

(Ireland) Act. The list of those detained under its provisions generally confirms this view, and fails to reveal their occupations. Suspects detained are listed in terms of names, counties, districts, dates of arrest and release, and crimes of which suspected.[48] The Act operated from March 1881 to September 1882. The final debate on introducing the Act took place in the House of Commons on 25 February 1881. On 28 February Forster returned to Dublin. On 2 March Harcourt pushed the ancillary Arms Bill through the House of Commons. On that day Florence Arnold-Forster wrote in her diary: 'The actual work of looking into evidence and preparing warrants begins, I believe, tomorrow.'[49] On 4 March she noted that

> the work of enquiring into cases for arrest has been going on all day, Lord C[owper] present but taking little part . . . partly on account of his deafness. The more the organisation and personnel of the Land League is examined, the more (according to Oakel) does the connection with Fenian and Ribbon Societies become apparent. In most cases the prominent Land League man is, or has been, prominent in other ways.[50]

An examination of the extensive correspondence surrounding the proposed arrests of a number of 'suspect persons', though not exhaustive, seems to confirm the thesis of Paul Bew and others on the social backgrounds of the active individuals.[51] It also seems to confirm the opinion of the fairly fanatical 'Oakel', Hugh Oakley Arnold-Forster.[52] On the other hand, since Oakel's opinion is almost a self-referential proposition, in view of his zealous commitment to his adopted father's opinion on all matters political, it is dangerous to set too much store by it.

Dublin Castle arrested those whom they believed to be involved. They believed that those who had formerly been prominent local Fenians and 'known activists', in the perennial euphemism of the Castle, were involved. One can therefore make certain comment about those that they detained. Whether those detained were those 'responsible' or not is debatable. Certainly those names most prominent in the local press and reported meetings were detained.[53] But again this no more than squares the circle as to whether they were in fact the persons responsible for 'criminal activity'. They were prominent and therefore arrested. Some, however, of those arrested do not appear to come into categories of Castle-deemed 'known activists' or Nationalist-press-highlighted Land League organisers.

The discussions, or written debates, outlined in the individual files of persons eventually detained and those whose detention was considered and then rejected, are more revealing.[54] The crimes of which detainees were suspected included: intimidation against rent, shooting and wounding, attempted murder, boycotting, firing into a dwelling, arson, malicious wounding, attacking dwellings, sending threatening notices, unlawful assembly, riot, treasonable practices, incitement to murder, murder, preventing the payment of rent, maiming cattle, assaulting and beating.[55] Most of the 995 persons detained under the Act in the period of eighteen months during which it operated were detained for 'intimidation against rent'.

Prominent parliamentarians were detained just like local activists. John Dillon was detained twice for alleged incitement to riot and assault and for preventing the payment of rent. Charles Stewart Parnell was held on suspicion of incitement of persons not to pay rent. He was held after the passage of the Land Act, from 13 October 1881 to 2 May 1882, when his release became contingent upon the so-called Kilmainham treaty. William O'Brien entered the lists under the heading of treasonable practices, and spent from 15 October 1881 to 15 April 1882, in Kilmainham where he drafted the 'No rent' manifesto. Thomas Sexton was detained for treasonable practices from 14 October 1881 to 23 April 1882. James O'Kelly MP was detained from 15 October 1881 to 2 May 1882 for suspected treasonable practices. Michael Boyton was one of the first to be detained on 8 March 1881 and he was held on suspicion of incitement to murder until 30 November 1881.[56]

The most startling aspect of the first month of the operation of the Act is the very low number of individuals detained; one on 7 March, five on 8 March, thirteen on 9 March, five on 10 March, nine during the rest of the month. From the files of those first considered it seems clear that many of those 'wanted' by the Castle quickly fled, chiefly to the United States.

That an Act acquired by such gnashing of Liberal principles should appear to accomplish so little in terms of individuals detained immediately after its passage seems strange. Strange, unless it is appreciated that its primary function was to act as a deterrent on future offenders, and to ensure 'control' in certain disturbed areas by a process of curfew and specific powers to search and break meetings. It was further intended to reassure nervous Liberals and the landlord interest, and so to pave the way for land reform. Membership of the Land League did not initially constitute a ground for detention as such, though the suppression of the Land League in October 1881 in response to its ambivalent attitude to the Land Act accelerated the pace of detentions.

The files of suspects highlight the nature of communication between Dublin Castle, the Royal Irish Constabulary both locally and nationally and the local Resident Magistrates, and illuminate that confused hinterland of 'reality on the ground' that has meaning in policy terms only as lists of names and statistics. It appears to underline Charles Townshend's point that government imposition neither conceded quickly enough on reform nor suppressed hard enough.[57] But while Townshend sees the relationship between government and people as one of imposition and resistance, it seems truer to suggest that the dialectic is a more complex game between government and Nationalist leaders, with respective grounds being contested – the hearts and minds of the population of Ireland, but also political opinion in Britain. Few specific concessions are demanded explicitly by Nationalist leaders in these years. Their aim is the exploitation of uncertain ground into which the administration blunders consecutively with repression and attempts at what is deemed to be required . . . 'a solution'. A dynamic and generative process, in which the interests of parties are transformed as a consequence of minute actions from day to day, becomes fossilised by the structure of administration into a static problem and solution. This is the language of the so-called 'Irish problem'. Replicated in the historiography of the period are the errors of the government's solidified construction of a single problem.[58] Even more distorting, however, is a depoliticised analysis of rural change that exaggerates the autogenerated internal dynamics of Irish society in this period and misses or ignores the dynamic connection between government policy and local action; that shirks from attempting to analyse consequent changes of mentalities merely because they can neither be counted nor proven.[59]

Certainly in these political terms the suspension of the habeas corpus, though dangerous and potentially lethal to the League, was its finest hour. Followed by suppression of the League itself in October this facilitated Nationalist leaders in crossing an easy bridge from the clear politics of land to the more sophisticated Home Rule rhetoric of the National League. The gains of 1879 to 1882 to the Home Rule cause were not primarily those of the Land Act. The true gains can be read in the language and rhetoric of William O'Brien's *United Ireland*. *United Ireland* constructed a unified Nationalist voice out of the images and exclusions, the hootings and groanings, hissings and booings and heckling of the former on-circuit performers.

Detaining fewer than a thousand men for under a year in conditions of remarkable comfort is scarcely brutality at its most obscene. However, in terms of public representations of the plank bed and the 'broken defenders of the people' no act more calculated to harden anti-government sentiment could have been imagined.

In August 1882 posters emblazoned in South Kerry played on the theme of the oppressed leaders:

> Traitors in the Camp. A year has now passed since you pledged yourselves. Have you adhered? Have there been among you base, sordid traitors, who have betrayed your interests by breaking that pledge? Men of south Kerry. Banish the land sharks from the society of honest men! Leave their corn uncut, their potatoes undug and themselves to wither under the people's curse.
>
> Their names, their human names,
> Shall hang on high,
> Exalted mid their less-abhorred compeers,
> To fester through the infamy of years.[60]

So while the government acquired the reputation for summary unwarranted harshness through what was publicly perceived to be relentless disregard for human suffering, the law officers at the Castle indulged in the perusal of the usual flow of information from every area of the country. The extent and detail of their reports on individual cases cannot be reproduced. Some impression of how the process worked, how decisions were arrived at, and the factors deemed relevant for detention can, however, be seen. In anticipation of the passage of the Act the Inspector-General of the RIC wrote to all County Inspectors requesting them to consult with the Resident Magistrates before making their recommendations on the state of an area. They had no direct control over the input of the Resident Magistrates into such decisions.[61] The RMs were separately instructed to give their impression on the state of the country to the Resident Magistrate's office in Dublin Castle. In certain areas the request for information had come from Hillier at the head of the RIC before 25 February 1881. Apart from details on whether or not it was the opinion of the local police that an area should be proscribed or placed under curfew officially, the main requests of the Castle were for the names, ages, occupations and general character of the individuals who it would be advisable to detain. Special forms were printed for the purpose of providing the necessary details.[62]

> The list on the form enclosed which reached you on 16th inst is to be filled up and sent so as to arrive at this office without fail on the morning of Wednesday 23rd inst. The inner envelope is to Colonel Hillier personally. Should it be necessary to consult your County Inspector before sending it you are to proceed at once to County HQ.[63]

The city of Cork is of some interest in revealing the types of urban individuals detained. The selection made by the Sub-Inspector of Cork city did in fact go through the County Inspector's office. The list recommended the detention of six suspects: John O'Connor, age 34, travelling agent, nationalist, and secretary of the Cork branch of the Land League, who was detained from 4 July 1881 to 20 May 1882 on suspicion of treasonable practices; C. P. O'Connor, age 40, described as a 'noted fenian' who was said by the police to be 'proposing to organise secret societies in case the Land League was crushed by government', detained from 28 October 1881 to 30 April 1882 on suspicion of preventing payment of rent; James Reynolds, a noted fenian and shop assistant who was not finally detained; Patrick O'Neill, a paid organiser for the League who was also not detained despite being described as a 'suspected intimate of Hare of Queenstown', a man apparently lost to history; John B. Heffernan, no further details given, detained from 12 May to 26 August 1881; and Patrick J. Murphy, detained from 6 July 1881 to 25 January 1882.[64]

From Galway RM, Ballinasloe, it was suggested in an official minute marked *Secret* that the area should be proscribed:

> I beg to record that my district be proscribed should the above become law. I have consulted the sub-Inspector and the Resident Magistrate, and

they both agree with me that the general state of feeling and *tone* of the community, as so far frequently exhibited, coupled with several outrages quite justify me, I believe, in this recourse. Also, over the bounds of the district on every side a more urgent feeling prevails – which of course may at any moment extend and equally embrace the locality.[65]

The Report advised the arrest of only one individual, Matthew Harris:

stationer, contractor for buildings on a small scale, at present the paid agent of the Land League. *NB* Harris has always been a dangerously clever man. Scarcely any doubt of him being connected with the general conspiracy. I believe his conspiracy still continues with that treasonable body. I consider any others too insignificant.[66]

Harris has been discussed in considerable detail by Lee, Bew and in every popular account of the origins of the Land League in the west, most recently by Donald Jordan. He was one of the earliest suspects to be detained, on 16 April 1881. The 'official crime of which suspected' was listed as 'inciting to assault', and he was held on that count until 3 February 1882.[67]

The more individual cases are examined, the more it seems apparent that the specific 'crime of which suspected' was often an arbitrary category; and that the individuals detained were in the main formerly known activists, a euphemism for Fenians, or those who had come to prominence through the Land League, and were deemed to be potentially powerful in the community.[68] A smattering of individuals genuinely suspected of serious crimes were cast in with this collection.[69] Essentially, the criteria of selection seem to have been influence and ability.

In 1881 moonlighting, a phenomenon later primarily confined to the south-west, particularly Clare, Kerry and the Millstreet area of Cork, had no substantial existence. As a widespread phenomenon it was not evident until after the foundation of the National League in 1882, though that organisation appears to have had little direct power in controlling it. Incidents like Maamtrasna in 1884 lend an air of general night-time brutality to *all* of the country, but in the context of the west, Maamtrasna was an isolated incident.

In 1881 intimidation against rent, boycotting and treasonable practices were the predominant categories used for detaining individuals. Such specifications as murder, shooting and wounding, and assaulting dwelling houses appear from the lists to be confined to the south-west, insofar as they existed at all at this time. Harris was ostensibly held on suspicion of a crime of 'inciting to assault', while Timothy Harrington in Tralee was held for almost a year from 3 June 1881 on ostensible suspicion of incitement to riot.

An examination of the case of an individual who was *not* detained, despite suspicion, gives some insight into the basis of decision. Reporting on F. S. Cleary of Ennis in County Clare, on 27 February 1881 the County Inspector wrote to Hillier:

Submitted in compliance with the Inspector-General's minute of 25 February in conjunction with Mr Carroll the sub-Inspector – I have conferred with Captain McTernan RM. I beg to annex a statement from the Sub-Inspector and also to state that though F. S. Cleary is secretary to, and took a very prominent part in the Land League movement, yet from enquiries I have been able to make I learn that he was the means of preventing in great measure 'boycotting' and other terrorism in the town of Ennis. At the present time he has not that great power with the people, and what influence he had is very much lessened. I consider that it would be more politic to stay any proclamation against him for the present, as at any time should it be considered judicious to do so, he can be arrested. But his arrest just now would have the effect of making of him a martyr and when he should be released after some months from gaol he would regain his old influence. Whereas, if he is treated as beneath notice, he is more likely to be forgotten in a short time . . . This power will hold good in 10 days or a month hence . . . much better effect on the population if at present the arrests were few. It is no doubt a great thing to have a strong coercive measure ready for any event, but it 'requires' a great exercise of judgement to exercise the power for the public good.[70]

This report by Smith, the County Inspector, was based on the fuller report of the Sub-Inspector, Carroll, who claimed to have 'minutely watched Cleary's acts and speeches for some time'. He claimed to have

observed him systematically to deprecate violence and intimidation . . . through his influence proposals to boycott traders in this town some time ago were not carried out . . . Though he has given certificates to certain people who sent to him for such that they could sell their produce without the censure of the Land League, I can ascertain no instance that he prevented anyone from either buying or selling to others on account of their not belonging to the Land League or violating its rules etc. I cannot trace to him or his influence any violence or intimidation nor do I see that he can be held responsible for such practice elsewhere by members of branches of the Land League throughout the county, though founded through his instrumentality. Were he liable to be arrested for his conduct, every secretary of a branch of the Land League in Clare would be equally so.[71]

Carroll had, however, failed to confer with the Resident Magistrate, McTernan, and received a firm rebuke from Anderson of the Chief Secretary's office reminding them that the instructions to confer with the RM were very explicit.[72] McTernan's views were succinct on the decision to put forward nobody for detention from the town of Ennis: 'I say he should have put forward the name of Mr Cleary of the *Clare Independent*'.

In the Galway East Riding, the numbers proposed for detention were higher. In the district of Loughrea Sub-Inspector Barry advised the detention of Martin O'Halloran of Clogherivaun, Kiltullagh, a 'dangerous and ill-disposed man'[73] and president of the Kilfalla branch of the Land League. The main ground of complaint against him was that he had held several secret meetings and a land court in his house, behind closed doors. He had also acted as an organiser of Lord Dunsandle's labourers. He was detained on 8 March, and so was one of the first six men to be detained under the Act. He was held until 19 April 1882 under suspicion of preventing payment of rent. Portumna, also in the East Riding, sent forward the name of no suspect, but advised that the district itself be proscribed under the Act.[74] Moylough proposed no names, nor did the Sub-Inspector demand proclamation of the district.[75]

In Athenry, Alan Bell, the RIC adviser, recommended that the district be proscribed and that Thomas Griffin of Gurteen be detained. Griffin was secretary of the Gurteen branch of the League and was stated to summon people before Land League commissions on charges of paying more than Griffith's valuation. As a consequence, no rent was paid. He had the further dubious glory of being a close friend of Matt Harris. Despite Bell's recommendation, Griffin's detention was temporarily rejected by the Castle, though he went on to a secondary list of those who were taken in the autumn when resistance to the Land Bill was at its height. He was then detained from 11 November 1881 to 12 April 1882, on suspicion of intimidation against rent.[76]

In Clifden the inability of either the County Inspector or the Resident Magistrate ensured that nine individuals, including three priests, who Forster was most reluctant to touch except through Errington in the Vatican,[77] were not detained, despite local knowledge of them as 'active': Rev. Rhattigan; Thomas Glougherty; Hubert Finneran; Robert Campbell, a dealer in game from Clifden; Cummis Coury, a stonemason; the Rev. Healy from Boffin Island; Rev. Flannery from Errismore; William O'Keefe, a shop assistant; Michael Logue from Cloone, a farmer.[78]

Woodford was proscribed, and John Kelly, the known organiser of a boycott against a blacksmith John Mara and John Mulloy, both of Ballygowan, were held from 8 July 1881 to 1 December 1881 for suspected boycotting.[79]

In the area of Galway town and rural, in the district of Dunmore, a number of individuals were recommended for detention with the agreement of the Resident Magistrate, Hill. The most prominent of these was Joseph Dalton from Milltown, in the district of Dunmore who, according to the confidential police report, was strongly suspected of the murder of James McDonagh of Dunmore and Milltown, and also of personally carrying out an attack on the police protection hut in Milltown. He was also alleged to have arranged the boycott of the Milltown constabulary. There 'can be no positive proof' the report states, but there was further information:

> He has always kept close and confidential company with the principal members of illegal societies, not only in Milltown and Dunmore, but

also in Claremorris, Ballindine and Tuam . . . personal motives in the assassination of McDonagh. Dalton is a very clever man.[80]

Dalton too was in the handful of those first detained. He was arrested on 8 March, though released on 16 July, under the officially listed suspicion of assaulting a police hut. Thady Ryan, stonemason and road contractor from Milltown, was also recommended for detention, and may be the Michael Ryan listed as being from the district of Dunmore on the detention lists, and held from 18 June to 2 October for 'sending threatening notices'.[81]

Michael Hawthorne from Williamstown, a 'stonecutter and a fenian who has maintained his influence with the people' was not detained despite being suspected of sending threatening letters to the parish priest; nor was Lawrence Kearns from Glenamaddy, 'a stonemason and a fenian'.[82] In the district of Gort nobody was recommended for detention, nor was the district proclaimed.[83] In the district of Headford a considerable number of recommendations were made. The most prominent was Patrick Furey of Bunatober, a farmer, miller and shopkeeper, 'a turbulent, disloyal man and an active member of the Land League' who was detained for incitement to riot on 9 March, though he was released in July.[84] In Galway West Riding nine men were recommended for detention by the Resident Magistrate, Blake. Only one of them, Patrick Kearney, was detained on 9 March, for 'inciting to arson'.[85]

Every individual file examined reveals that there was a scrupulous legal procedure for assessing prominence and culpability. Yet by definition the suspension of the habeas corpus pushed the administration in the direction of less scruple. As Cowper put it, they prevailed upon themselves to be less scrupulous.

Gladstone had agreed to the suspension of the habeas corpus with reluctance. He demonstrated his willingness to accept the Irish parliamentary party analysis of rural disorder by his acceptance of the recommendations of Bessborough. He made it apparent that he did not believe the Land League to be a criminal conspiracy, and acquiesced in an analysis that insisted that most, if not all, of the population were sympathetic to agitation. Whether his analysis was correct or incorrect is irrelevant. In introducing the suspension of habeas corpus, in defiance of his own analysis, he acted from a desire to carry his party on the Land Act.

Despite the complexity of his position, and the initial ambiguity and unease of Forster in administering a policy of arbitrary detention for which he had pressed, the image of the government *popularly* available in Ireland was that epitomised in the person of the hated 'Buckshot' Forster. Thus, though policy was formulated by an admixture of cabinet perusal of statistics and maps, allied to the emotional pendulum of Forster's increasingly erratic impressionism, it publicly had the face of absolute authority. The combination of this perceived repression with concession on land provided Land League organisers with a permanent momentum in their exploitation of 'government brutality'. So too the panic of government increased.

From Detention to Politics

> We are hampered in our action by an express agreement that we will not arrest any man unless we can say on our honour that we believe him to have actually committed or incited to outrage. This at first prevented us from attacking the leaders as vigorously as we might have done, but latterly some of them have been less cautious, and we have also prevailed upon ourselves to give a wider interpretation to our powers. For my part I should be inclined to interpret them very widely. It is hardly too much to say that in the present state of the country everybody who takes a part in the Land League, does, by the very fact of doing so, incite to outrage . . . The state of the country is very bad, after making every allowance for the exaggerations of the Press. Indeed these exaggerations are a proof of the uneasiness of public feeling. One of the worst points is the uneasiness that prevails in the south and west against the military and police. Worse still are the vast mobs that can be collected at a moment's notice. In the autumn individual assassination was the great danger. Now in addition to this is the danger of a sudden overwhelming, by sheer weight of numbers, of small bodies of police or military. One such catastrophe would be an incalculable evil. Besides the disgrace of the authorities it would lead to after attempts of the same kind, and might actually be the beginning of a small civil war, which could not be concluded without such an amount of bloodshed as would cause renewed bitterness against England for more than one generation.[86]

This was the analysis of 1881 advanced by the Lord-Lieutenant. Cowper has been painted as an alarmist and a coercionist in the Morley-edited myth. So too has Forster. But the more closely one examines the registered papers, the Irish crime returns, the lists of individuals detained, the correspondence of Forster and Gladstone, and the debates of the House of Commons in conjunction with one another, the more evident it becomes that the state of agreed crisis delineated by Cowper in the early months of 1881, intensifying through the autumn, was the reality accepted by all parties.

From the diary of Florence Arnold-Forster we see the situation as it appeared to a close observer and confidante of the Chief Secretary in Dublin. Throughout, Florence's perception is sympathetic and justificatory of her father's policy. Despite her bias, or perhaps because of it, the *Journal* is valuable as a source. Though intelligent, analytical and perceptive she feels so completely for her adoptive father that clearly, as perceiver of the 'Irish situation', she merely acts as a cipher for his views. Walking through the Phoenix Park with him in the mornings to Dublin Castle was her greatest pleasure. In London she walked with him from the family home to the Irish Office in Queen Street, or to the House if he was to face a barracking from the Irish members. Sitting in Mrs Brand's gallery of the House of Commons with the other Liberal ladies through every major debate of the year gave her a stark sense of the discrepancy between the 'sham debates on sham issues', that contrasted so severely with her beloved father's job of 'governing' Ireland. She was friendly with Thomas Burke and his sister Marianne; with her brother 'Oakel', who identified even more than she did with Forster, she talked politics. She knew Jephson,[87] Burke's Private Secretary, before becoming secretary to the Chief Secretary, and Horace West,[88] who was Forster's assistant private secretary. Her favourite Irish magistrate was Clifford Lloyd,[89] whom she saw as genuine and committed to the same cause as her father, the 'good of Ireland'. She met everybody who was anybody in both London and Dublin. In Dublin she moved from the National Gallery to the Hibernian Chapel, to St Ann's in Dawson Street with equal ease. She dined with O'Hagan, Law and Johnson. Her friend Charlotte O'Brien, daughter of William Smith O'Brien and *bête noire* of all Irish administrations, considered joining the Ladies' Land League in 1881. She was contemptuous of Cowper's perpetual closeting with moaning landlords, and amazed at the intricacies of Irish landlord life which resulted in a situation whereby her friends the Kenmares lived in terror of crossing their agent Samuel Hussey.[90] But what most clearly emerges from her diaries is the profound sense of Christian responsibility which weighed Forster down as he bore his dreaded burden: solving Ireland. She concurs in this view, yet is always amazed by the perceptions of her London friends:

> . . . with anyone to whom I speak it is the same story. As for the way people speak of Ireland and our experiences in Dublin during the past three weeks, one would think that we had been living in a barbarous country infested with brigands and assassins and on the verge of civil war . . . I can quite believe that if we had gathered all our impressions of the state of things from the London papers instead of from the facts in Ireland we should have been.[91]

Despite her intelligence, it does not seem to occur to Florence that if there is a great discrepancy between the 'facts in Ireland', and the 'story about Ireland' available in London that a part of this act of mistranslation might be contingent upon the nature of the information supplied by her father as Chief Secretary to London. Also that the 'facts' were not materially different in each case. It was merely that the list of outrages, tales of independent atrocities, reports of Land League horrors and crimes were something quite different to her when she lived in Ireland. For in Ireland there was a daily life that she lived that was peaceful, there was a social round, a circle of rural jaunts and a network of friends. Though many of them spoke of their disasters, this was superimposed on a pattern of stable life. However, in London there was no stable Ireland, merely this distillation of crime statistics and horrors, an impacting of statistics, people and events; a stationary, intractable 'Ireland'.

And Forster's letters to Gladstone and statements in the House fed this vision, because his only means of communicating the necessities of 'government of Ireland' was by appealing to the horrors. The Land Bill, introduced in April, was the central plinth around which Liberal strategy was concentrated.[92] Coercion had been 'sold' to the waverers on its account. Strangely, by the time of its introduction few Irish landlords seemed to be emphatically opposed to it, much to the disgust of the Tories.

As Florence notes, and as historians have suggested, the Whiggish element in the Liberal Party found it more than difficult to swallow. While the view of the 'defection of the Whigs' as a body in 1886 has now been largely revised,[93] it seems clear from contemporary sources that the Duke of Argyll was merely the tip of an iceberg of incipient discontent. There were few defections in 1881 but Cowper, Selborne and Hartington were not easily reassured. Spencer did not like the Act any better than they did, but clearly his sense of duty and devotion to Gladstone took precedence over his personal unease as a landlord suffering under the depression.

In London then, the tales of Ireland grew worse and worse, as did the behaviour of the Parnellites in parliament. In official announcements it was emphasised that the detentions, proclamations and curfews were not to *punish* malefactors, but to remove them from the community and so create a climate of defeat. The most sanguine landlords realised that compromise was essential, and refused to listen to the Tory line which was that concession was merely encouraging the growth of Irish nationalism, a cloaking mechanism for unannounced theft. As Lord Monteagle said to Florence it was clear

> that 'the levelling process' had begun in serious earnest, and that the relations between the classes in Ireland will never . . . for good or bad . . . be what they were again.[94]

On 27 May she spent the day 'blotting and turning over' 306 search warrants which her father was obliged to sign under the Arms Act. Though the overall intention of policy was to maintain a level of 'law and order' pending the trial and working of the Land Act, it seems quite clear that the daily pursuit of the former acted against the interests of the latter. Forster lived in a state of crisis management, and saw every event in the country as part of a grand design. He increasingly felt that London did not understand the realities of 'life on the ground'. In May, Clifford Lloyd was appointed as a special magistrate to cover the area around Kilmallock in County Limerick. He immediately came to the Castle to explain to Forster, Cowper, Burke, Naish[95] and Anderson[96] that more direct moves should be made to paralyse the local Leagues, the 'hostile powers in occupation' in his language.

Clifford Lloyd was merely one of a succession of old Africa and India hands sent to Ireland in different capacities in these years. All shared one characteristic, a deep inability to recall that Ireland was part of the United Kingdom with representatives in parliament, and not a far-flung colony. Their impatience was acute, their diligence real, and their infectious power considerable. Lloyd, striding around Limerick with recurrent malaria, or 'tropical ague', presents both a menacing and moving picture. Oakel Forster spent months with Lloyd in Limerick and his experiences there fuelled his views in his work on *The Truth about the Land League*.[97] But every anti-democratic slip that such individuals initiated was pounced upon by Nationalist MPs and turned on the Chief Secretary in the Commons. He then found himself hoisted by the earnest moral petard of John Morley's *Pall Mall Gazette*. This infuriated Forster, particularly as he saw a situation in Ireland whereby the 'ordinary law', so frequently invoked against him, simply did not work. The only group sympathetic to his plight were the Tories who demanded an enquiry into jury trials,[98] or rather into their usual failure to convict.

Forster, so absorbed by the situation in which he found himself, so intent in removing the Land League menace, was in the throes of forgetting that he was a Liberal. In many ways he was kept at arm's length by Gladstone. He acted as a conduit for all Nationalist aggression. 'Buckshot Forster' was depicted as a figure of sublime ugliness and crass stupidity and brutality. Joseph Biggar said in the House that Forster's reasons for setting out with Quaker relief missions to assist famine victims in the west of Ireland in 1847 had been to relish the sight of human suffering.[99] There is a pathos in Florence's anxious worries about the popularity of her father. She cheerfully repeats witless accounts by clearly demented landlords who tell her 'Mr Forster will in due course be the most popular man in Ireland'. His one public speech in Tullamore she sees as the beginning of the turning of the tide, the start of the end of Nationalist misrepresentation.[100] She has, for some reason that a Freudian analyst might uncover, a certain muted passion for Mr Dillon, arch-detractor of her father, whom she saw as a twinned lonely and passionate man. Mr Parnell she refuses to look at, indeed she never mentions him, except to say that on his re-entry to the House after Kilmainham he heightened the dramatic impact of her father's speech.[101] One is inclined to suspect that this 'king' of the Land League was too much competition for daddy to be permitted even to intrude on consciousness.

Several isolated events contributed to the success of Morley's campaign to discredit Forster. Despite the insistence of Forster's wife to the contrary it seems clear from a reading of Labouchere's biography,[102] and between the lines of Garvin's *Chamberlain*[103] that Chamberlain was not far removed from the plot.

Gladstone's battle with Parnell and the League was essentially political. He began his exploration in the matrix of rising and falling crimes rates, and the contingent paraphernalia of subsidiary statistics of evictions, reinstatements and disasters. However, from the time of his decision, reluctantly arrived at, to introduce the Land Act, Gladstone realised that in making such a concession he was in fact acknowledging the political validity of the Land League case.[104] Thus while Forster continued to inhabit a mental world of the League as ruffians, Gladstone though perhaps also considering them to *be* ruffians, seemed appraised of the magnitude of the step that he had taken. Gladstone's strength as a politician was partly derived from his ability, after careful, tortuous and exhaustive mulling, to make a decision. Slower colleagues assumed that the nature of the material mulled over determined the nature of the decision. The material perused usually related to the decision arrived at, but really his leaps were intuitive. Having made them he deemed them to be self-evident. In April Florence writes:

> An early call from Mr Seebohm and a slight discussion between him and Father over the new bill. Before leaving the dining room, in answer to some remark of Mr Seebohm about the extreme intricacy and difficulties of the Measure, Father observed that some of these came from the fact that Mr G had so many difficulties in his own mind.[105]

Throughout the correspondence between Gladstone and Forster in 1881, and into early 1882 there is a sense of indulgence on Gladstone's part.[106] He congratulates and supports Forster in the good work that he is doing. After the Land Act's passage in August 1881, however, it is clear that the outcome of the Act alone preoccupies Gladstone. He is disheartened by the initial response of the Land League at their September meeting. As the autumn progresses, however, and the tenants seem to show an independent willingness to go and present their cases to the Land Commission, he feels more optimistic.

Forster, on the other hand, remains oppressed by daily accounts of outrages and horrors, and begins from January 1882 to reiterate that something must be done. His line in effect was 'now that we have made the law just, we are called upon to put down lawlessness with a strong hand'.[107] He saw Gladstone's Leeds speech of October, in which he affirmed that 'the resources of civilization are not exhausted',[108] as an unequivocal statement of support for his own analysis. Yet if one studies Gladstone's speech carefully it is clear that Forster read there only what he wished to see. While Forster and the men in the Upper Castle yard, scrupulously reviewing detention cases at three-monthly intervals, saw themselves as besieged by a murderous and now illegal League, Gladstone was creating a method for dealing with the League's leaders by acceptance!

> Dangerous as that association has brought itself to be, it has many members and perhaps many local branches who have no object but the attainment of lawful and reasonable objects, and whose exertions and the credit of whose name and character others are endeavouring to pervert to purposes neither lawful nor reasonable.[109]

Gladstone was in effect keeping the way open for distinction between 'good' nationalists . . . and 'good' Land Leaguers . . . and bad ones. His agreement to the suppression of the League was not for the reasons articulated by Forster 'the defeat of chronic lawlessness and crime', but because the League was seen to be working in a fashion hostile to the success of his 'solution', the Land Act. Thus, if Forster had attended more closely to what Gladstone said rather than to what he wrote to Gladstone, he would not have found the so-called Kilmainham treaty so great a shock. For the Gladstone-Parnell rapprochement, whether treaty or not, of April 1882 was not an event that arrived like a bolt from the blue.[110] The extent of Forster's later hurt and Gladstone's subsequent unease, manifesting itself in an almost obsessive desire to justify his actions, sprang from a background of crossed communication.

The 'No Rent' manifesto, issued by the Land League on 19 October 1881, was a political move in the League's bargaining game with Gladstone. To have permitted the Land Act to work quietly and effectively would have removed the political centrality of the League. To have closed down on the boon of the Land Act in an unequivocal fashion earlier would have meant repudiating their political gains in acquiring it, while simultaneously alienating those tenant farmers who wished to gain from it. In October they were in a bind, since the tenants were in fact working the Act. Parnell was, at this stage, still directing Irish Nationalist action and, in the leap from the politics of land to the politics of higher political ends at Westminster, the stimulation of oppression by 'Buckshot Forster' was a clear temptation. Forster obliged. Gladstone agreed to Parnell's incarceration because he felt that Parnell might challenge the Act more seriously if left at large. The League then was suppressed, with massive propagandist value for William O'Brien at *United Ireland.* Parnell and Dillon were arrested, thus removing them from a very uneasy corner, and rendering them conveniently oppressed victims of Castle brutality.

The dislocation caused by the Land League suppression was enormous. The lists of those detained under the Protection of Persons and Property Acts swelled massively. When the Land Court provided for under the Land Act opened on 20 October in Merrion Square, presided over by the Commissioners O'Hagan and Vernon, the first day revealed that the weight of business, of tenants applying to have their rent levels arbitrated under the terms of the Act, was to be enormous. At the moment of official opening

> the clerk declared the Court open – by a slip of the tongue he called it the 'Court of the Land League', an announcement received with an outburst of laughter in which the three Commissioners joined heartily.[111]

By 26 October the Dublin court alone had received 1,800 applications, and the Sub-Commissioners appointed to peregrinate the country in groups of three, forbidden to enter into any social intercourse in the course of their ramblings, were clearly already in need of supplementation.

In the House of Commons on 9 February 1882 Forster justified his policy in Ireland over the previous five months.[112] Gladstone appeared to support him. Yet on 23 March, Herbert Gladstone wrote in his diary:

> ... talk with father about coercion. He agrees that our party won't stand the renewal of the present act. He told me what I had never heard, that he had all along been opposed to this kind of coercion by suspension of habeas corpus. He thought the action too big, wide and strong for it [coercion] to be successful. It is good versus secret societies but not against an open, organised, almost national conspiracy like the Land League. He would have altered the law in regard to inciting to break contracts and mischievous speeches and made these offences punishable by summary jurisdiction with severe sentences. I am sure he was right, but he declared that he was almost alone in his view in the cabinet.[113]

In a debate in the House of Commons on 28 March Forster said that the existing coercion act certainly had not succeeded to the extent they had hoped. He then hinted that stronger coercion measures might yet be introduced. His speech was, according to Florence, unprepared:

> ... the only thing clear is that Father is much annoyed, and that he will have to return to another long spell of the useless, irritating, parliamentary badgering, which is so specially trying to him at a time when he is anxious to be spending all his available time and practical energy in practical work in Ireland.[114]

Forster made his invitation clear:

> As Secretary to the Lord-Lieutenant, with a responsibility as much as man can have for the maintenance of law and order in Ireland, my business is to maintain it and to stop outrages, and that is the business of this House also. We cannot look forward to the future. Signs of improvement may be much greater than they are, but it may turn out that in order to maintain law and order, and to stop these murders and outrages which are a disgrace to our country and to humanity, that some stronger measures even yet may have to be passed. And if the House of Commons is convinced of the necessity, it will mind its business and pass them.[115]

Gladstone, according to Herbert, was 'much alarmed at Mr Forster's speech yesterday afternoon – not as positively wrong, but as far wanting in balance as to give a possibly erroneous impression in the wrong direction'. Herbert told his father that as a result of his tour of the country it seemed to him that the 'No Rent' manifesto had failed, and that the crime being then committed was 'more revolutionary in its character'; and that outrages were committed 'to prove the government wrong in coercing'.

Before Captain O'Shea made contact with Gladstone and Chamberlain on Parnell's behalf, Frank Hugh O'Donnell had been in touch with Herbert

Gladstone. They did not in fact meet until 22 April. By this date the O'Shea contact, negotiated by Parnell on leave from Kilmainham *en route* ostensibly to the funeral of his sister's son, had been initiated. O'Donnell was endeavouring to put himself to the fore as usual, but his views on the position of the Irish party tally with those laid before Gladstone. As Herbert Gladstone noted

> he told me that the Land Act was succeeding and if amended in the way of arrears would prove a single success: that the Land League [ostensibly suppressed] wishes to withdraw the No Rent manifesto which was now doing mischief: and that crime now due to ribbonism was shocking to Parnell, and they were afraid that unless the natural leaders of the people were released that the whole country would get out of hand.[116]

O'Donnell claimed that Sexton, Healy and company were no longer irreconcilable. Their main fear was of the potential consequences of the labourers being mobilised by old secret societies. According to Herbert Gladstone, Parnell had acknowledged that the labourers' agitation was growing dangerous and had promised to 'head it'. O'Donnell concurred, and emphasised that the aims of the Nationalist party were not for further agricultural dislocation; that they wished to return to a mainstream politics of Home Rule. O'Donnell apparently 'laid great stress on treating Irish members as Irish representatives – with kindness and courtesy, and thought that a convention of all Irish members would mark a new departure and be hailed with gladness'.

While O'Donnell's plenipotentiary status may be called into question, it is undeniable that the line he pursued with Herbert Gladstone reflects accurately the tenor of Parnellite strategy at the time; a demand that the Irish parliamentary party be recognised as the elected representatives that they irrefutably were, and removed from a language of English political excoriation that tarred them all as murderous ruffians. It is a demand for political negotiation. Chamberlain was informed of O'Donnell's interview, the substance of which he apparently conveyed to O'Shea when he met him later in the day. The interview was indeed without Parnell's authority.[117]

The Phoenix Park murders had a direct but not qualitative impact on Liberal policy. The decision on coercion and arrears had been made before Lord Frederick Cavendish's journey to Ireland, as had the decision to release Parnell and others. They did, however, substantially affect the tone of politics. The murders circumscribed the possibilities of friendly contact. They perhaps increased Parnell's nervousness about his IRB contacts on the fringes of the Invincibles.[118] Under Spencer the Liberals continued coercion, but it was coercion of a different kind. The Crime Prevention Bill of 1882 provided for a special tribunal to try cases that were bound to be dismissed by juries, for the extension of summary jurisdiction and the treatment of incitement to intimidation as intimidation. The Bill was to last for three years.

The structure of the magistracy was centralised and the special branch at Dublin Castle was reorganised under Brackenbury and his successor from August 1882 Jenkinson, 'an excellent Liberal'. That in fact was the nub of the argument. After Spencer's arrival in Dublin in May 1882 Ireland was governed sternly according to Liberal principles. Habeas corpus was no longer suspended, an indication of Liberal refusal to view the whole country as being in the grip of crisis. With the successful passage of the Arrears Act the 'crime statistics' fell rapidly. Spencer's alterations were administrative and practical – improving communication between Resident Magistrates and police, and further developing a structure of divisional magistrates. It was not a style of government found elsewhere in the United Kingdom, but it was 'Liberal'. The National League was permitted to develop openly as a political party. Nationalist MPs continued to excoriate the administration publicly, but recognised that they were deemed to be valid parliamentary opponents in the House of Commons. It was not a recognition that extended so far as to permit Gladstone to speak to Parnell directly, but then it was a change of mind and not of heart.

4 FREEHOLD IN VICTORIAN IRELAND

At this point it may be worth examining the assumptions that lay behind Liberal and Conservative policy on the question of Irish land, from the date of the passing of Gladstone's first Land Act in 1870 to the Conservative Land Purchase Act of 1903. In that light one can consider the wider question of the extent to which policy on land was formulated in response to the 'Irish situation', or in response to the political and ideological constraints within which Liberal and Conservative policy operated. This examination does not seek to provide a comprehensive account of so complex a problem, but to isolate the fundamental issues of principle involved.

The 'revisionism' in Irish historiography which detects the complexity of relations within rural society, the increased prosperity of the years between the famine and the depression of 1879–81, and the varied practices of landlords on individual estates, is committed to the debunking of all myths prevalent in late-Victorian Ireland with the exception of the central Conservative myth of the landlords as a preordained ruined class.[1]

In the Home Rule debates of 1886 and 1893 Conservatives intertwined their objections to Home Rule with fundamental arguments on the rights of property. It was the Land War in Ireland that had brought the issue of Home Rule to the surface. According to *The Times* there were a variety of ways of interpreting Irish agrarian outrage. Earlier in the century the phenomenon of ribbonism could be dismissed as a violence inherently 'politically illiterate'. But the organised union of Home Rulers, Land League and fenian sympathisers in the 'New Departure' and Land War of 1879–81 was clear in intent. Irish separatists were pursuing a policy of re-conquering Ireland for the Celtic race through an agrarian agitation sketched out by Fintan Lalor. According to classic Tory doctrine, Gladstone, by initiating a policy of agrarian 'reform' in his Land Act of 1870, had begun a process which undermined the status of property and, as a corollary, the integrity of the United Kingdom. How this argument developed is of great interest.

Though Ireland was England's first colony, the rhetoric of the Union proclaimed it to be an integral part of the United Kingdom. As such its significance in imperial terms was essentially symbolic. By being absorbed into the United Kingdom it became, in Conservative thought, an imperfectly assimilated backward fringe area within that United Kingdom. According to this analysis, one that is by no means untenable, Ireland was, in Arthur Balfour's articulation of Conservative party doctrine, an 'arbitrarily selected area within the United Kingdom'. Notions of nationality, upon which Irish nationalist rhetoric drew, were mere obfuscatory devices to mask the true nature of agrarian discontent – a desire to undermine property. By refusing to enter into the conceptual framework of their opponents, in marked contrast to some Liberals, Conservatives avoided the pitfalls of applying romantic neo-*geist*-like notions to the concept of the law. Liberal notions of bringing people into sympathy with the law were anathema to the Tories. The English law was a moral absolute, the matrix of civilised society, and the Irish, a notoriously wayward people, would simply learn through firmness to rise to its demands. Property and the law were the fundamental principles which Irish agitation sought to undermine.

Before the Land Act of 1870 Irish land law was not markedly different from English land law. Land was let to tenants by a variety of contractual and non-contractual arrangements – leaseholders, tenants-at-will, year to year tenancies. If it differed at all from the English model it was in the degree to which agrarian living was politically and personally perceived to be characterised by outrage and lack of sympathy between landlord and tenant, and by a lack of industrial alternatives within Ireland. Recent research has undermined most of the formerly cherished assumptions about nineteenth-century Irish agrarian society: it is now argued that tensions between large tenant farmers and their sub-tenants were at least as important as those between landlords and tenants,[2] that rural society was poor and undercapitalised for a variety of social and economic reasons; and that the caricature of the voracious self-serving absentee landlord is merely an artefact of nationalist demonology.[3] While such revisionist interpretations are economically 'correct' and interesting, it seems difficult to discount utterly contemporary accounts of landlord–tenant relations which fail to emphasise that mutuality of interests which social and economic historians so persistently perceive.

In the 1870 Land Act Gladstone perceived the dilemma of demand for tenant right in parliament and bombings in England to be the product of ills which contemporaries highlighted. These he sought to 'remedy' by introducing nationally, by law, the habit of tenure that was thought to be common in the north-east of the country, known as the Ulster Custom,[4] ostensibly characterised by the 'three Fs': fair rent, free sale and fixity of tenure. The new historiography claims that Gladstone confronted the fundamental economic problem of an undercapitalised economy by promoting the sectional interests of tenants and making Irish landlords the scapegoats for his Liberal conscience; also, that he was tainted by naive Liberal delusions – derived from Mill – of the survival of an atavistic clan mentality in relation to land ownership.

The revisionist economic argument runs like this. Irish agriculture was undercapitalised. Evictions took place, not arbitrarily but for non-payment of rent. Given the economic undercapitalisation of the society there was an inbuilt tension between conflicting views of what constituted a fair rent. What was fair to the economic necessity of the landlord was by definition 'unfair' to certain kinds of tenants, merely because they could never afford to pay it. Hence legislation to render eviction difficult, except in the event of non-payment of rent, was merely to evade the issue since eviction merely arose as a *consequence* of the non-payment of rent.

The Irish case was exceptional because it was believed that improvements on individual tenant holdings were not – as in England – made by the landlord but by the tenant. It was as a consequence of this that the notion of a tenant 'interest' in the land existed in the Ulster Custom. On departure the tenant in effect was entitled to compensation for such improvements as he had effected. In the works of historians like Barbara Solow this tenant 'interest' in the soil is merely a device for defaulting the landowner. She claims that tenant right was often 'sold' when in fact no improvements had been effected, when there was no need for a tenant entering into a property to compensate the outgoing tenant for his improvements. According to Solow, what is being 'bought' in this case is in effect the unexpired lease of the outgoing tenant. But no value would attach to this unexpired lease *unless* the land was in the first place being let at less than its market value. For example, she cites the case of a Kildare landlord, John La Touche, who appeared before the Bessborough Commission in 1881. La Touche denied the right of the tenant to sell his 'interest', though he was prepared to acknowledge his right to compensation for improvements:

> I would not allow him to sell because he has nothing to sell. I think the difference between what a landlord has let his land at, and what he might have obtained from another tenant, ought to be the landlord's.[5]

The new orthodoxy contends that, in rejecting the recommendations of the Tory-appointed Richmond Commission[6] and adopting those of his own Bessborough investigation, Gladstone effectively instituted in the 1881 Land Act a condition that was merely academic in the Act of 1870, and so laid the basis for a tenurial quagmire for reasons of expediency. Both of these commissions – one Conservative, one Liberal – investigated the situation in Ireland that had given rise to the extraordinary resistance to rent manifested during the 'Land War'. Even the Conservative enquiry found, after interviewing hundreds of witnesses, that real poverty and not mere political manipulation lay at the root of unrest.

The Richmond Commission had reported evidence of grinding poverty and inability to pay rent, at least in the west, in 1879 and 1880. That such poverty was used politically, both by those who partook of it, by those rich tenant farmers of the east who availed of the effects of its agitation and by nationalists, is undeniable.[7] The Richmond Commission suggested emigration, resettlement, drainage, fisheries and agricultural education. The poor subsistence farmers of the west, even in times of prosperity before the depression of the late 1870s, could not survive even when supplementing their incomes by migrant summer work in England and Scotland. The depression in England ended that. People living on the contents of American envelopes in an economy where the option of city migration did not exist, clearly had no future prospects within their society. Therefore, the revisionist economic consensus, inspired by Solow, coincides with contemporary Conservative thought by condemning the Liberal Bessborough Commission on the recommendations of which Gladstone legislated. By instituting an elaborate legislative apparatus in the form of a Land Commission to set rent levels, it is argued, Liberalism formalised a procedure which denied the economic logic of the market. Tenants could not afford to pay rent in times of recession, therefore that rent was to be reduced through judicial intervention. Tenurial tinkering was substituted for a coherent ability to follow the logic of the market.

What this interpretation, in its historiographical form as well as in its contemporary Conservative Malthusian emphasis, fails to recognise is the political. Ireland was in a state of anarchy in 1881. Policy was not determined by higher economic ends, but by the political demands of the situation. Tenants *did* flock to the land courts to have their rents revised in 1881 and in general succeeded in so doing. Gladstone's policy partially achieved its ends; ends composed of a pragmatic mixture of the desire for the expiation of Irish wrongs and, more importantly, peace.

The contention of Tory contemporaries and current historians is that the effects of the 1881 Land Act far outstripped its Liberal intentions. As prices continued to fall, rents continued to be reduced. Not merely that, but the notion of a tenant's 'interest' in his holding, by being legislatively recognised, was transformed in a fashion that had serious repercussions. It was intended to ensure that on departure a tenant could be compensated for his improvements by selling his 'interests', or by not being rented on the increased value of the holding, if remaining, by virtue of those improvements. In practice, it is alleged, it transformed the contractual integrity of property into a species of dual ownership. The landlord's right of eviction was circumscribed, his capacity to fix his own rents negated. In effect the landlord became encumbered by an unrealisable asset in a time of continued recession. Such at least is the revised analysis.

A consideration of the ten years that followed the Act of 1881 makes it difficult to accept this analysis. During those ten years Irish rents were reduced by a mere £1.4 million. In fact, since the fall in prices marginally outstripped that of rents, it is arguable that, since the Act stabilised rents, it in fact protected the landlords.[8] There is no evidence to suggest that the economic story of a broken-spirited landlord class is a product of legislation. That is not to deny the economic horrors of the landlord's financial constraints *or* their Land League induced social isolation. In fact, many of the landlord's economic difficulties related more to the further economic squeeze of 1886–87 than to any specifically Irish legislative circumstances. Had the period been one of rising, rather than falling, prices, the landlords could have benefited from the 1881 legislation. It did, however, mean that, though rents were controlled, the price of tenant interest was not. As the price for tenant interest soared, the large grazier tenants consolidated their holdings,[9] and began a new politics of exploitation. In effect, it is argued, the benefits of the legislation were being reaped not by the poor tenants in the congested districts of the west who had provided the dynamic for the Land War, but by entrepreneurial graziers who benefited from the fact that speculation was now conducted in the private, unregulated domain of tenant right.

The finalisation of the particular myth of the landlord's economic emasculation, which became a staple of Conservative thought, can be traced to ideas that became manifest during the Salisbury-led Conservative administration that followed the collapse of the 1886 Home Rule Bill.

It was during the period between 1885 and 1892 that Conservatism legislatively articulated a clear policy on Irish land. In analysing the discrepancy between the stated Tory position at Westminster and the reality of administration in Ireland, the contrast between the findings of the commission appointed to enquire into 'Parnellism and crime' and the policy practised by the administration between 1886 and 1892 is illuminating. The Special Commission, reporting in 1890 after an enquiry stretching over a year, described – after a ten-year interval – the Land War of 1879–81 as having been in no way attributable to distress and excessively high rents. It found, in utter contravention of the opinion *even* of the Conservative Richmond Commission that had reported at the time, nothing other than a vicious criminal conspiracy behind the activities of those years. It retrospectively found seven members of the Irish Parliamentary Party guilty of joining the Land League with the intention of severing the Union, ruled that the Irish members as a body had incited the people to intimidation which they knew led to crime, and that they had consistently refused to put themselves on the side of 'law and order'.

Despite this, however, the Conservative administration in Ireland after 1886, through its policy of aid to the so-called congested districts, through a Land Purchase Act in 1891 that built upon the limited credit extension of Ashbourne's 1885 Act, and a policy of social intervention, demonstrated in its policies a commitment to ameliorating problems to which its rhetoric denied existence.

In 1886 Salisbury's government appointed under the chairmanship of Earl Cowper, the former Liberal Lord-Lieutenant who had finally abandoned

Gladstone, a commission to enquire into the 1881 Land Act and to ascertain the extent to which its workings were affected, either by combinations to resist the enforcement of legal obligations – ultimately an indirect way of enquiring into the Plan of Campaign – or by an exceptional fall in the price of produce. The Land Commissioners and the sub-commissioners appointed under the 1881 Act gave detailed evidence to Cowper. Leaseholders, 'the flower of the Irish tenantry', had been excluded from the provisions of the 1881 Act, despite Parnell's protests at the time of Kilmainham, since contractual relationships forbade interference in Gladstone's scheme of things. Certain types of holdings (town parks, demesne lands and grazing lettings) did not partake of the clause in the 1881 Act which protected tenure: the granting of compensation for disturbance in the case of capricious evictions. So of the 499,108 holders of land in Ireland, according to the 1881 census, 150,000 or almost a third were excluded. Of the remaining 350,000 the majority were year-to-year tenants. Tenants could apply to the court of the Land Commission, created by the Act of 1881, or to the County Court to have a 'fair rent' fixed. The landlord and tenant could, on the other hand, enter into an agreement with the court, thus creating a judicial rent. This also entitled the tenant to unlimited tenancy of a farm for the fifteen-year duration of the judicial rent, provided that he paid that fixed rent. In the first five years of the Act from 1881 to 1886 over 176,000 rents were fixed. Overall, the rental reduction was eighteen per cent from a total rental of over £3,200,000 in 1881 to £2,600,000 in 1886. The Arrears Act of 1882 had wiped out the 'Land War' arrears.

In 1886–87, when agricultural depression intensified, politically directed combinations, particularly the Plan of Campaign, constituted themselves into external arbiters of rent and, in cases of deadlock where judicial rents had already been set, demanded reductions of the landlord. These so-called 'abatements' were to be determined by the tenants' ability to pay. If refused, the sum was paid into a fund to finance the maintenance of the combination. This was in effect the Plan of Campaign.

The depression had brought about a fall of almost twenty per cent in the agricultural capital of the occupiers. A reasonable reading of the evidence would then appear to suggest that since rent and price reductions were almost commensurate, the Land Commission was in effect implementing an equitable sliding-scale method of assessment. In effect the Land Commission was implementing a policy that in a politically integrated society would have occurred naturally. In England in the same period landlords did, in general, adjust their rents to adapt to falling prices. However, what the Plan of Campaign demanded was in excess of this.

Cowper's commission, appointed by Hicks-Beach as Tory Chief Secretary, was composed of Cowper, the Earl of Milltown, the barrister Chute Nelligan and George Fottrell, who resigned almost immediately after the swift termination of his career as a Land Commissioner.

Cowper, in 1887, was sympathetic to the conclusions of the Conservative commission of the House of Lords which had sat immediately after the passing of the 1881 Act. The questioning of that Commission, its policy and purpose were clear, perhaps best expressed by Lord Tyrone. In speaking of Irish tenants he had then said, 'They look to some political machinery or result to give them that which should come from their own industry.'

While most post-Solow interpretations highlight the danger of uncritically accepted hardship tales from the mouths of Commission witnesses, and suggest an emendation of their partial truth by a dispassionate examination of the social and economic statistics, they fail to recognise that commissions were not composed of individuals devoid of political intent. Cowper, now a Liberal Unionist, had a political role to fulfil – the discrediting of Gladstone's 1881 Act, passed during his own uneasy period as Liberal Lord-Lieutenant, and its fundamental premise about the right to judicial interference in rent on private property. But the notion of dual ownership as the logical corollary to such interference, a notion widely accepted at the time and now dogma, was a Conservative rhetorical response to interference in the sanctity of an owner's right to omnipotent control. It is here, in the Cowper Commission of 1887, that the seeds of all subsequent Conservative analysis and land policy are clearly stated.

The report of the Cowper Commission is a clear articulation of the principle implicit in the Conservative Ashbourne Act of 1885: a policy of land purchase. The report states that under the system of judicial rent revision the landlord has 'ceased to be owner' and, in the phrase that was to recur in all subsequent debate, had become 'an encumbrancer upon his property'. But it was not directly stated that the *principle* of judicial rent reduction was untenable:

> If the system now prevailing in Ireland was found in practice to work well, no theoretical imperfection would much signify, but the direct contrary is the case. The landlords consider themselves in an untenable position. The tenants as a rule have not much regard for the landlords as such. In the north they are generally indifferent to them and in the south they are often bitterly hostile . . . It would be impossible now, even if it were desirable, to restore the position of the landlord to what it is in England. Any move that is to be made must be in the opposite direction . . . There was never before in this country, nor in any other that we are aware of, so liberal an offer by the State to assist farmers to become landowners.[10]

Formerly, it was alleged in Nationalist rhetoric, tenants had no incentive to invest because their rental would be increased commensurate with their gain through investment. Now the Conservative retaliatory argument was that no landlord could afford to invest in land when such investment as he made would be appropriated by the tenantry. Tenants, while availing of the

principle of judicial interference, objected to the inflexibility of that interference in the face of continued depression.

The Cowper Commission claimed that its rejection of the 1881 Act was not based upon *theoretical* objections. This, however, is precisely where the Conservative objections lay. This 1887 Commission of enquiry went into laborious and impenetrable discussion of the principles of valuation held by the Land Commissioners in setting fair rent – hundreds of pages of apparently lucid analysis of the relationship between valuation and rental, the injustice of applying Griffith's valuation of the 1850s to the economy of the 1880s. But a detailed reading of this material reveals that all apparently reasonable economic analyses were – from Conservatives, Liberals, Nationalists and Irish landowners, agents and tenants – mere cloaking mechanisms through which to advance their respective desired political ends. The Irish Parliamentary Party and the Land League had demanded rents set in accordance with Griffith's valuation in 1879-81. This was manifestly absurd since the valuation, set for income tax in the 1850s, was at least twenty per cent below the real value of land in 1881. Rents were, however, 'too high' and Griffith's valuation was a convenient political rallying cry. Conservatives, by seeking to demonstrate that it was the absurd working of the 1881 Act that they found objectionable – shoddy standards by which the sub-commissioners set rents – implied that their objections were merely to a system that was unjust, inadequate and inoperable. In fact, the system worked quite smoothly.

It is when one turns from the debate that was ostensibly about land to the wider rhetoric, demonstrated on the issues of Home Rule and law and order, that the real nature of Conservative thought and the basis on which land policy was formulated is to be found. Adjectives like dark, vituperative, sinister and murderous reverberate through every public speech and every Commons debate on the issue of Ireland. *The Times* throughout the period maintained a pitch of anti-Irish invective that was astonishing, not merely in its verbal range: 'The ignorant Irish imagine that Home Rule will mean that nobody has to pay for anything'. In the British press Ireland was a wasteland in which the forces of civilisation were fortified behind demesne walls, behind army garrisons and Royal Irish Constabulary barracks. Outside these gates lurked thousands of duplicitous wretches, cattle maimers, murderers, congenital liars and, orchestrating the squalid chorus, a partnership: the banners of the priesthood and self-seeking Irish MPs. It is at this point that the duality of Conservative thought on Ireland becomes apparent. As Balfour said, 'Bills for the Better Government of Ireland', the full title of the Home Rule Bills, were in effect euphemisms for the worse government of Britain. For imperial purposes Ireland had to be retained.

This necessity demanded, on the one hand, the rhetoric of Ireland as an integral part of the United Kingdom. On the other hand, the rhetoric proclaimed Ireland to be a savage and different place. In effect Ireland was a nuisance and a burden. More nineteenth-century governments had fallen on 'the question' than on any other single issue. From the time that obstruction was initiated by Biggar and Parnell Ireland occupied more time in the Commons than any other matter of policy. As Salisbury wrote in 'Disintegration' (1883):

> On Tory principles the case presents much that is painful but no perplexity whatever. Ireland must be kept, like India, at all hazards: by persuasion if possible, if not by force.

To concede, as the Liberals did, not merely on the question of separate nationhood, but on fundamental principles of property and the law, was untenable and unforgivable: if the Irish could not be retained by English notions of property and the law then the problem lay not, as Liberals sought to imply, in the English law and English notions of property: it lay in the Irish character. That was the essential division between retrogressive and redundant Liberal sentimentality and Tory self-confidence in the rightness of English standards. The untenable interference with property enshrined in the 1881 Act was to be dismantled. In effect since, in the words of Cowper, that could not be 'gone back upon'; the only possible resolution from the Conservative point of view was the purchase of land by tenants. That presented some difficulties: the apparent lack of interest on the part of Irish tenant farmers in purchase, and the lack of demonstrated desire on the part of the landlords to sell.

These difficulties were removed in the period from 1887 to 1903 in response to considerations at Westminster and in Dublin Castle that were primarily political rather than social and economic. The policy of the brief period of Liberal government in the years 1892-95, combined with a landlord realisation that local government reform was unavoidable, catalysed the decision of the Irish landlords to cash in on favourable terms; not, as Conservatives at the time and historians now, proclaim the *economically* untenable situation to which Liberal legislation had consigned the landlord class.

5 PARNELLISM AND CRIME:
CONSTRUCTING A CONSERVATIVE STRATEGY OF CONTAINMENT, 1887-90

Cleared in the face of all mankind beneath the winking skies,
Like phoenixes, from Phoenix Park (and what lay there) they rise!
Go shout it to the emerald seas – give word to Erin now,
Her honourable gentlemen are cleared – and this is how:–

They only paid the Moonlighter his cattle-hocking price,
They only helped the murderer with counsel's best advice,
But – sure it keeps their honour white – the learned Court believes,
They never give a piece of plate to murderers and thieves.

Their sin it was that fed the fire – small blame to them that heard -
The 'bhoys' get drunk on rhetoric, and madden at a word -
They know whom they were talking at, if they were Irish too,
The gentlemen that lied in Court, they knew, and well they knew.

'Less black than we were painted'? – Faith, no word of black was said;
The lightest touch was human blood, and that, you know runs red.
It's sticking to your fist to-day for all your sneer and scoff,
And by the Judge's well-weighed word you cannot wipe it off.

Hold up those hands of innocence – go, scare your sheep together,
The blundering, tripping tups that bleat behind the old bell-weather;
And if they snuff the taint and break to find another pen,
Tell them it's tar that glistens so, and daub them yours again!

If black is black or white is white, in black and white its down,
You're only traitors to the Queen and rebels to the Crown.
If print is print or words are words, the learned Court perpends:–
We are not ruled by murderers, but only – by their friends.

'"Cleared" – in Memory of a Commission'
Rudyard Kipling

It is not the first time that you have poisoned the bowl and used the dagger against your political opponents in that country [Ireland] where you could not overcome them in fair fight.

Charles Stewart Parnell, July 1888

Analyses of English policy towards Ireland in the years from 1879 are both detailed and fragmented. The proliferation of contemporary accounts and the publication of a large number of biographies and surveys in the past twenty years has lent to the historiography a quality of finality.[1] The publication in the past decade of studies that seek to explore the 'land question' in terms of peasant mobilisation have answered the questions deemed to be important by those who pose them.[2] Questions of policy are seen to be answered separately, or to be explored through the magnifying and distorting mirror of the Cooke and Vincent school.[3] Liberal policy towards Ireland is seen to be understood and resolved. The 'coercion and conciliation' thesis of L. P. Curtis, that Conservatism began 'killing Home Rule by kindness' after the defeat of murder by Arthur Balfour's calming coercion measures in 1887 provides a neat conclusion to a period of disorder.[4]

Because of the drama of the Home Rule Bill 1886 is considered to be *the* important year in the evolution of Liberal and Conservative policy towards Ireland: the Liberal intent to pursue a policy of Home Rule, the defection of the Whigs, and the adoption by the Conservatives of the high imperial ground through their public rhetoric on the issue of Ireland. By undermining the significance of Ireland in that year, and proclaiming it to be merely an issue around which political groupings reconstituted themselves, Cooke and Vincent have concluded that the issue of Ireland was never important as a 'thing in itself' in English politics.[5] Attempts to refute this view invariably enter into the 'facts' as presented by Cooke and Vincent. This is history written as detective novel with multiple-choice endings – each new letter shifts the story, producing a different optional resolution, but the plot, the characters and the decision as to what was important remain in the control of the minds of the original authors. In writing about the Special Commission[6] most historians have adopted a consensus verdict: that the Commission was an error of judgement on the part of Salisbury's government.[7] But as Sir Joseph West-Ridgeway wrote to Balfour in 1890, commenting with amusement on the depression of the uninitiated, 'He [the Irish Attorney-General] is utterly demoralised by the present phase of the Parnell Commission and regards a change of government as a certainty . . . The curious thing is that all along we have anticipated a collapse of *this* part of the case with equanimity. I do not, therefore, understand this panic'.[8]

The significance of the Special Commission has been distorted by the extent to which historians have viewed it as a sprawling anomaly that represents a failure of judgement on the part of the otherwise astute Conservative administration of Ireland after 1886. This analysis conforms to the judgement of Randolph Churchill at the time: a view that emphasises the embarrassment of Conservative politicians and the extent to which, by their association with *The Times*, they compromised their case.[9] As a corollary to this historians have accepted the view of the Conservative administration after 1887 that was posited by the Conservatives at the time; the view that Arthur Balfour's role in 1887 was to bring Ireland back from a state of chronic lawlessness into which Land and National League violence had plunged it. According to this view Balfour succeeded where Hicks-Beach and Liberal predecessors had failed – in redeeming Ireland from League-orchestrated chaos.

The accepted view of the Conservative administration of Ireland after 1886 is that, having attempted reasonable measures under Hicks-Beach, the Conservatives were finally forced to recognise the essentially intractable nature of Irish violence and to defeat it by force before embarking upon a constructive policy of ameliorative social reform. This interpretation is facilitated by the apparent disjunction between the 'high' politics of Westminster in 1886 and the realities of Irish administration before and after that date. Thus, in the historiography there is an apparent lacuna for the years 1883 to 1886 in Ireland. The historiography has particular emphases: the violence of the Land War of 1879 to 1881, the 1881 Land Bill, the Kilmainham treaty, the Phoenix Park murders and the necessary Crimes Act, followed by an Arrears Bill. Studies of the Liberal Irish administration after 1882 are few.

The chief-secretaryships of Trevelyan and Campbell-Bannerman are rarely written about: it is as if for those years from 1882 to June 1885 the domestic condition of Ireland is an irrelevance. With the singular and significant exception of Maamtrasna, politics is conducted in the rarefied atmosphere of Westminster. But these are the years of the politicisation of the Irish Nationalist Party, years during which that party's leaders endeavoured to distance themselves from violence and forge a constitutional political identity, committed to the achievement of Home Rule. Their language was of political change and their tactics were devoted to fighting their cause at Westminster. On going to Ireland as Lord-Lieutenant in June 1885 Carnarvon, acting on the advice of the Permanent Under-Secretary, advised an end to the Crimes Act and an abandonment of coercion. The 'crimes figures' for these years would seem to confirm the correctness of such an analysis.

L. P. Curtis, in the standard work on Conservatives and Ireland, while acknowledging the significance of Ireland in imperial terms, essentially writes a history of these years on the assumption that the Conservatives were doing what they said they were doing – necessarily defeating crime in Ireland before proceeding to ameliorative social measures. Thus the state of Ireland is said to be what Conservative rhetoric proclaimed it to be in 1887 – one of anarchy and near disintegration.

The Cooke and Vincent thesis on 1886 is tenable if it is accepted that significant political activity took place where they see it as having taken place – in the private correspondence and conversational exchanges of politicians. Like literary critics of a discredited generation they see political rhetoric as a thin and obfuscatory patina behind the screen of which 'real' political action takes place. Thus the political rhetoric of 1886 can be dismissed as irrelevant.

The public language of politics is subverted by nudging reminders of the infinity of private intrigues that contribute to the truth behind its foundation. Public language then is barren and meaningless, essentially a lie, and history, the search for 'truth', is concerned with what *really* happened behind the scenes. Not merely is that view philosophically naive, in that it posits a recoverable 'truth' behind a smokescreen, but it also involves a fundamental failure to recognise the salient and essential characteristic of the political: the degree to which its meaning is defined only when it becomes a public act through language. By definition the focus of such analysis is microscopic and necessarily static. Process or change cannot be accommodated by an analysis that is exclusively concerned with unravelling private motivations, one that considers 'real' politics to be over at the moment that its labyrinthine hinterland gives way to public language or public action.

The Conservative Party in 1886 carefully orchestrated a rhetorical onslaught on the notion of Home Rule for Ireland. Having committed themselves to a public expression of the Irish incapacity for self-government they were no longer in possession of the political choices that preceded the language of 1886. Public political language is not a redeemable temporary expedient – it is an irrevocable political act that changes the nature of political reality. Goschen had made the definitive point when he said:

> Is the imperial parliament bound to listen to the voice of the majority of any particular portion of the Empire, and to come to a conclusion in accordance with that voice![10]

Moreover, Ireland presented an even more complex problem:

> . . . with views of the majority of the Irish people with regard to some of the chief principles of legislation are different to those of the inhabitants of England and Scotland . . . the attitude of the Irish people, partly from history, perhaps partly from the misgovernment of their country, for which we are paying so heavy a price, towards laws which are recognised in other countries, is a hostile attitude and different from the attitude of most of the nations of Europe.[11]

But to Gladstone agrarian crime was

> a symptom of a yet deeper mischief of which it is only the external manifestation!

Moreover:

> If we, the English or the Scotch, were under the conviction that we had such grave cause to warrant . . . action as is the conviction entertained by a large part of the population in Ireland I am not at all sure that we should not, like that part of the population in Ireland, resort to the rude and unjustifiable remedy of intimidation![12]

In 1886 the Home Rule debate placed the question of Irish self-government in what Victorian politicians called the 'realm of practical politics'. The Irish Nationalist Party at Westminster, organised on the structure of the National League, was a democratic, constitutional reality in English political life. The democratic process ensured that the Irish party was perceived to be electorally bona fide, a group worthy of political cultivation. The defeat of Home Rule in the Lords was politically irrefutable, but the Home Rule party was sufficiently committed to the parliamentary process to see its future role as defined within parliament.

Within two years, in an action constitutionally unprecedented, this perception was utterly changed. All of the leading members of the Irish parliamentary party were in effect 'tried' before a special commission, constituted by Act of Parliament on the following charges:

(i) That the respondents were members of a conspiracy and organisation having for its ultimate object to establish the absolute independence of Ireland.

(ii) That the immediate object of their conspiracy was, by a system of coercion and intimidation, to promote an agrarian agitation against the payment of agricultural rents, for the purpose of impoverishing and expelling from the country the Irish landlords who were styled the English garrison.

(iii) That when on certain occasions they thought it politic to denounce certain crimes in public, they afterwards led their supporters to believe that such denunciation was not sincere [a charge chiefly based on the 'facsimile' letter of 15 May 1882, alleged to be signed by Mr Parnell].

(iv) That they disseminated the *Irish World* and other newspapers, tending to incite the sedition and the commission of other crime.

(v) That they, by their speeches and by payments for that purpose, incited persons to the commission of crime, including murder.

(vi) That they did nothing to prevent crime, and expressed no bona fide disapproval of it.

(vii) That they subscribed to testimonials for and were intimately associated with notorious criminals, defended persons supposed to be guilty of agrarian crime, supported their families and made payments to secure the escape of criminals from justice.

(viii) That they made payments to persons who had been injured in the commission of crime.

(ix) That the respondents invited the assistance and accepted subscriptions of money from known advocates of crime and dynamite.[13]

The contention of this chapter is that such a transformation reveals the central meaning of Conservative strategy in Ireland after 1887, and that without an awareness of its implications no satisfactory understanding of the development of Irish nationalism or the emerging imperial strategy of Conservatism is possible. More particularly it contends that the real aims of Arthur Balfour's chief-secretaryship can only be understood in the light of such an awareness.

The National League, as had been noted in Royal Irish Constabulary District Inspectors' reports for late 1885, was anxious to emphasise its essentially political status. During the election of 1885 National League officials:

> drilled their supporters as to the procedure for voting so that they should make no mistake. Their zeal and devotion to the national cause are quite remarkable.[14]

After Kilmainham and the formation of the National League, the aims of the Nationalist parliamentary party had been to set a distance between themselves and the worst excesses of rural agrarian discontent. Indeed, as the machinery of the Land Commission substantially revised rents, and as the Arrears Bill took effect, in 1883, the political significance of the 'land question' receded, at least until the bad harvest and falling prices of 1885 and 1886. The tensions in the Conservative cabinet of January to June 1886 on the issue of coercion were shelved in the compromise of the Queen's speech which suggested that special powers could be invoked legislatively if the ordinary law did not suffice.

Salisbury was continuing to hold the balance between Hicks-Beach and Churchill on the one hand – with Carnarvon as a grim reminder of the potential dangers of such ambiguity – and on the other his own strongest sentiments as expressed in the 'Disintegration' article of 1883[15] and parodied in the wounded passages of Cranbrook's diary.[16]

The post-Home Rule Conservative administration was, however, significantly different. Despite Churchill's self-aggrandizing role as mediator between Hicks-Beach and Salisbury it is difficult not to see a certain distancing in Salisbury's reserved and wry 'appreciations'.[17] Hicks-Beach, in Ireland, still clung to the assumption that the game was the same as previously; that coercion would be used if and when serious crime seemed to warrant it, and that simultaneously the legitimate grievances of an oppressed tenantry would be appeased. Parnell too, by immediately proceeding with a Tenants' Relief Bill, was seeking to treat the continuing agricultural depression as a functional issue that required resolution lest it erupt in violence which the National League could not control.

Ironically, it was to be the trump card of earlier dealings with Gladstone – 'deal with me or Captain Moonlight will take my place' – that was to undo the Nationalist strategy. For in dealing with Salisbury, Parnell was confronted by the reality of which his own public image was merely a mask – a man of infinite coolness, caution and patience. Parnell gave the appearance of control, of a long-term strategy. It was this quality that gave him his uncontested, if galling, superiority over excitable and unstable peasants like Healy. In Irish terms he was the urbane, unruffled aristocrat and, indeed, so he appeared on the Westminster stage. Confronted by the reality he was merely a simulacrum.

Hicks-Beach grew frustrated and irate in Dublin as the cabinet refused to listen to the force of his position when he warned that economic conditions would lead to a renewal of violence outside even Nationalist control. The Irish committee of the cabinet was essentially a cipher: Salisbury, Hicks-Beach, Churchill, Matthews and W. H. Smith. Hicks-Beach was effectively negated, Churchill was fully occupied in feeling important as a superannuated inter-mediary; Matthews, presumably included to give Churchill an even more reassuring sense of control, was meaningless, and W. H. Smith was absolutely 'sound'. The institution of the Cowper Commission, the only concession to Hicks-Beach's demands, was designed, in the long term, to investigate agrarian grievances, despite Hicks-Beach's view that its real role was to prop up the landlord interest.[18] According to Ashbourne, despite the existence of 'crime figures', it was impossible to make any firm statements about the state of Ireland.

> Some parts are bad, others indifferent and others again in a fairly good state. Kerry is the worst. Clare possibly is next in badness, Limerick is bad and in parts nearly bankrupt. Other counties are some degree better. Rents in some districts will be paid fairly; in others with substantial reductions; in others not at all.[19]

The contention of the Nationalist parliamentary party was that, unless measures were taken to reduce rents judicially, violence would erupt among the tenants in the most distressed areas. While the parliamentary party had been organised upon the structured grievances of an oppressed tenantry in 1879–81, they had no desire to become the hostages of 'Captain Moonlight' in 1886-87, hence their desire to have agrarian grievances swiftly resolved.

To Hicks-Beach the Irish land problem was an economic one. The land-lords were being crushed by an irrefutable economic imperative. Rents required to be reduced because, particularly in the south-west, tenants could not afford to pay them. Rooted in Dublin Castle and deluged as he was by a documentary avalanche of police reports on every aspect of the life of 'crime' in the country, he nonetheless declined to take up the high ground of the rights of property and enforcement of the law. The appointment of Sir Redvers Buller to 'pacify' the south-west was a triumph for Salisbury, but, as Buller's letters to Hicks-Beach and evidence to the Cowper Commission revealed, his first-hand experience of conditions there undermined his efficacy. He saw violence as springing from the intolerable economic condition of tenants in the counties of Clare and Kerry particularly: instead of merely putting down 'disorder' as instructed, he assumed the role of tenants' apologist.

He saw the weapon of the boycott as rooted in the private sanctions of an impenetrable community. Though politicised and 'named' by the Boycott case of 1881, it essentially sprang from age-old regulatory rituals. Its politicisation and organisation from 1879-81 had, however, transformed its potency. Despite the language of Dublin Castle reports – which spoke of a primeval and incomprehensible peasantry – the Nationalists' 'dupes', local newspapers, intercepted letters and National League communications present a different view.[20] Literacy was high, newspapers like *United Ireland* and the *Kerry Sentinel* were widely read. The machinery of the Land Commission since 1881 had ensured that most tenant farmers could analyse valuation, rental and prices with considerable skill. In short, as Joseph Lee has noted elsewhere, if the Irish peasantry were distinguished in any sense, it was in the degree to which they were highly politicised and litigious. Land Commission and Land Court litigation had effectively created not merely a career circuit for aspiring barristers, but also a form of unwitting public education.

Balfour was appointed Chief Secretary for Ireland on 7 March 1887. On that day *The Times* published the first of the articles that were to be known as 'Parnellism and Crime',[21] in which allegations of criminality were made against Parnell, the Land and National Leagues, and the Irish Party. A debate, which had been apparently resolved before 1886, was suddenly reopened. On 18 April, on the second reading of the Bill, *The Times* published a facsimile letter signed by Parnell and linking him with the Phoenix Park murders. Balfour immediately announced an enquiry into these allegations.

Balfour's 'campaign' in Ireland began with the passing of the Crimes Act. It was to be over a year before the Special Commission was constituted to investigate allegations made in the course of the O'Donnell libel case. This has led historians to mention as an aside the publication of the articles and letters in March 1887, indicating that they may have helped to swing wavering Liberal/Unionist support behind the Bill. Balfour's Irish policy, his commitment to ordering chaos is then examined. When the intractable twelve-volume report of the commission is mentioned on its publication, it is accepted as an embarrassment to the Conservative government. The vindication of Parnell on the single issue of the Pigott forgeries is presented as the 'failure' of the *Times* case. In short, Parnell's brief hour of glory and triumph on the issue of approval of the Phoenix Park murders is treated as the salient reality, Sir Charles Russell's devastation of Richard Pigott as the apotheosis of the Irish nation.[22]

The question then posed is how the Conservative government could have ill-judged such an issue; whether *The Times* was in fact 'tipped' by the Conservatives to print the articles and letters on the crucial Crimes Bill dates; whether William Henry Joyce was telling the truth when he alleged that he was responsible for directing a Castle operation to cull from the police reports of a decade earlier, incriminating evidence on nationalists to substantiate the *Times* case.[23] Doubts will always be cast on Joyce's story: he was a bitter and disappointed man. A careful reading of the extensive Balfour papers does, however, reveal his considerable importance to the Irish administration at the time.[24] But a debate around imponderables cannot be conclusive. It can perhaps be said that the absence of any written record in the private correspondence of those responsible for Irish government on so important a question is surprising.

A debate on what *is* known may, however, prove more useful. The English Attorney-General appeared on behalf of *The Times* at the insistence of his colleagues. In an unprecedented legislative departure a special commission was constituted by act of parliament. In defiance of all legal practice 'incidental' incriminating evidence produced by *The Times* in the libel action brought by O'Donnell was transposed into the charges which the 'Irish nationalist conspiracy' was to face. Elected members of parliament were 'tried' on criminal conspiracy charges for events that had taken place almost a decade earlier. The commission, constituted by the Conservative government, was structured to enable 'evidence' to be given by selected members of the Royal Irish Constabulary. Even if Soames of *The Times*[25] received no direct assistance from Dublin Castle, the fact that *The Times* was given powers to subpoena, complete with relevant 'records', any member of the constabulary, and hence have indirect access to all of the crime papers of government, is remarkable in itself.[26] The sheer quantity of material supplied to *The Times* and the rambling and interminable nature of the Attorney-General's case contrived to ensure that the investigation would be as long, as extensive and as comprehensive as possible.

To see such a monumental exercise as a 'mistake' on the part of the Conservative government is strange. Moreover, the delight with which the Conservatives treated the report's publication scarcely indicates any regret at its progress or conclusions.[27] Substantially it had succeeded in establishing precisely what it had been constituted to establish: that nationalism and crime were one and the same thing.

The constitutional achievement of the parliamentary party between 1882 and 1886 was effectively negated. Interminable details of horrific barbarity, particularly in the south-west, were neatly juxtaposed with information that branches of the Land or National League had been set up, or had met near the scene of the crime. Sir Charles Russell's 'skill' in breaking down Piggott, a man already on the point of collapse, appears to have masked his forensic incompetence for the remainder of the proceedings. In short, nationalists felt pleased because a letter that nobody politically informed, not even Salisbury, believed Parnell to have written was demonstrated not to have been written by Parnell and, perhaps more characteristically, relished the cathartic thrill of hearing 700 years of Irish history unfolded by Russell. More understandably perhaps, the temptation retrospectively to view Parnell as having been triumphantly vindicated immediately before his catastrophic fall is irresistible. Thus the Special Commission can be seen as Parnell's finest hour in stark contrast to his subsequent defeat.

But the enquiry was only incidentally about Parnell. It was about the nature of the movement of which he was leader, and about the focus through which its development since 1879 was to be seen. It recast the terms of the debate about Ireland, and was a vital ideological underpinning to Balfour's declared mission in Ireland. The National League, which in 1886 had been the political organisation of the Home Rule movement, was transformed in two years into a suppressed criminal conspiracy. The role of the commission was systematically to demonstrate that a criminal conspiracy was, in fact, precisely what the National League had always been. In this it succeeded.

It showed the Land and National Leagues as contiguous conspiracies uninterrupted since 1879, except for those periods during which a Crimes Act was vigorously enforced in Ireland. That the Liberals and the Irish poured scorn upon its findings was irrelevant. It was intended – secondarily – for public consumption, but primarily as an irrefutable, judicially sanctioned 'legal' document which demonstrated to the Conservatives themselves the rightness of their adopted position. It provided an ideological justification for their chosen analysis of the nature of Irish agitation, and made coercion a demonstrable ideological necessity, and not merely a governmental expedient. But above all it effectively stymied the future political evolution of 'nationalism'.

The tension within the Nationalist Party from the time of Kilmainham onwards had been between those who viewed compromise with the English government as the 'great betrayal', and those who believed, particularly after the passing of the Arrears Bill, that the 'land struggle' which they had availed of, organised and monitored, was an uncertain weapon. Parnell's strategy was, while continuing to evoke the spectre of 'Captain Moonlight' as a bargaining counter, to battle constitutionally for Home Rule. He never fully carried his party with him in this, as the Plan of Campaign demonstrated. Nor, indeed, was it in the interests of his conception of the constitutional struggle to have the 'land issue' at boiling point. Hence his immediate, reasonable requests to the Conservatives for a Tenants' Relief Bill in late 1886. But Salisbury was a very clever man. Manifestly, the way to defeat the Nationalist party was by exposing the tensions within its position. Hicks-Beach's agitation about what 'ought' to be done in Ireland was the hectoring of a political innocent: he did not recognise the extent to which the necessary corollary to the anti-Home Rule rhetoric of 1886 was the utter discrediting of 'nationalism' in Ireland. The land question and Captain Moonlight could potentially hoist the Nationalists with their own petard. The verbal battle of 1886 had tainted the Irish with criminality, duplicity, murder and savagery.

That language had created a reality in which future constitutional bargaining with Nationalists was ideologically impossible for any Conservative and Liberal–Unionist government. The Special Commission was constructed to render the Irish parliamentary party constitutionally impotent, since it established them all as criminals.

> One hand stuck out, behind the back, to signal 'strike again',
> The other in your dress-shirt-front to show your heart is clane.[28]

What distinguished Conservative coercion after 1887 from coercion that preceded it was not its greater success, or the fact that it was followed by ameliorative measures, but rather that it refused to distinguish between different kinds of nationalists. The constitutional party, the cattle hougher, the back street assassin, the boycotter, they were all the same: criminal because they were nationalist.

Balfour's coercion was no more or less successful than earlier coercion. Its single success was in defeating boycotting. On any other level his talk of defeating crime was dubious. When Balfour came to Ireland it was peaceful with two exceptions: the south-western counties where 'crime' – mostly intimidation and boycotting and moonlight murder – had been outside the control of the Nationalist Party for years,[29] and the Plan of Campaign which was always confined to particular estates and which would never have reached its dramatic crescendo but for the nature of the terms of the Crimes Act. These terms, by suppressing the National League, provoked a confrontation between 'all' of nationalist Ireland and the 'forces of law and order' in precisely the kind of set piece calculated to underline the equation of crime and nationalism. This equivalence was simultaneously demonstrated in all of the daily newspapers through reports on the transactions of the Special Commission. Dillon and O'Brien, with characteristic shortsightedness, played their allotted roles. Parnell was constitutionally impotent as he hovered beneath charges of the approval of murder. The debate was recast.

The extraordinary nature of the structure of the Irish administration facilitated that political recasting. The reports of the Royal Irish Constabulary are remarkable documents. With the possible exception of France, no European country was so intimately documented. Not merely were all agrarian returns made through the RIC, but on the basis of county inspectors' confidential reports divisional commissioners appointed under the Crimes Act sent detailed monthly accounts to Dublin Castle, monitoring the level of agrarian discontent, of violence and local dissatisfaction. These, together with figures of evictions, crimes and outrages, were studied by the Under-Secretary and Chief Secretary, were quoted in debates in the Commons and Lords, and formed the basis on which the state of the country was assessed and policy justified.[30]

This was very far removed from the primitive machinery of unsolicited

Resident Magistrates' reports on which Forster had relied in 1880. The structure had grown up during the Land War and was refined by the creation of 'areas' under Spencer.[31] Instituted by the Liberals to provide 'solid information' to substantiate garbled reports, the system itself became a weapon of propaganda. Crime figures had always been thrown back and forth indiscriminately during coercion debates and had provided party political ammunition, but the form and content of reports under Balfour substantially altered. Returns headed *Fifteen Years of Agrarian Crime – the Effects of Agitation and the Result of the Crimes Acts* provided the format through which crime was assessed.[32] The negation of all variables in the statistics of crime other than the presence or absence of a Crimes Act posited a view in which, since the foundation of the Land League and the beginning of the Irish nationalist conspiracy, violence was seen to be the constant norm, held down only by the firm lid of coercion.

Criminality was then the corollary to nationalism, its essence and effect. The intricate reports of the period before 1886 gave way to litanies that invariably concluded with statements to the effect that 'the demeanour of the people is much improved'. Undoubtedly intimidation and boycotting figures dropped dramatically when it was appreciated that non-jury trials would not result in automatic acquittal. Davitt's 'Charter of the Land League' of December 1880 had stipulated that those who 'betrayed' the policy of the League by bidding for a farm from which a tenant had been evicted for non-payment of rent, 'should be looked upon and shunned as a traitor to the interests of his fellow tenant farmers and an enemy to the welfare of his country'.[33]

Any Land Leaguer who participated in serving ejectment processes, assisting at evictions or who purchased stock or produce at sheriffs' execution sales was to be ostracised. But by August 1882 Nationalist journals had recognised that such exhortations had taken on their own dynamic:

> It is difficult to believe that any section of our fellow countrymen would be so blind to reason and to common sense as to believe their interests could be advanced by the commission of so heinous a crime as that which we record today, and yet all the circumstances of the cruel deed force upon us the conclusion that it was inspired less by private malice than by a misguided wicked belief that it could advance a public principle. It is sad to reflect for a moment that such a feeling could obtain in Ireland, and it is particularly discouraging at a time when bold efforts are being made to teach the people the virtue of self-reliance, and point out to them the road to liberty by means which heaven can approve of.[34]

William O'Brien's *United Ireland*, the most valuable source for an understanding of the emerging tensions within the nationalist position from 1882, reveals the ambiguities of that position in a perspective utterly at variance with the 'high' view. It is the disintegrating control of nationalism from 1881 that emerges most clearly. It was those cases which the National League executive had felt most uneasy about that provided *The Times* with the wealth of their case. Since the *Times* case was that boycotting and intimidation were both brutal, inhuman and League-orchestrated, Soames chose the 'worst' cases from the copious crime records of these years.

The Curtin murder case at Castle Farm in the midst of the Tralee, Castleisland, Killarney triangle, was one of the most barbarous and complex stories of these years. The Curtins were substantial, 'respectable', educated tenants on a 160-acre farm held from Lord Kenmare. On 13 November 1885 two killings took place on the farm, that were eventually to drive the family from the neighbourhood. They were also to create considerable anxiety in National League headquarters in Dublin, and to arouse a level of interest perhaps only equalled by the Maamtrasna murders. From the point of view of *The Times* no more ideal case could have been chosen to illustrate the brutality of the boycott as an instrument. The extent to which ostracism was relentless and compassionless, and the degree to which, despite the summary powers of the law, information was something that the community was skilled at keeping to itself, was manifest. To *The Times* this demonstrated the tightness of the grip of fear in which the National League held the people. But the evidence of Sergeant Francis Meehan of Farranfore, who replied to the question about whether or not he obtained help from the local community with an unequivocal, 'none whatsoever', is perhaps more revealing in demonstrating the extent to which the Royal Irish Constabulary lived civilly among people who revealed little or nothing to them.

Four or five men called to Curtin's house on the night of 20 November 1885. The family heard the arrival of the men 'from the parlour'. The National League branch in Fieries was set up in March or April of 1885. Curtin was a vice-president of the League and both of his sons were members. At the time of his death, though he himself had paid his rent to Lord Kenmare, he was apparently negotiating on behalf of the tenants for 'an abatement'. The 'boys' who called on the night of 13 November were on a mission for arms, though it is clear that there were other matters at issue which are unlikely ever to come to light. Quite what happened within the house that night is unclear. Curtin was shot dead and a young man in his early twenties, one of the raiders, was also shot dead.

Sir Charles Russell, speaking from an 'official' briefing, emphasised that the murder of John Curtin had never been classified by the police as an agrarian crime. Russell claimed that the dispute was not about land. The 'boys' raiding for firearms were neighbours' sons. John Curtin fired the first shot, killing Timothy Sullivan, the son of a local widow. He was then shot himself. One of the Curtin daughters, Lizzie, gave evidence before the tribunal. After the shootings four servants in the house refused to fetch the police, though they did 'go for a priest'. The only people who witnessed the killings were the family and the moonlighters, one of whom died.

What *is* clear is the treatment that the family received after the event. John Curtin's funeral was sparsely attended. After the funeral the family were rigidly boycotted. Though they had always bought their supplies from Cork, they had purchased smaller items locally. That became impossible. Their workmen left the farm. Their horses could be shod only in Tralee or Killarney. On the roads and in the village the family were 'hooted and shouted at, called informers and murderers'. Even the local parish priest, Father O'Connor, displayed more sympathy for the widowed mother of Timothy Sullivan. Stones were placed on the road before them and groups stood by the side of the road to watch 'to see us pass them, and kept hooting and shouting the whole time'. Ballads were composed about the family and publicly posted. Two Sundays after the trial in December 1885 the family's pew in the chapel at Fieries was smashed. The attempt to replace it was greeted by a further assault when the carrier was beaten while the new pew was smashed at the chapel gate. Two men were sentenced to fourteen years penal servitude at the trial for Curtin's murder. It was after this verdict that the intense boycotting and persecution of the family began. On the day that the pew was smashed the Curtin's herdsman for thirty-two years came and handed over the key of his cottage. He claimed to be afraid to stay.

In January 1886 the National League headquarters in Dublin became seriously alarmed about the Curtin case. John O'Connor, the MP for Tipperary who knew the family, had attended Curtin's funeral. Davitt came to the area but visited the family of Sullivan, while not coming to the Curtins. His alleged purpose was to end the intimidation which was providing the League with highly unfortunate publicity at a time when its activities were politically concentrated on constitutional politics. Finally Alfred Webb, the treasurer of the National League, intervened.

His letter, headed with the League's Abbey Street address in Dublin, was circulated to local League branches:

> Private. To some of my nationalist friends.
> My dear Sir,
> Can nothing be done to save Mrs Curtin and her family from outrage . . .
> I spent last Sunday with the family.
> I will never forget my experiences.
> Were I now to relate them they might be used as arguments for
> coercion . . .
> It is the duty of all Nationalists openly, unequivocally and effectually to
> stand by the family.[35]

In February 1887 the farm was put up for auction. There were no bidders. It was later purchased for a quarter of its value by a man in the neighbourhood.

What this demonstrates is that the offences for which Irish Nationalist politicians were held to be answerable encompassed every private vendetta of a peasant society. Yet, the nature of the intense observation to which Irish rural communities were subject, together with the practice of constant monthly scrutiny of 'crime figures', facilitated the mergence of all rural crime into the murky, all-encompassing fold of 'nationalist conspiracy'. If the role of policy in a society is indicative of the nature of that society, then Ireland was, from 1880, a society in which the permanent scrutiny of civilian populations was the paramount reality.

From 1879 to 1886 Irish nationalism had evolved from a crude agrarian base to a sophisticated political strategy. The achievement of Arthur Balfour's Irish chief-secretaryship was to negate that development and remould the nature of the Irish challenge to a parody of the confused agrarian conspiracy of 1879–81. In this he was facilitated by the personal enmities that existed within the parliamentary party. For Dillon and O'Brien were men with fixed goals but no strategy.

Balfour presented to the cabinet in April 1889 a memorandum prepared by Jenkinson in 1883, to which he attached considerable importance:

> I have always held that our policy in Ireland during the last three years could only make matters grow worse and worse and was not an honest one towards the people of Ireland. Our government of the country was neither one thing nor the other. It had the pretence of being a constitutional government and we were not honest enough because while we set our faces against Home Rule we gave free licence to the press and allowed it to vilify and abuse our administration and to educate the people to believe that Ireland never can be prosperous unless it has a parliament of its own. We also allowed the National League to rise up on the ashes of the Land League and to cover Ireland with its branches and its organisation. Depend upon it, the time has now come when the present state of things can no longer continue, when we must make up our minds to the adoption of one of two courses. We must have recourse to what is called the 'strong arm' policy or we must boldly acknowledge the principle of Home Rule and give Ireland gradually if possible a separate parliament.[36]

Jenkinson, in 1885, reported on the now low level of violence. His comments of 1885 were also circulated at the same April 1889 cabinet by Balfour, with emphasis on the role of Parnell. Though violence was low in September 1885, Jenkinson said that:

> At the same time the feeling against the English government and the landlords was never worse than it is now. I do not hesitate to say that were it not for the faith which the people have in Mr Parnell and for the influence which he and his party exercise over them, there would be an outbreak of serious outrages in all the worst and most distressed parts of Ireland . . . It is a most serious consideration that the peace of Ireland depends upon the influence and position of Mr Parnell and upon the forbearance of the Extremists . . . Any words which may lessen Mr

Parnell's influence or dash the hopes which at the present time fill the hearts of the Irish people . . . We may be quite sure of this: that unless Mr Parnell succeeds in obtaining during this next year Home Rule or a promise of Home Rule he will either fall from power and lose all control or he will have to place himself at the head of a revolutionary movement.[37]

In May 1889, a month after the discussion of these memoranda in cabinet, Balfour wrote to West-Ridgeway:

There is a curious lull in politics both here and in Ireland . . . I hope it is not a lull that precedes a storm but there are rumours about (more or less well authenticated) that if the Judges find against the Parnellites they will give up during the remainder of the Parliament the constitutional game altogether and will return to Ireland and promote a recrudescence of crime and outrage. If there is any truth whatever in these rumours they are partly satisfactory and partly disquieting.[38]

The reasons for the end of Parnellism as a political movement have been sought in the confusion and bitterness of the Parnellite split of 1891. It is in Committee Room 15 or at the hands of Gladstone that the causes of the defeat of Parnell and hence Parnellism have been analysed. But Parnellism was not merely the movement led by Parnell. It was the term used to describe the slow evolution of Irish constitutional nationalism.

Parnell's reluctance to involve himself in the Plan of Campaign was due to his unwillingness to move retrogressively in his political tactics. In contrast to this, William O'Brien placed the material concerns of the tenants above political ends. Dillon however – choleric, dyspeptic and devoid of judgement – relished the politics of unreality on which he began to lead in 1887. Tim Healy was the *petit-bourgeois* opportunist *par excellence*, delighted to be at Westminster, retaining his distilled vitriol for the election circuit of 1891.

The investigations of the Special Commission had effectively destroyed Parnellism. The crude tactic of equating Parnellism with crime worked. By bringing every residual cattle hougher and informer to the same level as the parliamentary party, the sophisticated loose and undefined network that Parnell held together effectively collapsed. By recasting the debate in terms of defeating crime, which was, of course, synonymous with Parnellism, the viability of the parliamentary party as a political force at Westminster was at an end. The respect with which Gladstone, and indeed Hicks-Beach and Churchill, had treated the Irish at Westminster before 1887 gave way to a Conservative view whereby their status as politicians was treated as a manifest joke. Balfour, in correspondence with West-Ridgeway, displays certain fundamental beliefs: that Irish politicians always lie, that their antics are amusing, that structures like New Tipperary are a fitting monument to their absurdity.[39] In the police intelligence this perspective was mirrored by the reports on their 'dupes', whose fluctuating propensity for 'breaking out' was monitored on graphs of crime figures. Balfour changed personnel where he could. District Inspectors soon learnt the type of report that was expected from them. 'Extracts from speeches from prominent nationalists' became a euphemism for the rantings of any townland activist. The rhetoric that came up from the level of the *sans-culotte* 'groaners' and 'hooters' was certainly alarming, 'Keep the snake from amongst you . . . put a brand on him . . . the sign of the cross between you as you would with the very devil from hell'.[40]

The achievement of the Conservative administration was effectively to undermine the constitutional pretensions of Irish nationalism, to claw back ground conceded politically in the past. 'Parnellism and crime' was the text around which this mission was accomplished. Arthur Balfour confessed to thinking that his years in Ireland had been the most important of his life. He was right. In these years all of the central strategic necessities of the retention of power in the face of emerging nationalism were developed: the absolute equation of nationalism with crime, the removal of political effectiveness from constitutional nationalists, the deployment of 'new' personnel to tighten up the regime, the ridicule of existing officers seen to be corrupted by their environment. But most important was the recasting of the debate in terms of defeating crime, a perspective into which historians have been more than willing to enter.

Parnellism was dead because it was politically bankrupted by the Conservative strategy of containment after 1887. The Special Commission dismantled the nationalist alliance by publicly examining its entrails. By seeking to prove that they were not 'criminals' the parliamentary party had already lost the game. The drama of the battering ram was diversionary.

On a letter from West-Ridgeway to Balfour in December 1890 is scribbled:

> We want P. to win because his success will break up the Gladstonian alliance and be a smashing blow for the priests.

The letter itself was circulated to the cabinet, annotated by Balfour:

> Parnell is falling entirely I fear into the hands of the extremists. Last night P. N. Fitzgerald ['the leading IRB organiser', AJB] was on the platform and Clancy, the sub-sheriff ['a physical force man', AJB] and Holland, the Invincible have been his lieutenants. The moderate men will hold aloof and I fear he will fall. He made a very telling speech last night but he was very excited, jumping about the platform and thumping the table. But this was nothing to his excitement at the *United Ireland* office today when he found he had been outwitted. He was in a terrible state of excitement and showed it to everyone.[41]

Parnell's fall into the hands of the hillside men in 1891 is commonly represented as evidence of the desperate mental confusion into which his personal dilemma had forced him. His rejection of constitutionalism, his repudiation of Home Rule – both are seen as the follies of a sick man. This is, of course, part of a view of Parnell's last years that posits adultery as a degenerating malaise. Parnell's lack of apparent political activity after 1887 may have, in part, been due to his personal circumstances. It is more likely to have come from his horrified and powerless observation of the dismantling of his achievement. He was sufficiently shrewd not to be deluded by the significance of his Pigott vindication. It is perhaps valid to suggest that his final rejection of constitutionalism sprang not from hysteria but from lucidity. For Parnell's version of constitutional nationalism was effectively dead before Parnell's fall. The irony is that the minutiae of that tragedy have diverted attention from the real triumph of Conservatism.[42]

6 THE FORMATION OF CONSERVATIVE POLICY, 1886–87

> Some parts are bad, others indifferent and others again in a fairly good state. Kerry is the worst. Clare possibly is next in badness, Limerick is bad and in parts nearly bankrupt.
>
> Ashbourne to Salisbury, 18 July 1886

The Case of Kerry Stated

In terms of what Joseph Lee has characterised as an agitation calendar the Land War in Kerry erupted eighteen months after Mayo. In an attempt by the lawyers of *The Times* and their government supporters to establish the Land and National Leagues as sustained criminal conspiracy, the case of Kerry was vital. The first Land League meeting took place there, in the town of Castleisland, in September 1880. The government case was that it was as a consequence of this meeting that agitation began that was to make Kerry the most notorious county in Ireland.[1] In the Commission appointed to investigate the allegations brought to the surface by 'Parnellism and Crime' the evidence available to *The Times* through government sources was exceptional, even by Irish standards. The full archives of the Royal Irish Constabulary and stipendiary magistrates' reports had been opened for the *Times* case. The appointment of 'special commissioners' to pacify the south-west provides an additional source of information with which to compare the official record as put forward by the Commission. The special commissioners were Major General Sir Redvers Buller for the years from 1886 to 1887,[2] and later Major General Sir Alfred E. Turner.[3] Their presence emphasised that the state of the county was a matter of high political and policy concern. Kerry was an area where the statistics of agrarian outrage clearly demonstrated a dramatic rise from September 1880, when the first Land League meeting was addressed in Castleisland. Hence, Kerry substantiated, or potentially substantiated, the government contention that conspiracy was at the root of disturbance. In 1878 there were five agrarian crimes in Kerry. In 1879 the figure was thirteen. In 1880 the figure was two hundred and ninety eight, of which only sixty six occurred in the first nine months of that year.[4] Kerry was also exceptional in that two of Parnell's most loyal lieutenants, Timothy and Edward Harrington, were from Tralee, from where they ran the highly influential newspaper the *Kerry Sentinel.*[5] It also had some of the largest landowners in the country, in particular the Kenmares, and the most notorious land agent in Ireland, Samuel Murray Hussey.[6] Hussey, in his reminiscences, romanticises Kerry as the county of the great Elizabethan settlements, names that still owned the land of the county – William and Charles Herbert, Valentine Brown (the family name of the Kenmares), Edmund Denny, after whom the main street of Tralee was named, Captain Conway, and Roland Blennerhassett, whose family occupied the area around Muckross House, the old Norman family of Fitzmaurice-Fitzgerald – the Lansdownes.[7]

The violence that was to make Kerry notorious through the 1880s was concentrated in a triangular area marked by three main towns of the county: Tralee, Killarney and Castleisland. Castleisland was a town remarkable for little other than its weekly market, and its dramatically wide main street.[8] It was also the opening town for the road to Cork through King Williamstown, later Ballydesmond, an area notorious in the 1830s. It was in response to trouble at that time that a road had been cut over the mountains to Cork, to open up what had formerly been bandit country. The name of Castleisland was, however, to acquire, during the eighties, a familiar ring in both Houses of Parliament, in Dublin Castle consultations, and in cabinet meetings. It became a name almost as notorious a Maamtrasna, a byword for acts of savage brutality, agrarian atrocity, murder and lawlessness. The aim of the Special Commission's investigation of that notoriety was to demonstrate that this brutality was Land and National League orchestrated and controlled, and that it was intimately directed by the Irish Nationalist members of Parliament under the guiding hand of Parnell.

In August 1888 Salisbury had discussed with Balfour the extent to which the government should assist *The Times* in prosecuting the *Times* case:

> The question . . . if we light on valuable bits of evidence are we to give those to the *Times* or not . . . is not I think capable of a general answer. It must be decided with a view to the peculiarities of each case. There may be grounds for not sitting, if the evidence in question is not of a conclusive kind, or if the mode of getting it cannot be explained. If, on the other hand it has come naturally into your hands – and still more if it clearly fixes someone's guilt we shall be fulfilling our obvious and elementary duty in facilitating the proof of it before the Commission.[9]

The role of the Conservative government in the Special Commission has been observed.[10] By looking more closely at the case made about Kerry, several questions of fact and perception can be explored. Firstly, the question to which the Commission was ostensibly seeking an answer: the degree to which the League was a criminal conspiracy and secondly, and more remotely, the role of the police in monitoring crime, their role within the society, and the impact of their reports on the Dublin Castle administration and on London.

The 'prosecution' case consisted of the evidence of Royal Irish Constabulary officers who had served in the north- and mid-Kerry area from 1879 to 1887. The official lists of outrages prepared by the RIC,[11] and each individual case was highly detailed, had been 'culled' for appropriate cases, and the relevant parties to these cases had been subpoenaed to appear before the Commission in London. Appropriate quotations from the *Kerry Sentinel*, penned by Harrington, who was both League organiser and Nationalist MP, were also produced to demonstrate exhortation to violence from the top.[12] Police report notetakers' accounts of Land League meetings were read to the Commission, details of agrarian outrages were expounded upon by close cross-questionings of witnesses – land agents, paid informants, victims of attack, boycotted caretakers and relatives of the dead. Though these cases were specifically selected to establish a connection between Land League organisation and violent attacks, and are as such biased or weighted sources, they nonetheless represent an exceptional documentary insight into the nature of rural unrest. The RIC reports can provide such an insight if carefully read, though evidence presented to the Commission provides, obliquely, a clearer view of the relations between government policy, the League and the local population.

The area discussed is one of little more than ten square miles, though some of the cases took place outside this core area. Another source which illuminates the politics of the area is the late William Feingold's essay on the Tralee Poor Law election of 1881.[13] The cases cited by the Commission are, when compared with the list of outrages for the period, representative. In this analysis the focus attempts to set aside the concerns of the Attorney-General. It tries instead to provide a window onto the self-representations of those who acted and were acted upon, their attitudes towards politics and the law, the extent to which they were intimidated into certain actions, and the extent to which they intimidated. Whether it illuminates, as intended by the Commission, the extent to which they acted under Land and National League orders or merely availed of the climate of uncertainty to pursue old wrongs is debatable. It seems clear that there was dislocation and eviction in Kerry from early 1880 and that, at least initially, it was provoked by sharp agricultural decline.[14]

Alexander Bennett was land steward on the estate of Arthur Blennerhasset, owner of 12,621 acres in the county at a valuation of £4,157 in 1873.[15] The agent for the estate was Samuel Hussey who, in addition to managing his own fairly modest estate of 3,000 acres, was agent for vast tracts of Munster.[16] Bennett, an Englishman who had lived on the Blennerhassett home estate at Ballyseedy since 1869, gave evidence about the murder of Patrick Cahill on 22 June 1882 in the townland of Mount Nicholas. Ronan, acting for *The Times,* reminded Bennett that in November 1880 Timothy Harrington and

John Kelly had made speeches at a Land League meeting at Ahane, a mile from Mount Nicholas, at which they protested against an eviction carried out by Hussey.[17] In fact the original event that precipitated the organisation of the Land League in Kerry was a bitter battle between Hussey and certain tenants. According to Bennett, Poff, the tenant of a farm at Mount Nicholas, was evicted by Bennett in 1881. In swift succession, those that Bennett put in to 'care for' the farm, departed, presumably in response to boycotting and intimidation; Fitzgerald left within months, and a man called Keefe, who was fulfilling the same function on three other farms from which tenants had been evicted, after he had been fired upon. They were succeeded by John and Thomas Clifford. On 6 November 1881 John Clifford reported to the RIC the shooting of his brother by 'Moonlighters', as they were locally called – men who came with blackened faces in the night. Bennett visited Thomas Clifford and found him

> sitting on a chair by the side of the fire, and a coat thrown over his shoulders; four bullets went clear through his thigh and another one went and lodged in his backbone.[18]

The Cliffords, not surprisingly, refused to continue on the farm and were replaced by Patrick Cahill. On 14 June 1882 Cahill reported that he had been fired at, and was granted police protection. On 22 June he was dead: found on the roadside at a spot between his house and what had formerly been Poff's farm. An ejectment decree had been obtained against Poff for non-payment of rent in May 1880. His eviction took place in May of the following year 1881. He was tried at Cork for the murder of Cahill and hanged, late in 1882.[19]

Clearly there were certain men who could be relied upon to occupy farms from which tenants had been evicted. By mid-1882, most of them were under police protection. The same Thomas Clifford, who figured in the Poff case, came to prominence again a few months later. On this occasion he was employed to herd and care for the farm from which the tenant, Pat Driscoll, had been evicted in October 1882. Driscoll had been a tenant of Blennerhasset, as was Clifford's father. Both farms were within two miles of Ballyseedy. Clifford tended the Driscoll farm by day, and stayed on his father's farm at night. Late on the night of 6 November eight masked men came to his father's farm. They shot him once in the thigh. Before leaving, the last man

> raised the stock of the gun over my head and said next time I go to this place, the next night they visited me they would cut off my head.

Nobody was charged with the attack. Clifford claimed to have no knowledge of the Land League in his area, and to harbour no suspicion of League complicity in his shooting. He himself, held, in 1889, five acres from

Blennerhassett, since the death of his father. His rent had been reduced by the Land Court appointed under the 1881 Land Act from 5 guineas to £2 a year.[20]

John Culloty was a rent-warner and tenant on the estate of the Misses Mary and Anne Busteed in the division of Carker, about five miles from Castleisland. Theirs was a relatively small estate of 1,685 acres, with a valuation of £644 in 1873.[21] On 3 August 1883 he left Carker to live at Ballaghantouragh. From the date of the founding of the Land League in 1880 the attitude of his neighbours changed. He said:

> I found that they did not want any rent warner as far as paying rent . . .
> In 1880 the people were very much against paying rents and considered the rents very high according to the speeches made.[22]

But their attitude to him personally, or certainly their behaviour, did not change until 5 October 1881 when he accompanied a bailiff Fitzchallor, acting for Miss Busteed's agent Mr McCullen, to serve writs on the estates. Culloty's role was to identify the tenants to the bailiff. Before this date, in June 1881, Culloty had attended a Land League meeting at Knocknabue addressed by 'clergymen and farmers'. At that meeting the speakers urged that a nearby farm from which tenants had been evicted 'should stop their idle', and Herbert, the estate agent, was denounced. They said that 'they would make him a remarkable man, though they would not touch a hair of his head'. Later, at a Scartaglin meeting after Sunday Mass, a man in the crowd called out Culloty's name, 'and I left and went home'. Before going to serve the bailiff on 5 October

> a friend came to see me and said he was afraid I was doing myself great harm.

After assisting the bailiff 'offences were thrown in my face about it'. He heard stories of what had happened to others and became afraid to stay in his house at night:

> I would walk out and lie in the ditch, or I would walk out some distance from my farm to the cowhouses.

When he tired of that he built a hiding place in his own house. On 12 March 1882 a group of men called in the small hours, told his wife that they were members of the RIC and held a gun to her face. One of the men said to her that Culloty had boasted 'next time he would serve writs without a bailiff's assistance'. He had in fact said this to a friend Michael Daly, at a fair in Castleisland in October. After this incident Culloty had police protection at night. A month later, three nights before there was to be an eviction for the writs that had been served in October, two disguised men 'shot and fired' his leg, which was later amputated. One man, David Fleming, was sentenced to thirty years for the attack. When Culloty was discharged from hospital all of his neighbours boycotted him:

> On the morning of 6th May there was a notice found in the Ardtully road near the bridge, offering £100 reward for any man's name who did anything to me.[23]

In 1887, five years later, Culloty was still boycotted. He lived entirely in an island of police protection, outside the pale of his own community. In August 1883 he had moved to an evicted farm in Ballaghantouragh, thus confirming his status as outsider. When his child died in 1886 a coffin was obtained only through the influence of the District Inspector of the RIC. When he claimed criminal compensation for injuries before Judge Lynch in Tralee, the Poor Law Guardian who defended the claim against him was Timothy Brosnan, a member of the Land League's Castleisland branch. Local gossip claimed that the attack on him had no agrarian base, and was carried out by the relatives of a servant girl whom he had seduced.[24]

Daniel Leahy, a tenant of Lord Kenmare's from Scarteen near Killarney, was shot dead in his home on 21 August 1882. In questioning his widow the *Times* counsel tried to establish a connection between his death and his second cousin Jeremiah Leahy, who was secretary of the Land League branch at Fieries near Farranfore.[25] But the *Kerry Sentinel* of 22 August 1882 published an article that seemed to indicate a very strong desire to distance the then National League from such attacks:

> Another shocking murder has been contributed to the roll of crime which records our national disgrace and this latest bloody deed of assassination is contributed by Kerry . . . Our duty as public journalists is simply to raise our voices in protest against the bloody deeds that are fast bringing disgrace upon our land and to caution our people that as they value life or liberty they must unite in stopping the progress of this fearful demon of blood . . . Is it by dark deeds of blood that any section [of Irishmen] can hope to advance the interests of their country. It is difficult to believe that any section of our fellow countrymen would be so blind to reason and to commonsense as to believe that their interests could be advanced by the commission of so heinous a crime as that which we record today.[26]

United Ireland revealed the ostensible 'reason' for his death.[27] Up to nine months before his killing, Leahy had been not merely a tenant, but a minor agent, on Lord Kenmare's estate. He would have been one of many, since the estate was one of the largest in the county, with an acreage of 91,000 and a valuation of £25,252. Lord Headley, a substantial landowner in his own right with 12,679 acres, held a grazing farm of fifty acres from Kenmare at

Lecabane. This he sub-let some weeks before the killing. The farm, from which the tenant had been evicted, was put up for auction at a sheriff's sale. It was purchased by a man called Daniel Cronin from Gortalea. The sale was annulled without explanation after completion. The farm was granted to John Cronin, a son-in-law of Leahy's, whose influence was assumed to have been used to annul the previous sale.[28]

The most important Kerry witness for *The Times* was Maurice Leonard, a Justice of the Peace for Killarney, and chief agent for Lord Kenmare since January 1886. He was educated abroad and then 'bound' to Samuel Hussey from his return in March 1875 until November 1876 when he became assistant agent on Kenmare's property.[29] He made it part of his duty to know about the Land and National Leagues. It was, he claimed, unknown for anyone to be 'punished for paying rent' before the meeting held by O'Donoghue and Parnell at Listry in 1881. Punishment for taking a farm from which tenants had been evicted was also unknown, he claimed, before the 'No Rent' manifesto. Since the 'No Rent' manifesto was later than many of the cases already cited, this seems rather odd. Almost all of the crimes attributed to 'Captain Moonlight' arose from one or other of these 'offences'. O'Donoghue's Killarney meeting of 9 January 1881 was, he claimed, the signal for the evicted farmers' campaign. Before that date caretakers would process evictions without police protection or public interference. There were private quarrels between tenants about land-holding, but 'nothing of an organised character'.[30]

Leonard was a young man – thirty-six in 1888: a mere twenty-three when he returned to the country in 1875, five years before the trouble began. The expression 'land grabber' he dated to 1885. He stated that from November 1879 to April 1880 there were people 'blue with hunger'. 'Crime', when it did break out in 1880, was, he claimed, confined to those areas that were relatively well off. In 1881 when the League was established, the Rathmore district was where crime began. Crime stopped after the passage of the Coercion Act in 1882. Leonard did *not* mention the conciliatory Arrears Act, which was passed at the same time, thus removing one of the main grievances of tenants. In other words, his analysis insisted that it was repression and not concession that proved effective. The 'improvement' he alleged, had lasted until September 1885, when William O'Brien, editor of *United Ireland*, Tim Healy, Edward Harrington and a Roman Catholic clergyman from America, came to Killarney and made violent speeches. This marked the 'official' establishment of the National League in Kerry.[31]

In October and November 1881, at the time when Parnell issued the 'No Rent' manifesto from Kilmainham, Leonard claimed that Land League courts were actively regulating behaviour on the Kenmare estate. The proceedings of these 'court' sessions were published by Harrington in the *Sentinel*. Leonard held to the view that 'there was a terrorism actually extending and overshadowing the whole of this district, by reason of the action of the Land League courts'.

Martin Cullinane was one of three brothers in residence in a Kenmare holding at Ardwainig near Farranfore. In 1881 an ejectment order was made against them and executed. An arrangement was made with Leonard whereby one of the brothers, Michael, the wealthiest of the three, was to become the official holding-tenant to whom the brothers, who were to remain on their existing properties, were to pay rent. After the agreement the new tenant came to Leonard. His ears had been slit. He said: 'Look what the boys have done to me for taking the farm, sir'. He told Leonard that he had been summoned to the Land League court.[32]

John Cuirnane, a tenant at Dromahegmon (sic), in the Killarney division of the Kenmare property, was legally 'proceeded against' for non-payment of rent. He was defended by Broderick, the local Land League solicitor. Cuirnane was nonetheless evicted. A notice was posted in the centre of Killarney:

> To the farmers of Kerry. Take notice that you will not propose Mr S. Hussey for the lands of Dromahegmon, near Killarney.
>
> > At your peril.[33]

The complicated nature of the relations between tenants and agents was illustrated by the case of Patrick Murphy. In October 1879 he came to Leonard, and requested that an order of ejectment be instituted against his holding to enable him to dislodge a creditor O'Callaghan, who had attempted to call in his debt by taking possession of his (Murphy's) holding.[34] Since Murphy owed merely twelve months' rent, the county judge declined to bring an order of ejectment, and merely dismissed the case with costs. At Murphy's request, ejectment had, however, been secured, by application to a Dublin 'superior court'. O'Callaghan was evicted. Having taken possession in the interval, before the local court's decision, Murphy was reinstated as caretaker. During 1880 and early 1881 Murphy was involved in 'agitating in the district'. Leonard, aware of this, called upon him to pay up and redeem his land, since the six months legal period for redemption had passed. Failure to do so would result in reletting.

Leonard proceeded to relet to a new tenant who paid a £120 entry fine. His bailiffs and a young assistant, Perrot, went to execute a caretaker's summons against Murphy. They met with every resistance. This, according to Leonard, was unprecedented. Before 1881 he had never met with such resistance.[35] The bailiff was instructed to remove doors and windows from the house. Leonard implied that the fire which burnt it to the ground had been started by Murphy's wife. Certainly neither he nor Kenmare had authorised it. On the following Sunday a group of five hundred people led by Edward Harrington, brother of Timothy, tried to erect a Land League hut on a road on Kenmare's estate. This action had been authorised by a Dublin Land League meeting chaired by Sexton on 24 August.[36] Two hundred troops were sent in to 'protect the peace'. Leonard claimed that he and about sixty labourers 'hunted them off the road'. The hut was finally erected on the farm of William Daly of Dromreag. Daly pulled it down after the crowd dispersed, and some nights later was customarily warned, again by 'ear clipping'.[37]

'Poor John O'Keefe' of Lisbawn paid his rent to Leonard on 25 October 1881. On 27 November he was shot in both calves. On the same day John and Michael Cronin of Maughantoorig paid their rent. They were shot on the same night as O'Keefe.[38]

Leonard in his evidence before the Commission discussed a variety of cases, attempting in all to demonstrate that attacks were clearly under the direct control of the League. Jeremiah Callaghan of Ballynamanagh paid his rent through his daughter, Mrs Lynch in December 1881:

> Mr Linnord, my father have sent me with the balance of a gale's rent, himself would be afraid to come with it as he is no Land Leaguer. Please make no remark in presence of anyone in the office but give me a receipt'.[39]

Callaghan had been a tenant for years, since a middleman's rent fell in, and before 1881 always came personally to the office to pay.

In November 1881 the son of Patrick Lynch of Inchicullane, a substantial tenant who held two farms at Duneen and Coolcorcoran, wrote to Lord Kenmare from the Oratory of the Holy Family, Grosvenor Square, Manchester, enclosing his father's rent:

> The most honourable and courageous course would be to pay it himself but the poor man cannot repress this feeling of terror which those midnight marauders have caused to spring up in his mind.[40]

Nonetheless, the son availed of the '25% reduction granted on the current gale', and enclosed a cheque for £35 allowing for that deduction.

Jeremiah Leahy, already referred to, was secretary of the Fieries branch of the National League. On 9 August 1884 Sergeant Cornelius McCarthy, who had been stationed at Farranfore barracks since January 1883, searched the home of John MacMahon of Bushman, who had succeeded Leahy as secretary of the League branch. The search took place in the presence of District Inspector Paston Crane, and was authorised under the Protection of Person and Property Act (1882).[41]

They found a letter from Leahy, written before he fled to America in January 1883. The letter was addressed to MacMahon:

> Enclosed is a list of the Fieries collection for Parnell . . . You can enquire of Mr Harrington if the funds will be turned over to the National League and if so send up whatever balance you may have in hand. I will send you a cheque for the remainder at the first opportunity, that is if I am not arrested in Queenstown, which I dread very much. I need hardly tell you what a wrong that would be, but there is nothing but wrong in the

present day. Do not mention a word of this to anybody living, as if it became known to the police they might arrest me at once. Goodbye, old fellow suspect. Write often and send me papers.[42]

Thomas Lyons, a large shopkeeper from Tralee, in a letter to Samuel Hussey dated 27 October 1881, paid the rents of two tenants who had previously paid openly.[43] Daniel O'Connor of Lisheen wrote to Hussey on 29 December 1881 pointing out that

Donoghue who was served [with a writ] with me was attacked the second night after leaving your office.

Both he and Donoghue were willing to pay rent

but want your honour to allow us some time, at least till peace is restored in the locality.[44]

O'Connor felt that he was already unpopular and envied in his locality because of his role as agent for Tivy, the Cork butter merchant, and had no desire to make matters worse for himself.[45]

Arthur O'Keefe from Fortwilliam, who purchased his interest on the Kenmare Killarney estate in 1877, went through an elaborate ritual whereby, despite having paid his rent secretly, he feigned the role of protesting tenant up to the point of eviction.[46]

In Glangrasteen three tenants who were able and willing to pay were afraid to do so. The arrival of Miss Reynolds of the Ladies Land League in Killarney in 1882 was 'the signal for chaos in Rathmore and Glangrasteen'.[47] On the night of the eviction of these three tenants shots were fired into the deserted houses. Leonard, however, claimed that all of the other tenants in that townland had paid their rents, which makes it more than surprising that League-induced fear inhibited these three from so doing. Immediately after, the eviction rent and costs were paid, and the three were reinstated.

An even more elusive case was that of John Moynihan of Bauard who used the sophisticated John O'Keefe as intermediary. Moynihan was pursuing a similarly tortuous path of paying secretly though he was apparently already subject to public odium in his townland of Rathmore. This dated from his ability to pay rent in November 1880, when all of his neighbours where either unable or unwilling to pay:

When I came home they began to vent their indignation against me and I was held up as an enemy, even in Rathmore, A notice was posted 'The Black Sheep of the Parish' and under that notice the names of the Cronins, of John Keefe of Lisheen and mine appeared. I earnestly entreat you will not tell anyone of my having paid any rent, as it is a sentence of death. I have my brother James at my house, but if you are

> against it I shall have him removed, as I should not do anything that
> would be hostile to the interests of the Earl of Kenmare.[48]

Cornelius Leahy of Keanasup had made over his farm to his son-in-law, 'keeping a reservation for himself'. When they were all evicted in January 1882 for non-payment of rent Leahy alone was reinstated as caretaker, on condition that he did not bring his son-in-law and daughter in to the farm. For complying with this injunction, he was shot at night in both legs, for which he later received £100 compensation under the Crimes Act.

The questions that the Special Commission posed and sought to answer on the nature of the connection between Land and National League incitement to outrage could not be proven. That connection was, however, deemed to be demonstrated by the reiteration of witnesses on the connection between League meetings and outrage. It seems clear that the vendettas pursued and tabulated by the constabulary were about a general repudiation of authority into which they had little insight. In Kerry, contrary to the government contention, the Land League lit the fuse to a powder keg but had little direct control of the explosive forces unleashed. The Leagues – Land and National – acted through local organisation into which pre-existing groupings and interests cohered to pursue old grievances in a new language, with new opportunities and methods.

Another view of the politics of land and violence in Kerry was provided by government appointees.

Unwelcome Analysts:
Tories out of Step – Hicks–Beach and Redvers Buller

Major-General Sir Redvers Buller 'pacifier of the African bush' was appointed to suppress moonlighting and boycotting in the south-west shortly after the return to office of the Salisbury administration in August 1886. He was appointed to take command of the civil and military forces in the Millstreet area of Cork, in Kerry and in Clare.[49] Working in close consultation with Sir Michael Hicks-Beach, the Conservative Chief Secretary, his early months in the job coincide with a hiatus in Tory policy. Home Rule had been defeated: the process of stripping the Dublin Castle administration of neo-Liberal influences, in particular the Under-Secretary Sir Robert Hamilton, had gently to be approached.[50] Buller, a professional soldier with colonial experience, on leave from the Adjutant-General's office, was to provide an antidote to the ambiguity that was seen to have characterised Liberal policy towards law and order in the period leading up to the introduction of the Home Rule Bill in 1886.

Buller on the ground proved, however, to be an unpredictable instrument. Intended to counter Hicks-Beach's earnest and governmentally unpopular belief in the gravity of the renewed agricultural depression of late 1886,

Buller and Hicks-Beach, in fact, turned into a team at one on most matters of substantive analysis. An examination of their appraisal of events in the half year preceding Arthur Balfour's arrival in Dublin highlights the extent to which Balfour's appearance in Dublin Castle marked the adoption of a dramatically new and clear line on the way in which the 'Irish question' was to be viewed.

Buller, alarmingly, did not immediately enter into the 'law and order' role for which he had been appointed. He combined his necessary tour of the Royal Irish Constabulary and army structures with a taste for economic, social and historical analysis that Salisbury viewed with distaste.

In September Buller wrote to Hicks-Beach from the relative splendour of the Railway Hotel in the Victorian town of Killarney:

> I have now seen four of the police districts and probably the four worst – Castleisland and Killarney in Co Kerry – and Kanturk and Millstreet in Co Cork – of these the first and the last are I fancy the worst. Castleisland has 21 derelict farms and 23 from which the tenants have been evicted, but which are now occupied by caretakers under police protection. Millstreet has scarcely one evicted or derelict farm and the crime there is due to quarrels among the tradesmen and their having combined to boycott the most successful of their fellows in order to obtain his trade. The usual results have followed in each district the formation of a branch of the National League, boycotting and intimidation with consequent night attacks and assaults. Castleisland is actively bad. Millstreet is at present quiescent – the reason I fancy is that the raiders in Castleisland come from separate farms and are harder for the police to watch than those in Millstreet who are of the town and are therefore more easily controlled by the police. In both districts rents are being fairly paid but the people are poor.[51]

According to Buller:

> The country is lawless and has been badly and loosely governed, and the National League has got full hold of it, and this same National League has got into low hands and is in most places working for family feuds in private interests. There is no faith in the government whatever, no man will give evidence, most of the lawbreakings that occur are never reported or even heard of by the police, for fear the sufferers should be made to prosecute.[52]

Buller was not dismissive of the competence of the police, but felt that, despite their efficiency and discipline, they were ill-adapted to their task. They are

> really efficient and are doing their best, but they are a Military body, they live in Barracks and do not mix with the population so they hear but little of what goes on.[53]

He had an ostensibly clear view of what was required:

> I believe that I shall be able to improve the police work in detail: out-
> rages are said to be decreasing and I think that they can be lessened still
> more by slight alterations in the police system which I am gradually
> carrying out.[54]

He thought that he could greatly improve the level of police work by
reordering the deployment of men. The only remedy was, he believed, to
establish a wise, kind but strong government in 'these western districts':

> Pass a special act; give power to try offenders taken within, outside the
> district; give power to examine before trial; and to suppress branches of
> the local League if thought necessary. I am no longer in favour of the
> total suppression of the League.[55]

Hicks-Beach was sympathetic to Buller, but he felt it necessary to restrain
Buller's excessive zeal in reorganisation. Buller was quick to reassure him
that changes were not being made without reference to Dublin Castle, that he
was constantly in consultation with Waters of Jenkinson's department and
was not making any changes between the 'special' and 'regular' members of
the constabulary. He had not adopted that system in his division, and Waters
agreed with him. He had long discussions with Waters on the demerits of the
existing system and possible remedies. He found Waters a 'clever, good man
who would doubtless, with his knowledge of the existing system, be able to
formulate better reforms'. Both agreed on the inadequacies of the existing
system. He emphasised to Hicks-Beach that, although he appreciated his
statutory independence, he would not attempt to make changes or introduce a
system which would be in conflict with the aims of the Government of Ireland,
or affect other districts, without full consultation with the authorities in Dublin.

On the subject of 'power to change place of trial' he was aware that, though
Kerry offenders could be tried by a Cork jury, Cork juries were already
protesting. He thought that, given the lawless state of the country, an
unknown place of trial might act as a deterrent. The power to enquire before
arrest he thought most valuable. It seems that most of the worst murders in
Kerry in 1882 were solved by such means.

In a letter outlining these points, written in September 1886, Buller put
forward this view of the National League:

> I think that anyone coming here at first would be, as I was, astounded at
> the direct connection between outrages and the National League, but
> further enquiry led me to the opinion I explained in my last, viz. that if
> you could settle the farmers, the National League, now passing to the
> shopkeepers, would soon be discredited – and it was better to wait for
> that if we can wait, than to make it a martyr and revive its popularity –
> of course the question is: Can we preserve society while we wait? I am

not yet prepared definitely to answer that question in the affirmative – If the section of the Crimes Act (the 7th I think) which deals with boycotting and intimidation and allowed trial summarily by the Resident Magistrate could be revived that would be the best, but I fancy this was too much to ask – If also the power of search warrants under the Peace Preservation Acts could be extended and the power of being restricted to particular houses, and for ten days, were made more general, that also would help us enormously . . . The real question is the land question – settle that and you can settle the country.[56]

The provision for land purchase provided in the Tory Ashbourne Act of 1885 had been well responded to in Kerry, and Buller felt that this response was partly due to National League influence:

In Kerry there are a very large proportion of the farmers who can pay rent most, if not all, that is due from them, but there are many who cannot pay at all: the National League centres, where in good hands, are apparently encouraging tenants to pay and to purchase – I am told, but have no means of verifying it, that £250,000 of land has been sold to tenants in the county of Kerry this year. In other districts, however, where National League centres are not so well led, there can be no doubt that they are supporting the farmer in a refusal to pay, or to demand when they do pay enormous reductions, this latter with the view of lessening the future purchase money to be paid for the property. The year has been a bad one, the people are poor and short of money. In kindly managed estates, Lord Ventry's, Lord Carte's, Lord Listowel's, W. Hewson's, there are many, I believe the majority in those districts, of farmers who are three and four years in arrears, a tenant told me the other day 'It is £80 they're asking, sure I would as soon pay £800' – this makes them unwilling to pay even what they can. Money, being short of employment and this all adds to general discontent.[57]

Buller was not in doubt as to the culpability of the Liberal government:

In considering this state of things with a view to its amendment, one must recollect that the past Governments have not been strong: indeed, I should say have been very slack. Men of very low character have been appointed JPs. The Local Government Board have been very slack in looking after the Board of Guardians; everybody I have spoken to in Kerry comments upon the weakness of the Kerry County Court judge O'Connor Morris. The country is strewn with low publications, and the proprietors of these to get a trade encourage every sort of devilment: and further it is evident to me that during the last six months many of the police have been preparing for Home Rule and to a certain extent following the advice of the unjust stewards – a great number of farms are practically out of cultivation and many police are locked up in them protecting caretakers and so forth . . . it seems to me that to do anything with this country we must have:
1. Summary powers for Resident Magistrates in cases of boycotting and intimidation and of language inciting to the same, and of forcible entry

or retainer. I do not think the punishment need exceed two months at the most but it must be summary.

2. Powers should be given to the police to attend all meetings even if in private houses; I think this would suffice to draw the teeth of the dangerous leagues.

3. Power to change venue . . .

Then as to the land. I do hope you will see your way to do the following this session:

i. Encourage Lord Ashbourne's Act if necessary, I mean allow more money.

ii. Add a clause providing for compulsory purchase of head rents.

iii. Add a clause allowing that if the majority of tenants in a divided townland purchase the landlord may be relieved of the whole of his interest in that townland by the state.

iv. Allow leaseholders to obtain judicial rents.

v. Take power to stay eviction and also foreclosures and proceedings by mortgagees, Head-rent landlords and others . . . *The real fact is that the land is charged with more money than it now can pay* – So far as I can see most landlords have had their pound of flesh long ago . . . My earnest recommendation to you is to support Parnell's Bill which is meant to be a coercive act for the people, both acts are wanted – and then next session introduce a good Land Purchase Bill secured by a coercion act of a good but mild nature which should coexist with the purchase act.[58] [my emphasis]

Buller moved on his tour from Killarney to Ennis, and from there to Kilkee where he based himself at Moore's Hotel. He decided that the situations in Kerry and Clare were not comparable, and ought preferably to be handled separately. Jenkinson was *not* apparently happy to rely exclusively on Buller's judgement, and Buller demonstrated no resistance to 'the Castle' sending 'a man' to report separately to Jenkinson. Buller thought that in Kerry the violence was 'local and purely agrarian'. In Clare, on the other hand,

> the people are not so congested and perhaps a little better able to pay, anyhow there is not the same combination against the payment of rent and certainly not the same bad feeling against agents and landlords: but there is apparently a dangerous secret society.

In Kerry most murders were clearly agrarian but 'in Clare they have been mysterious, for no assignable cause. At present I have found no peg whatever on which to hang a theory'. Buller's impression was, however, that:

> an agent sent to Kerry would have to ingratiate himself locally with small local bands of farmers' sons and rowdies who are moonlighting – while in Clare he would have to get in to a very closely organised and most dangerous society.[59]

Clearly the Dublin Castle man, sent by Jenkinson, was to be discreet and unobtrusive:

> It will be for Mr Jenkinson to say which line the man is best suited for. I think in any case he should have special means of communicating with

me through a third party and that for the present at any rate it would be better that I should not even know him by sight.[60]

Buller was more concerned by the continuing Curtin saga:

> I think the government ought to take the responsibility of their fire insurance. Mrs Curtin told me the other day that they had paid a premium to the 'Imperial' for thirty years, but that office had now declined to continue it on the grounds of great risk of incendiarism, and so her buildings are now uninsured, which she said was a great anxiety to her.[61]

He had also dropped his intention to revise the structure of the Secret Branch, controlled by Plunkett and Byrne, in view of the temporary nature of his own appointment.

One case which he encountered in the course of his Clare travels was to have serious implications for the future:

> In County Clare there is a certain landlord Colonel O'Callaghan – who is what is here described as very obnoxious to his tenantry, and who is certainly in respect to them a hard, overbearing man – his tenantry are withholding their rents and demanding reductions which up to the present he has refused. He has taken out processes against many tenants, say about 40 or 45 in all; of these some few could pay but many really cannot. If Colonel O'Callaghan proceeds in these processes to evictions there will, I think, undoubtedly be very serious disturbance. Colonel O'Callaghan has been more or less boycotted but now gets labour, all his men have, however, given undertakings to leave his service should he act on these processes. Colonel O'Callaghan's life is at present undoubtedly in serious danger and he has personal protection. He is a determined man and promises that he will be a dear bit of clay to anyone who shoots him. The district is a very lawless one, indeed, there was a serious disturbance here in 1881 – the battle of Bodyke caused by resistance to some distraints made by Colonel O'Callaghan.[62]

What Buller wanted to know from Hicks-Beach was if Colonel O'Callaghan were to call on the sheriff to proceed, should police protection be given to the sheriff:

> And also should the evictions be assisted? It will probably require a large process to carry them out: most of the tenants cannot really pay and there will be a great social disturbance.[63]

Relations between Hicks-Beach and Buller, and the London view of Buller, were not improved by newspaper coverage of the tour. Buller had succeeded in having O'Connor Morris replaced by Judge Curran, and anticipated the next sessions with considerable hope. He was *not*, therefore, pleased to have his word impugned by the reports of the Nationalist press. Being maligned publicly by the Nationalists almost drove him to sympathy with the landlord case. In speaking about the money being spent on police protection in Kerry he concluded, 'in fact the law is impotent and an enormous expenditure is being incurred to conceal its impotence'.[64]

By 29 September, however, Buller was feeling more optimistic:

> When I last wrote I was taking credit for some small successes but I had better luck since – On Sunday the police in Castleisland arrested five men, armed and with disguises, who were, I believe, about to attempt a murder. It was a very satisfactory business and it was worked entirely on information, and Mr Davis the District Inspector and Sergt O'Donnel the Police Sergt who worked the matters deserve the greatest credit. It will give heart to the police who wanted success, and will also, I hope, make the moonlighters who had long enjoyed impunity distrustful of each other and more ready, therefore, to secure safety by informing. It was also cheap – £20 in advance – to be returned if no information was forthcoming, and security was given for this. £30 more if magistrates committed, and £50 more or £100 in all on conviction. I think these were, for a county in which information has been almost impossible, fair terms and five men, two of whom are notorious ruffians, was a better bag than I hoped for.[65]

By early October Buller was commiserating with Hicks-Beach on the state of his health, discussing details of the sale of Sir Rowland Blennerhasset's estate under the Ashbourne Act, requesting that Hicks-Beach's secretary Caulfield return copies of all significant memoranda:

> I do not know whether reports about the government's intentions regarding local government for Ireland are anywhere near the mark but while you are considering the subject, I would mention that it appears to me the Sheriff system is antiquated and works badly. I do not think it right in Ireland especially that a man selected at haphazard should be the man really responsible for executing writs and decrees. The Under-Sheriff in this country is not at all the sort of man for the work and is really trying merely to make as much money out of the business as he can. But apart from individuals it appears to me to be an important office that ought not be left to the haphazard choice of a sheriff who is only an annual officer.[66]

Though Buller had theoretical independence in reaching decisions in his district, he consulted Hicks-Beach on detail:

> I send you the report I promised you on the Douglas and Kilgobnet purchase of Sir Rowland Blennerhassett's tenants. It would appear that the priest's remarks were justified. But in Kerry one can never be quite certain 'til one has heard both sides two or three times over.
> As I told you Dr Haggard, the agent of the estate is one of, I think, the greatest rascals in Kerry: I heard the other day, and I thought it a great

compliment, that one of his gang said in Tralee they would give £2,000 to get me out of Kerry. I return you Miss Lucy Thompson's note – it is true that some of the police at Fenit House do some work other than protecting her; and it is true that Fenit is convenient to the harbour works and consequently there is an advantage in having the police there – in fact, I think the harbour when completed will necessitate the removal of the police barracks from Spa to Fenit – but Miss Thompson has also a great deal of attention protection, and even takes her policemen at the public expense to Dublin. The case of the farm is this: she evicted a lot of tenants and let the evicted farms to the Property Defence Association at a high rent, these farms are protected by police. In these circumstances I don't think she is right in saying that the seven men are the only men that can be counted to her. In short, I may describe her letter generally as a clever piece of special pleading. She is one of the hardest managers in Kerry and is largely responsible for the state of the county.[67]

Though the general tone of October communications was optimistic, Buller emphasised that boycotting had not diminished.

Apart from that the situation was not bad. Ideally, he felt that there should be legislation for Ireland in the coming session, but also felt 'that the Eastern question must now be of more importance to the government than the Irish one'. On the other hand,

I feel that now is the moment to strike. Landlords are making large concessions, while they continue to do so the party of disorder are feeling that these concessions are loosening their hold on the people; will they rest quiet under this feeling?

On coercive legislation he remained confused:

If I was recommending for myself alone I would ask for higher powers than I did, but great powers make weak men tyrants, and you must consider your agents: I am thoroughly convinced in my own mind that Clifford Lloyd and Blake did under the Coercion Act an infinity more harm than good. Where will you get in Ireland agents to trust with full powers? And these agents would be worked by Sir R. Hamilton, a clerk of clerks, whose soul is red tape and whose idea of initiation is the avoidance of responsibility.[68]

At the same time, on specific issues, he indicated an increasing propensity to discard exceptional measures and provisions. He agreed to the removal of the gunboat at Dingle. He wrote to Sir Andrew Reed to say that he

need not fill up the vacancies in the Kerry police as they occur, as since we have reduced a good deal of the protection there really are more police in Kerry than are immediately required; of course I don't know that I may not want them all and more at Christmas, but at present there is no pressure.

On 15 November he wrote to Hicks-Beach in his usual terms about the Kerry landlords:

> The fact is that the bulk of the landlords do nothing for their tenants but extract as much rent as they can by every means in their power, and the law helps them; and the tenant, even if an industrious, hardworking man, has no defence. Landlords are not evicting now in Kerry but they are distraining cattle where they can and a distraint punishes a tenant really more than a process of eviction, if the latter is not pressed home.
>
> The leases in Kerry, the customs and the tradition are all those of rack-renters – there are only two resident landlords in Kerry who are not bankrupt and most of the large absentee landlords are not much better. What chance has the tenant under the present law? No, you must alter the law if you are . . .[69]

Buller's clear anti-landlord sympathies, while congenial to Hicks-Beach, were not popular in the cabinet. The question of disposing of Hamilton was sufficiently pressing to make Buller's odd line in exculpation of the tenants irrelevant. This was not the case when he moved to expressing them in public to the Commission set up to investigate the workings of the 1881 Land Act, chaired by Lord Cowper. As has already been seen the Commission was not without political purpose, a fact underlined by the type of witnesses called – landlords, agents and neo-governmental officials. The most influential of the commissioners appointed – Cowper himself, Sir James Caird and the Earl of Milltown – all agreed in viewing the 1881 Act as a plot to default landowners of their legitimate rights.

Appearing before the commissioners in Killarney, at a public session on 11 November 1886, Buller announced that he believed that in the three counties for which he was responsible, despite the existence 'in certain localities of an organised stand against the paying of existing rents', the rent generally was being well paid. Such non-payment as existed was, he said, due to inability to pay. In response to landlord adjustments (extracted primarily by tenant pressure, though this fact Buller fails to mention publicly) tenants had paid the reduced rents: and those who had not done so were, he claimed, unable to do so.[70] Buller here appears to share a view of the country that even the Conservative cabinet had substantially held in early 1886; a stance rendered redundant by the decision to oppose Home Rule in April of that year. A. B. Cooke and John Vincent delineate Hugh Holmes's assessment of the state of Ireland in November 1885, a year earlier, as revealed to Carnarvon:

> Many tenants cannot pay.
>
> Those who can pay will where landlords press them, mainly because they dread to be put to cost of legal payment – and they remembered what had occurred before. He spoke to Naish on this subject lately who agreed and said that what is now said of the probably non-payment of rent was true for the last three or certainly two years.

As regards the state of the country he believes that crime will be about the same as last year with perhaps some slight increase of moonlighting owing to the long nights.

That boycotting is rather on the decrease, and that much of it is now due less to agrarian or political causes as to individual jealousies, quarrels etc. And he added that the complaints of boycotting come now very often from members of the National League rather than agents or landlords.[71]

For Buller to articulate such views in private correspondence with his Chief Secretary was one thing. He went further and expressed these views publicly. Hicks-Beach had no choice but to rebuke him, particularly in view of the fact that in response to Hicks-Beach's recommendations Buller had been appointed Under-Secretary to replace the unsatisfactory Hamilton. Buller wrote to Hicks-Beach, asking if he wished to withdraw the offer of the under-secretaryship because of the uses to which his evidence had been put by the Nationalist press. The reply was unequivocal:

I have seen *United Ireland* and it does not 'make me desirous of changing my mind'. Whether it will have any greater effect on my colleagues, I cannot say; but I do not think so; a day or two will tell.

If either you or I had known you were likely to become Under-Secretary, we should doubtless have agreed that it would have been better, whatever your opinion might be, that you should have given no evidence before the Commission. As you did, however, I know of no reason why I and my colleagues should trust you less, for having said to the Commission what you have said to me. But as I shall be questioned about it, I should like much to know (if you can remember) precisely what it was that you *did* say – as Lord Milltown failed to hear correctly. He certainly has acted, to my mind, very improperly in writing such a letter. But I can do no more than say as much, civilly, to Lord Cowper, to whom I am writing on another matter tonight.[72]

Conservative Policy: The Post–Home Rule Bill Hiatus

Hicks-Beach's assessment of the cabinet response to Buller was not an informed one. From the date of his arrival in Ireland Hicks-Beach had grown increasingly estranged from the details of high politics in London. On his appointment to the Irish chief-secretaryship he had been one of the most weighty, if not the most senior, colleagues with whom Salisbury had to treat. The Irish office was a strange choice for so senior a politician. In the light of the centrality of Ireland to the structure of a sustained Unionist alliance after the Liberal split of 1886, the Irish post was, however, crucial. Salisbury needed Liberal Unionist support to stay in office. Locating Hicks-Beach in Dublin also had the useful ancillary virtue of removing him from Salisbury's direct sphere of influence. In making the appointment Salisbury appeared to give Hicks-Beach *carte blanche* on policy, even permitting him a veto on the appointment of the Lord-Lieutenant who Hicks-Beach insisted should be an Irishman, Lord Londonderry.[73] Hicks-Beach pleased the government's Liberal Unionist supporters in that he was traditionally associated with a constructive and, in Tory terms, Liberal line on Ireland. Despite Randolph Churchill's atavistic line during the Home Rule fracas, it had always been clear that within the Tory party he and Hicks-Beach represented those who were sympathetically interested in Ireland.[74] Salisbury bought himself time with the Liberal Unionists by the appointment. Hicks-Beach was firmly opposed to coercion, and his appointment was generally read as indicative of what Cooke and Vincent call a 'soft words and hard cash' policy: a continuation of the Tory policy that determined their pre-Home Rule administration.

Hicks-Beach wrote to Salisbury when considering the office in July 1886:

> You will agree that I could not be expected to take such an office unless I saw my way to doing some real good. Without that I could not take up again the petty and irksome detail which constitute much of the work of the office . . . I have thought much on the subject of an Irish policy since we met. I have not, so far, been able to see my way to do any real good. I am not even at all sure that you would approve of my ideas as to the lines on which the humbler task of 'keeping things going' should be attempted.[75]

Salisbury had not formulated an Irish policy in mid-1886. He was absorbed by the issue of the consolidation of his own leadership and of yoking in Randolph Churchill. At the Carlton meeting of 27 July 1886 Salisbury, with Hicks-Beach seated beside him, announced his intention of dealing with current business in parliament in August, and then adjourning until the new year when the government would be in a position to state its Irish policy.[76]

What the correspondence between Buller and Hicks-Beach most clearly demonstrates is (a) that their shared view was one of acceptance of the existence of genuine hardship as the precondition of violence in the south-west, (b) an agreement that a sliding-scale revision in Land Commission rents set for fifteen years, as demanded by Parnell, was reasonable and would prove effective in reducing outrage, (c) a belief that the suppression of the National League was unwise and unnecessary, and (d) the view that a mild coercion bill alone would suffice to cope with an unrest that was viewed as both localised and diminishing.

Within a month of Hicks-Beach's removal from the Irish chief-secretaryship and his replacement by Arthur Balfour in March 1887, that perspective on Ireland had begun a process of revision. Redvers Buller did survive Balfour's arrival in Dublin, and, indeed, continued as Under-Secretary in the Castle for some months. His personal relations with Balfour were good and they worked amicably for a period. But Buller, despite his African and Indian background, had formed an opinion on the nature of Irish rural disorder that could not be accommodated to the new Tory spectacles through which Ireland was viewed after 1887. His successor in the south-western division, Major-General Sir Alfred Turner, accepted the revised Balfour analysis.[77] Buller's successor as Under-Secretary, Joseph West-Ridgeway,[78] was, despite the similarities in their career profiles, infinitely more suitable to Salisbury and Balfour's revised analysis. Though Irish, West-Ridgeway claimed to know nothing of the country, an advantage of immeasurable proportions for developing a proper approach to Irish administration, as Balfour blithely informed him.

A memorandum on the Plan of Campaign was prepared by Hicks-Beach for the cabinet of 13 January 1887. It recommended a mild but firm response to the Plan of Campaign:

> A conspiracy indeed must, it is presumed, be always punished by indictment; and if facilities were given to have criminal juries and a change of venue in criminal trials the law against conspiracy could be fairly enforced in Ireland.[79]

The memorandum continued by stating that together with this power, and the power to punish verbal incitement to violation of the law and boycotting, 'the Executive could deal with the open promotion of such an agitation as the Plan of Campaign'.

Yet by March 1887 Balfour had constructed an analysis that effectively rendered such a mild response redundant. Nowhere is the shift more evident than in the contrast between the communications of Balfour and Turner with those previously held between Hicks-Beach and Buller. Turner wrote to Balfour through Browning of the Chief Secretary's office. He reconstructed the presentation of the returns of crimes, so that boycotting cases, police protection rotas and numbers of National League branches appeared on single tables. He recommended in July 1887 that the whole of the south-western division be proclaimed, and that every specific power available under the Crimes Bill should be put into action. In contrast to Buller he saw a 'vile conspiracy against property and the Empire seething against us'.[80]

'Bravo, *The Times*, how it is scoring, it ought to be raised to the peerage'[81] Turner wrote in July 1888. He urged Balfour to remove Dowse, who was playing to the Nationalist gallery. Dowse did not have to live in Kerry and be 'hooted by these brutes':

> Cannot you muzzle that vulgar popularity-seeking old buffoon Dowse? . . . He is scaring some of these weak-kneed RMs whom it is hard enough to keep up to the collar without that old clown to make things more difficult.[82]

Balfour wrote on 25 March 1887:

> I should very much like to have conclusive proof (I do not mean) legally sound, but *morally* conclusive proof – proof which would suffice to

convince a commission of the House of Commons of O'Brien's and
Dillon's deliberate plan of causing riot and bloodshed if it suited their
parliamentary game.[83]

The Special Commission provided this 'moral proof'. In the proceedings of
the Special Commission the case of Kerry up to and including 1887 proved
vital, and Turner was in a position to congratulate himself in 1892 on having
facilitated a new perspective on how Kerry in particular, and the south-
western division generally, 'the most dangerous part of Ireland', should be
presented and handled.

7 THE TRANSFORMATION OF THE LAND QUESTION

Though the principles upon which land policy were to be conducted were clear by 1886, it was during the succeeding two decades that the question was resolved. The accepted view of its resolution is that a peasant proprietorship popularity demand was finally acceded to. This view emphasises the final 'success' of the peasant struggle – the natural consequences of the land struggle being the destruction of the landlord class. Outlined in Arthur Balfour's Bill of 1891, the purchase policy reached fruition in legislation promoted by Gerald Balfour in 1896 and George Wyndham in 1903. Questioning of this view centres around a debate on whether or not Conservative policy was committed to 'killing Home Rule by kindness',[1] though recent work does acknowledge that purchase was seen as the rescue of the landlords as a class.

John Morley's Liberal chief-secretaryship of 1892–95 represented an aberration in what would otherwise have been an uninterrupted period of Conservative policy and administration from 1886–1906. For these three years the Unionists of Ireland feared not only for their land but for the security they had enjoyed under Balfour.[2] Underlining the revocation of the Crimes Act, interfering with the resident magistracy, Morley provoked an outcry in Ireland, equalled only by the rhetorical storm that Gladstone's Home Rule Bill of 1893 was creating at Westminster. The Home Rule debate, as Salisbury told northern Irish Unionists, centred around the question of whether they were prepared to countenance the subjection of their prosperity, their industry and their lives to the absolute mastery of their ancient and unchanging enemies.

In relying upon the anti-Parnellite and pro-clerical groupings of Dillon and Healy to support his policies, Morley was circumscribed in his actions:

> Easy in comparison was Balfour's position. He had only to think of enforcement of the law. I have to think how, while enforcing the law, I shall not leave my nationalist allies planted in a position which they cannot defend on Irish platforms, and which will turn them over to their Parnellite foes.[3]

His impotence was highlighted by the fact that, despite concessions on the law, the constabulary and the evicted tenants, he was treated with barely concealed contempt by the majority of Nationalists. The huge rallies of

Conservative and Liberal Unionists vowing never to concede Home Rule on platforms all over Britain in 1893 presented a more inescapable reality to most groupings in Ireland than did the Liberal exercise of a Home Rule Bill which was doomed to failure in the Lords. For the Catholic middle classes the spectacle of stymied Home Rule at Westminster was not inspiring.

But when Morley toured the country to, in his own words, 'give flesh to the blue books', these were not the people he met. Nor did he join Asquith and Haldane in their sentimental procession on the anniversary of Parnell's death in October. Ivy days had little appeal as he faced the Parnellites' first active defiance of the law, meeting in their thousands on an evicted tenant's farm.

His allies, the anti-Parnellite parties of Dillon and Healy, supported his Evicted Tenants Commission. The so-called evicted tenants were the 'casualties' of the Land War, but more particularly of the Plan of Campaign. To replace them on the farms now inhabited by caretakers and emergency men would not be easy. To the Conservatives it was more evidence of the Liberals' willingness to reward vice and penalise virtue. In the Lords, when throwing out the Bill proposed by the Evicted Tenants Commission, Salisbury and Hartington reached a pitch of resistance unequalled even by Balfour, Goschen and Randolph Churchill on the Home Rule debate in the Lower House.[4]

The ties that bound the Irish peers and landowners to the Conservative party were not merely relevant to imperial integrity. They had material and palpable reality in the landed estates that they owned. Lansdowne, Londonderry and St John Broderick were merely the tip of a complicated undergrowth of minor peers, family connections and intermarriages. It was not just Conservative peers and Irish landlords who lost confidence when the Liberals were in; the constabulary, the magistracy, the whole legal apparatus had no confidence. Morley was an 'old woman' who could stand firm on nothing. As Balfour was informed later, Morley 'didn't even realise that police informers had to be paid off on release'.[5] As Lady Waterford informed Morley he simply did not know:

> I had some instructive talk with her about the Irish . . . She had come over full of illusions, they had slowly been dispelled. Call the Irish imaginative! So they are on one side, or on the surface; in substance they are not imaginative at all – they are sordid and prosaic, love no part of it, an affair of so many cows; sentiment, not a spark of it . . . they are actors, and they all know they are actors; and each man knows that the man to whom he is talking is not only playing a part but knows that he knows that he is playing a part. They cannot help lying and they have no shame, not merely in being found out, but in being known to be lying as the words come, fresh from the lips. Man, woman and child, they are soaked and saturated in insincerity.[6]

Balfour conducted an extensive correspondence on the issue of an Evicted Tenants Bill, a correspondence that illuminates Conservative policy on land at this time.[7] Since the Evicted Tenants Bill proposed the voluntary resettlement of thousands of tenants at a cost of £250,000 Balfour politically saw no reason why the Lords should not summarily dismiss it. The premise of this piece of Liberal legislation was unacceptable; it was that the evictions had been unjust and the law inequitable. It was a policy of reward for the Irish MPs 'and their dupes', the concession of which would have again permitted that perspective on the land which six years of Conservative rule since 1887 had sought to terminate.

The policy of post-Balfourian constructive Unionism was based on the premise that such inequities as existed in the Irish land system were the products of poverty and ignorance. The provision of public monies for the amelioration of such grievances was ideologically acceptable. It was not, however, acceptable to propose – as did the findings of the Evicted Tenants Commission[8] – that the law and the landlords were culpable. St John Broderick conducted private talks with Tim Healy who suggested that, if the Lords acted summarily in the matter, and:

> if all comes to nothing and the League funds (for maintaining the evicted tenants) will not keep them through the winter, he of course prophecies an outbreak of crime and agitation to which he will contribute in his usual way.

Healy did, however, suggest that if the Lords were prepared to propose an amnesty on the issue, they could, 'fairly require any amnesty to include the tenants being encouraged to purchase by himself and his colleagues'.[9]

Despite the Conservative political commitment to land purchase, a mere 30,000 holdings had been disposed of in this way by 1891.[10] In marked contrast to this, 354,890 judicial rents had been set by the Land Commission. Morley's own investigation of the process convinced him that, contrary to Conservative wisdom, set rents continued to be excessive, that tenants were rented on their improvements, and that the notion of a fixed rent for fifteen years in a period of sustained agricultural depression militated against the interests of the tenant, and that it was as a consequence of this iniquity that the Plan of Campaign had endured on target estates for the period from 1886–92.[11]

The purchase policy of Conservatives, which Gladstone described as 'dangerous and mischievous', formed no part of a Liberal land programme separate from Home Rule. For Gladstone, purchase and Home Rule were irreversibly linked. Morley proposed to legislate merely to increase the efficiency of the existing system, ameliorated by a commitment to resettle the evicted tenants. But, when the Liberals fell in 1895, Gerald Balfour's Purchase Act of 1896 sought to bring policy back to the line pursued by Balfour before 1892.[12] It was, however, a small-scale proposal. The only landlords who availed of its provisions were those whose economic base was elsewhere, those who wanted to leave Ireland for social or personal reasons, or those so heavily mortgaged as to reap financial benefit by escaping ruinous payments. It was not economically viable for solvent landlords to sell. Since most landlords had only a life interest in their estates they were compelled to invest in trustee securities at low rates of return. The purchase terms were not sufficiently attractive to induce them to do so. The measure, like all previous purchase measures, was ineffective.[13]

But in these years the nature of Conservative alliances in Ireland changed. Gerald Balfour closely associated his administration with improving landlords and agricultural reformers who constituted themselves in a body during the recess of 1895, known as the Recess Committee. The committee consisted of individuals from the co-operative movement like Horace Plunkett, northern industrialists, landlords like Lords Mayo and Monteagle, and, for a time, John Redmond, and resulted in the creation of the Department of Agricultural and Technical Instruction.[14]

The idea on which it was founded was admirable: a belief that since matters of policy had been resolved, and since Home Rule was 'not an issue', all classes should co-operate in improving the efficiency of agriculture. In effect, despite the eulogies that have been written about this particular union of hearts, it was politically ineffective. Most landlords viewed Plunkett as a crank. Irish Nationalists saw him as a well-intentioned, if effective, paternalistic bore. To Dublin Castle he was the authentic 'middle voice' in Irish politics, and his analysis of a vast range of topics was treated as dogma. Essentially his policy and that of his associates confirmed the Conservative analysis of the problem. Augustine Birrell, writing a few years later, described Sir Louis Dane, a leading light in the movement, in the following terms:

> His views are typical – he is of course an anti-Home Ruler at heart, thinks nationality all humbug and Romanism a creed for coloured men, and that all that is wanted is beneficent rule on Anglo-Indian principles, Plunkettised a little to suit the locality. The parliamentary situation with 80 odd MPs no more exists for him than it did for Anthony of blessed memory.[15]

Dane's particular contribution to policy in later years was a series of articles and letters which sought to prove the identical nature of the problems of Ireland and the Punjab: 'In both cases we have a fine, manly but rather hot-tempered and litigious population'.[16]

Most of the IAOS extortions, which informed the Department of Agricultural and Technical Instruction, seemed to imply that substandard agricultural produce lay at the heart of agrarian problems. Though well-intentioned and economically *correct*, it ignored the extent to which all questions relating to the land had been for so long entwined with opposed political beliefs that it was almost impossible to view any problem in strictly economic terms in view of the cluster of associations that obscured it. Undeniably, agrarian economic grievances had fuelled Irish Nationalist ends. But the Conservative policy of viewing all agrarian unrest as the product of Nationalist orchestration had the ironic effect of facilitating the Nationalist transformation of legitimate economic grievance into Nationalist feeling. Policy was formulated on the basis of cumulative misunderstanding and creative misreadings.

The Irish Parliamentary Party during the period presented a squalid frontage of internecine invective and, as Healy's letter to St John Broderick testifies, a willingness to trade individually and collectively with the Tories for short-term gain. In 1900 the party finally reunited after the Parnellite split of 1891. It was not that the divisions had healed; it was merely that the ludicrous spectacle they presented contrasted too unfavourably with the commemorations of 1798 and the appealing simplicities of cultural nationalism in Ireland. The fiery rhetoric of the 1880s had given way to the Westminster manner. Though Irish society had changed immeasurably in those fifteen years, largely as a consequence of Liberal and Conservative legislation, Nationalist MPs remained confined in their narcotic task of translating Ireland into English terms in the House of Commons.[17]

As Paul Bew has demonstrated, the main reason for reuniting the Irish party was the fact that failure to do so, and to absorb William O'Brien's United Irish League, could result in replacement by it. The UIL developed out of the grievances and poverty of western tenants who were being squeezed out of the land market by large graziers. The graziers were acquiring an increasing share of available land to fatten their cattle for export. It was a profitable business and could be effectively conducted by letting land on eleven-month leases. This suited the landlords, since such leases were not subject to judicial rents. O'Brien politicised these demands by proposing the compulsory purchase of these grazing lands and the transplantation and resettlements of the tenants. Re-enacting his career of a decade earlier O'Brien organised a tightly knit movement in the west.[18] At the same time T. W. Russell was demanding a policy of compulsory purchase in the north, where landlords were unwilling to sell. It was only in the north that there was a general desire by tenants to purchase.

George Wyndham then, in proposing a scheme of voluntary land purchase, effectively had what all previous Conservative schemes had conspicuously lacked: a popular demand, albeit from disparate sources, in the country. On this basis he set out to devise a final scheme of purchase. Most of his ideas were formulated in close cooperation with Balfour during 1901.[19] Compulsory purchase was agreed to be unacceptable. It would be resisted by both landlords and tenants with the exception of the O'Brien/Russell factions. But the reasons for voluntary purchase were precisely those that had been advanced confidently by Conservatives since 1881:

> Under the existing system the value of Irish land must be continuously depreciated; the landlord cannot be expected to improve the land; the

tenant may be expected to deteriorate it and even on the best estates certain occupancies will be perpetuated which are centres of lawlessness and rallying grounds for fresh attacks on the capital value of Ireland's chief asset.[20]

The technical details of the existing system which Wyndham proposed to abolish were fully understood only by a number of former Land Commissioners. The landlords' stereotype of the general valuation powers of most sub-commissioners was less than laudatory. This was back to the old argument, on the unreliability and politically motivated nature of assessing value and rent. In the words of Wyndham:

The Land Commission is in a poor state . . . Judge Meredith has lost his nerve. Murrough O'Brien is a crank . . . So long as he can come in after agreement between landlord and tenant and cut down the purchase money the landlords will not sell. Who would risk going to the workhouse on the decision of one eccentric gentleman with disloyal proclivities.[21]

Therefore the Land Commission and procedure must be reformed.

Wyndham's greatest repository of historical detail was the old Land Commissioner and land law and valuation expert, Wrench. But as Wyndham told Balfour, communication with Wrench now had to be conducted through the medium of an ear trumpet. Wyndham had central aims: to make the price of purchase annuities cheaper than existing judicial rent so that tenants, however indifferent to the idea of purchase, would buy; and to make the system of purchase so financially attractive to the landlords that failure to sell would mean considerable financial loss. In view of the fact that he was dealing with considerable numbers of various types of tenants, the proposal was to introduce the Land Commission as a buffer zone to purchase estates in their entirety, and then resell. This was a continuation of the type of activity already conducted in the so-called congested districts of the west where the Congested Districts Board purchased property, improved it, and then sold it to tenants. Wyndham also felt that any land settlement had to be accompanied by efficient law and order. Sir Andrew Reed, Considine and Chamberlain at the head of the RIC, seemed desultory. Detailed weekly surveillance reports were still forwarded to the Castle on every area in the country, but they were reports of an indifferent character:

What has happened is this. The local police to keep up an appearance of zeal have smothered the Castle with reports by one man who witnessed something at a window and by information accepted on the strict understanding that it was not to be used. They know as well as the Attorney-General that such evidence is worthless; and they add to it a pious opinion that the speech made 'will have no effect'.[22]

Hicks-Beach at the Treasury was tolerant of Wyndham's proposals. He had changed since his years in Ireland. 'Hicks-Beach feels we ought to help the landlords if a legitimate method can be found'. Eager to promote 'a machinery by which administration and capital could be brought back into an industry from which both were banished from the Act of 1881', Wyndham was adamant: 'This is surgery I admit. But I prefer surgery to medicine'.[23]

While immediate circumstances conspired to facilitate such legislation in 1900–03, and while it was in effect desirable to Nationalists, the essential dynamic for such a settlement came from a Conservative analysis that had remained substantially unaltered from the initial objection to infringements on the rights of property and concession to Irish pressure that they believed to be inherent in Gladstone's 1881 Land Bill. There is little evidence to substantiate their analysis of its disastrous economic consequences for landowners. But the gradual diminution of county control, particularly in the Local Government Bill of 1898, the bill that, in Healy's words, made all landlord influence 'end at his demesne gate', served to highlight the psychological sense of entrapment experienced by the landlords as a class, a sense experienced by small estate owners like the Bowens in Cork and the Leslies in Monaghan, and the owners of vast tracts. Though ostensibly economic, then, the land settlement was in effect political. It was less that Irish landlords pressed for such a settlement than that, when presented with so economically irresistible a possibility, they found it difficult to demur. As a class they had generally trusted implicitly in English Conservative government and accepted its analysis of their plight.

The Irish Landowners' Convention in October 1902 adopted an ostensibly hectoring tone towards the government: 'The government have shown themselves unwilling to grant the landlords' claim to compensation for the grave injuries inflicted on them by past legislation.' The land purchase legislation which is usually represented as a consequence of the pressure put on Wyndham by this spontaneous coming together of landlords in the Land Conference of 1903 was in fact fully thought out before either the Landowners' Convention *or* the Land Conference ever met. Indeed, there is reasonable ground for the suspicion that Shawe-Taylor, the man who came from nowhere to initiate the conference, was in fact prompted to do so by Wyndham.

The purchase scheme of 1903 was highly successful. It resulted in nearly 300,000 sales. By 1914 an estimated two-thirds to three-quarters of farmers owned their holdings. Most landlords stayed, having retained their demesne farm. It was, however, a political solution to the question of Irish land, which had consistently been perceived by Conservatives and others as a political question. The Conservative analysis which had always been that nationalism was an ideological cloak for defaulting landowners of their rightful role may well have been correct when first articulated. What was even more true, however, was that the 'land struggle', as it was called, had provided the raw material out of which a popular idea of nationality had been constructed. Though ironically the public role of the land question began in the articulated demands of poor western tenants, and concluded in 1903 with the concession of peasant proprietorship, it considerably distorts the role of ideas in the issue to assume a straightforward relationship of cause and effect. The 'solution' finally achieved was a response to rescuing a landlord class from a dilemma in which Conservative analysis proclaimed them to be embroiled. Its desirability to sections of Nationalist opinion is undeniable. It was primarily however, a testament to enduring Conservative belief in the rightness of their analysis of the Irish situation. The present historiographical assessment of the 'ending' of the landlord class in Ireland merely perpetuates the analysis which Conservatives imposed at the time.

CONCLUSION

The Cooke and Vincent thesis that Tory policy on Ireland was a product of internal English party high political manoeuvre may be true. What is truer, however, is that the policies of Tory and Liberal governments materially altered the structure of Irish society. Balfour's view that the Irish Free State was nothing more than 'the Ireland that we made' was in certain respects undeniable.

For the political positions adopted and the political decisions made by both Tories and Liberals created the framework of Irish Nationalist political manoeuvre. The tensions within the Liberal Party in the years from 1880 to 1881 determined and facilitated the fashioning of a self-image useful to Irish Nationalist MPs. By representing violence as Nationalist or Land League conspiracy from the date of the decision to prosecute Parnell and friends in late 1881, despite private reservations about such an analysis, the Liberals gave the Parnellites a political advantage. For the aim of the Parnellite party was to create through their rhetoric a situation in which, in the minds of the majority of the population, the politics of the next field became synonymous with the politics of the independent land of Ireland. Perceived oppression facilitated that representation.

By contrasting the complexity of the actual responses of the Dublin Castle administration, and the discussions of Liberal politicians, with the crudity of their public action, the contingency and indeterminacy of the course events took is illuminated. It has been suggested that the structure of Irish administration, in its capacity to gather information and the categories through which such information was collated, acted not as a neutral filter of 'facts' but as an actual determinant of how the problem was to be seen. The propensity of both Liberals and Tories to speak about an 'Irish problem' stereotyped every minor difficulty of a complex society. That perception was derived from the structure of administration in Ireland and the nature of communication between the Dublin Castle administration and the House of Commons, the press and the cabinet in London. The perpetual analysis of 'the situation' in statistics of crime figures and their 'balancing weight of eviction figures' created an ostensible logic in all political decisions. Thus Gladstone justified his political decision on land in 1881 in terms of neutral factual necessity. The contrast between the findings of the Richmond and Bessborough Commissions in 1880–81 on the same ostensibly neutral 'facts' is here crucial. The decision on land in 1881 by the Liberals was the decisive turning-point in their formulation of a policy on Ireland. The suspension of habeas corpus in early 1881, while publicly presenting the Liberals as oppressors, in fact provided the genesis for Gladstone's subsequent treatment with Parnell at Kilmainham. Liberal unease at being compelled to administer the law through the suspension of its usual protections convinced Gladstone of the idea that Ireland was held 'by force'.

The Liberals' perspective on land, the ostensible theatre of grievance, was crucial in determining their gradual shift towards Home Rule. The Tories on the other hand had, from the date of the passing of the 1881 Land Act, added to their original analysis of Irish disorder as trumped-up nationalist conspiracy on a teetering economic base, a declared rhetorical conviction that infringement of the status of property was one side of a coin, of which the other was the undermining of the Empire. Gladstone had 'stimulated the appetites of these gentlemen' by concession. After 1882 Gladstone treated the Irish MPs at Westminster as legitimate, if distasteful, political opponents. To an extent, for reasons of political manoeuvre, the Tories appeared to do the same thing. But the Conservatives' decision to oppose Home Rule in 1886 closed their options.

The conclusion of this work is that the direction of the land question between 1879 and 1903, while posited upon Nationalist action and rhetoric, was unpredictable in its outcome, and was directed as much by the nature of Liberal and Conservative analyses and policies as by Irish action. The public political responses of the Liberals in 1881 and the Tories after the defeat of Home Rule in 1886 facilitated a crude process of amalgamation of Nationalist and land grievances. The concentration in recent accounts of the period on internal differences within the Land and National League movements suggests that high politics, and the decisions reached at a high political level, operated in a separate world from the local. On the contrary, the structure of Irish administration – particularly the centralisation of the police and the constant mapping, graphing and monitoring of what was proclaimed to be a single unified problem – provided a dynamic connection between high and low politics. Only by recognising the contingencies and unpredictabilities of that refracting connection can a cultural determinism be avoided and the nature of the politics of late-Victorian Ireland understood.

Notes and References

Introduction (pages 1–10)

1. For example, Pat Lynch, *They Hanged John Twiss: A Tense and Dramatic Episode of the Irish Land War* (*The Kerryman*, Tralee, 1982); Michael Sheil and Desmond Roche (eds.), *A Forgotten Campaign and Aspects of the Heritage of South-East Galway* (Woodford, 1986).
2. John B. Keane, *The Field* (Cork, 1966); John McGahern, *Amongst Women* (London, 1990); Tom Murphy, *Conversations on a Homecoming* (Dublin, 1986).
3. Patrick Kavanagh, *Collected Poems* (London, 1964).
4. Patrick Kavanagh, *The Great Hunger* (Dublin, 1942).
5. Kenneth H. Connell's, *Irish Peasant Society* (London, 1968) now disputed in some detail, was the first to advance this view.
6. C. Arensberg and S. T. Kimball, *Family, Life and Community in Ireland* (Cambridge, Mass., 1968). See also Hugh Brody, *Inishkillane, Change and Decline in the West of Ireland* (London, 1973).
7. See Margaret O'Callaghan, 'Language and religion: the quest for identity in the Irish Free State, 1922–32' (unpublished MA thesis, University College, Dublin, 1981).
8. For an overview of the main lines of debate see Margaret O'Callaghan, 'Irish history, 1780–1980', *Historical Journal*, 29, 2 (1986), pp. 481–95.
9. On the relative wealth and poverty of Irish landlords and tenants see W. E. Vaughan, *Landlord and Tenant in Ireland 1848–1904* (Studies in Irish Economic and Social History, 2, 1984); L. P. Curtis, jr., 'Incumbered wealth: Landlord indebtedness in post-famine Ireland', *American Historical Review*, LXXXV, 2 (April 1980), pp. 332–68; W. J. Lowe, 'Landlord and tenant on the estate of Trinity College, Dublin, 1851–1903', *Hermathena*, CXX (1976), pp. 5–24; Cormac Ó Gráda, 'Agricultural head rents, pre-Famine and post-Famine', *Economic and Social Review*, V, 3 (April 1974), pp. 385–92; Cormac Ó Gráda, 'The investment behaviour of Irish landlords, 1850–75: some preliminary findings', *Agricultural History Review*, XXIII, 2 (1975), pp. 139–55; O. Robinson, 'The London companies as progressive landlords in nineteenth-century Ireland', *Economic History Review*, 2nd series, XV, 1 (August 1962), pp. 103–18; B. L. Solow, *The Land Question and the Irish Economy 1870–1903* (Cambridge, Mass., 1971). For the most comprehensive and stimulating study of the nature of landlord–tenant relations see James S. Donnelly, *The Land and the People of Nineteenth-Century Cork: The Rural Economy and the Land Question* (London, 1975).
10. To move from economic relations to social relations between landlord and tenant, and the question of group mobilisation and the internal politics of the Land League see Paul Bew, *Land and the National Question in Ireland 1858–82* (Dublin, 1978); Samuel Clark, *The Social Origins of the Irish Land War* (Princeton, 1979); 'The importance of agrarian classes: agrarian class structure and collective action in nineteenth-century Ireland', in P. J. Drudy (ed.), *Ireland: Land, Politics and People* (Irish Studies 2, Cambridge, 1982); Samuel Clark and James S. Donnelly, jr. (eds.), *Irish Peasants: Violence and Political Unrest 1780–1914* (Wisconsin, 1984); David Fitzpatrick, 'The

155

disappearance of the Irish agricultural labourer, 1841–1921', *Irish Economic and Social History*, VII (1980), pp. 66–92; David Fitzpatrick, 'Class, family and rural unrest in nineteenth-century Ireland' in J. Drudy (1982); W. L. Feingold, 'The tenants' movement to capture the Irish Poor Law boards, 1877–1886', *Albion*, VII, 3 (Fall 1975), pp. 216–31. For a political study based on a belief in the political centrality of internal tenant divisions in the post-Parnellite period see Paul Bew, *Conflict and Conciliation in Ireland 1890–1910: Parnellites and Radical Agrarians* (Oxford, 1987). For a view of the politics of landlord–tenant relations as revealed in local contexts see K. T. Hoppen, *Elections, Politics and Society in Ireland 1832–1885* (Oxford, 1984); also K. T. Hoppen, 'Landlords, society and electoral politics in mid-nineteenth-century Ireland', *Past and Present*, 75 (May 1977), pp. 62–93, also published in C. H. E. Philpin (ed.), *Nationalism and Popular Protest in Ireland* (Past and Present publications, Cambridge, 1987), pp. 284–319; Donald Jordan, 'Merchants, "strong farmers" and Fenians: the post-Famine political elite and the Irish Land War', in Philpin (1987).

11. A number of excellent studies were made by American scholars in the decades after the political independence of the Irish Free State. Many presented the 'story' of the Land War as a 'necessary' step in the defeat of the landlord class. Others, like that of Elizabeth Hooker, were US Treasury funded and designed to assist federal policy-makers in their dealings with US tenant farmers during the Depression. See in particular Elizabeth R. Hooker, *Readjustments of Agricultural Tenure in Ireland 1800–1923* (Princeton, 1930).

12. See the *Journal of Statistical and Social Inquiry Society of Ireland*. Hancock's repeated contributions to statistical developments can be seen in every edition of the *Journal* from 1875. See also the *Preliminary Report of the Richmond Commission*.

13. W. E. Vaughan, 'Landlord and tenant relations in Ireland between the Famine and the Land War, 1850–1878', in L. M. Cullen and T. C. Smout (eds.) *Comparative Aspects of Scottish and Irish Economic and Social History* (Edinburgh, 1977).

14. In particular Donnelly, *The Land and the People of Nineteenth-Century Cork*, and Bew, *Land and the National Question*. That revised view seems to be most substantially summarized by K. Theodore Hoppen in *Ireland Since 1800: Conflict and Conformity* (London, 1989).

15. L. P. Curtis, jr., 'Incumbered wealth: Landlord indebtedness in post-famine Ireland', *American Historical Review*, LXXXV, 2 (April 1980).

16. This point is most forcibly made by W. E. Vaughan in 'Landlord and tenant relations in Ireland between the Famine and the Land War, 1850–1878', in Cullen and Smout (eds.), *Comparative Aspects of Scottish and Irish Economic and Social History*, pp. 216-26. Repeated in his most recent publication: *Landlords and Tenants in mid-Victorian Ireland* (Oxford, 1994).

17. Now a pervasive assumption in the literature; see Solow, *The Land Question and the Irish Economy 1870–1903*.

18. See for example, David Fitzpatrick's exhortation: 'Let statistics be used as the hammer for shattering Irish self-deception.' David Fitzpatrick, 'The geography of Irish nationalism 1910–1921', in C. H. E. Philpin (ed.), *Nationalism and Popular Protest in Ireland* (Cambridge, 1987), p. 431.

19. As Clark and Donnelly pointed out in their introduction to *Irish Peasants* (Wisconsin, 1984) there is no comprehensive study of agrarian movements and rural violence in late eighteenth- and early nineteenth-century Ireland. The

following titles are, however, helpful: Michael Beames, *Peasants and Power: The Whiteboy Movement and their Control in Pre-Famine Ireland* (Brighton, 1983); Galen Broeker, *Rural Disorder and Police Reform in Ireland 1812–36* (London and Toronto, 1970); N. J. Curtin, 'The transformation of the Society of United Irishmen into a mass-based revolutionary movement, 1794–96', *Irish Historical Studies*, 24 (November 1985), pp. 463–92; J. S. Donnelly jr., 'Hearts of oak, hearts of steel', *Studia Hibernica*, 21 (1981), pp. 7–73; J. S. Donnelly, 'Irish agrarian rebellion: the Whiteboys of 1769-76', *Proceedings of the Royal Irish Academy*, 83, C, no. 12 (1983), pp. 293–331; J. S. Donnelly, 'Propagating the cause of the United Irishmen', *Studies,* 9 (Spring 1980), pp. 5–23; J. S. Donnelly, 'The Rightboy movement, 1785–88', *Studia Hibernica*, 17 and 18 (1977–78), pp. 120-202; J. S. Donnelly, 'The Whiteboy movement, 1761-65', *Irish Historical Studies*, 21 (March 1978) pp. 20–54; G. E. Christiansen, 'Secret societies and agrarian violence in Ireland, 1790–1840', *Agricultural History*, XLV, no. 4 (October 1972), pp. 369–84; Marianne Elliott, 'The origins and transformation of early Irish republicanism', *International Review of Social History*, XXIII, part 3 (1978), pp. 405–28; Joseph Lee, 'The Ribbonmen', in T. D. Williams (ed.), *Secret Societies in Ireland* (Dublin and New York, 1973); Patrick O'Donoghue, 'The tithe war, 1830–1833' (unpublished UCD MA thesis, 1961); Patrick O'Donoghue, 'Causes of opposition to tithes, 1830–38', *Studia Hibernica*, no. 5 (1965), pp. 7–28; Patrick O'Donoghue, 'Opposition to tithe payments in 1830–31', *Studia Hibernica*, no. 6 (1966), pp. 69–98; Patrick O'Donoghue, 'Opposition to tithe payment in 1832–33', ibid., no. 12 (1972), pp. 77–108; Angus Macintyre, *The Liberator: Daniel O'Connell and the Irish Party, 1830–1847* (London, 1965), pp. 167–200; Oliver Mac Donagh, *The Hereditary Bondsman: Daniel O'Connell 1775–1829* (London, 1988), and *The Emancipist: Daniel O'Connell 1830–1847* (London, 1989); Stanley H. Palmer, *Police and Protest in England and Ireland 1780–1850* (Cambridge, 1988); G. C. Lewis, *On Local Disturbances in Ireland and on the Irish Church Question* (London, 1836); Maureen Wall, 'The Whiteboys' in Desmond Williams (ed.), *Secret Societies in Ireland* (Dublin and New York, 1973), pp. 13–25; J. Smyth, *The Men of No Property* (Dublin, 1991).

20. Michael Beames, *Peasants and Power: The Whiteboy Movements and their Control in Pre–Famine Ireland*, p. 34.
21. Ibid., p. 207.
22. William Nassau Senior, *Journals, Conversations and Essays Relating to Ireland* (2 vols., London, 1868).
23. George Paulett Scrope, *How Is Ireland to Be Governed?* (London, 1846). See his notation of songs of the peasantry, for example:
   'Our gentry who fed
   upon venison and wine,
   Must now on old lumpers
   And foul claret dine.'
24. *Minutes of evidence taken before the Select Committee of the House of Lords appointed to inquire into the state of Ireland, more particularly with reference to the circumstances which may have led to disturbances in that part of the United Kingdom*, HC 1825 (181, 521), ix.
25. *Report from Her Majesty's commissioners of Inquiry into the state of the law and practice in respect to the occupation of land in Ireland*, HC 1845 (605), xix, 1.
26. In particular the works cited in note 19 of this chapter.
27. See W. J. McCormack, *Ascendancy and Tradition in Anglo–Irish Literary History from 1789 to 1939* (Oxford, 1985), pp. 97–168.

28. Maria Edgeworth, *Castle Rackrent* (London, 1800). See also Maria Edgeworth, *The Absentee* (London, 1812).
29. For the most influential statement of this analysis of the origins of the Land War see T. W. Moody, *Davitt and the Irish Revolution* (Oxford, 1981). See also 'The new departure in Irish Politics, 1878–79' in H. R. Cronne, T. W. Moody and B. Quinn (eds.), *Essays in British and Irish History in Honour of James Eadie Todd* (London, 1949); F. S. L. Lyons, *Charles Stewart Parnell* (London, 1977); Conor Cruise O'Brien, *Parnell and his Party 1880–90* (Oxford, 1957).
30. *Freeman's Journal*, 20 September 1880.
31. See Appendix III.

Chapter 1 (pages 11–30)

1. Lord Rosse as quoted in K. Theodore Hoppen, *Elections, Politics and Society in Ireland, 1832–1885* (Oxford, 1984), p. 409.
2. See R. B. McDowell, *The Irish Administration 1801–1914* (London and Toronto, 1964) for an overview of the structure of courts of law, in particular pp. 104–63.
3. For an account of the politics of the conflicting relief agencies see R. F. Foster, *Lord Randolph Churchill: a Political Life* (Oxford, 1981), pp. 50–3. The Marlborough Committee, organised by the Duchess of Marlborough, was viewed with suspicion by Parnell. As he said to William O'Brien, it was well known 'that the government is going to fight the famine – or is it the League? – from behind the Duchess's petticoats'. The rival Mansion House Relief Fund was set up in reaction to the Marlborough effort by the Lord Mayor of Dublin and Dwyer Gray of the *Freeman's Journal*. As Foster notes, Randolph Churchill reminded his mother of the potential political consequences of her charity. 'In the absence of full details it would be inadvisable for you to give the great weight of your name to such proposals . . . it must not be forgotten that the nature and extent of Irish disorder is a matter on which there is very great difference of opinion, and that those persons who assert that it is extreme are in many cases persons who have connected themselves with land agitation of a serious nature. By engaging in and initiating an appeal to the public to subscribe to the relief of Irish distress you will entirely corroborate the premises of these agitators and to a certain extent excuse their acts.' The politics of relief agencies, as Foster reveals, did not end there. James Gordon Bennett's New York fund was added to the other two, and the Society of Friends set up their own non–party fund to avoid further political bickering. See also Dublin Mansion House Relief Committee, *The Irish Crisis of 1879–80: Proceedings of the Dublin Mansion House Relief Committee, 1880* (Dublin, 1881).
4. For a view of the Tory cabinet's Irish policy in late 1879 see Nancy E. Johnson (ed.), *The Diary of Gathorne-Hardy, later Lord Cranbrook 1866–1892: Political Selections* (Oxford, 1981), pp. 427–34. It seems clear that the decisions on measures to be taken were made by Beach, Cross and Gathorne-Hardy, in consultation with Lowther.
5. For the views of Dublin Castle in the spring of 1880 see Foster, *Lord Randolph Churchill*, pp. 50–7.
6. The introduction of the Westmeath Act (34 and 35 Vic., c. 25) of 1871 was remarkable for being one of the few occasions on which habeas corpus had been suspended in response to agrarian conspiracy. In this case the conspiracy, it was

alleged, was Ribbonism. The suspension of habeas corpus was unknown in Ireland before 1791. It was suspended in the autumn of 1796, and held in suspension by a succession of six further acts until 1805. Since 1805 it had been suspended in 1822 for six months, in 1833 for one year and in 1848 for over thirteen months. It was suspended in 1866, and continued in suspension until 1869, in response to the perceived threat of Fenianism. In these years 1,131 people were detained under the Act. The Peace Preservation Act of 1875 (38 Vic., c. 14) was the 'extraordinary' legal measure in force in 1880. It was, however, due to expire on 1 June 1880. The Westmeath Act had expired in 1877, but the 1875 Act had prolonged certain sections of the act of 1870 together with certain sections of the Westmeath Act, i.e. provision for: (1) the levying of extra police costs on the 'affected' districts, at the discretion of the Lord Lieutenant; (2) power to control the licensing of arms and powers of search; (3) the holding of sworn enquiries into any felony or misdemeanour; (4) searches for evidence in cases of threatening letters; (5) the arrest of absconding witnesses; (6) compensation for victims of outrage and (7) the continuation of the Oaths Acts of 1819, 1823 and 1839. London, Public Record Office, subsequently cited as LPRO, Cab. 37/2, no. 23 of 10 May 1880. See also, on this question, two superb articles by Richard Hawkins: 'Liberals, land and coercion in the summer of 1880: the influence of the Carraroe ejectments', *Galway Archaeological and Historical Society Journal*, xxxiv (1974–75), pp. 40–57 and 'Gladstone, Forster and the release of Parnell, 1882–88', *Irish Historical Studies,* xvi, no. 64 (September 1969), pp. 426–34.

7. *Royal Commission on the depressed condition of the agricultural interest: Minutes of Evidence taken before Her Majesty's commissioners on agriculture,* vols. 1 and 2: [C 2778–1] HC 1881, xv and [C 3096] HC 1881, xvii; *Preliminary report from Her Majesty's commissioners on agriculture* [C 2778] HC 1881, xv; *Final report from Her Majesty's commissioners etc.* [C 3309] HC 1882, xiv, known as the Richmond Commission.

8. The other members of the commission were Sir William Henry Stephenson, Robert Nigel Fitzhardinge Kingscote, John Clay, Mitchell Henry, James Lennox Napier, Robert Peterson, Bonamy Price, John Rice, Charles Thomas Ritchie, Benjamin Bridges, Hunter Rodwell, William Stratton and Jacob Wilson.

9. The Irish preliminary report was presented to both Houses of Parliament on 1 January 1881. *Preliminary report from Her Majesty's commissioners* [C 2778] HC 1881, xv, pp. 841–48.

10. Ibid., p. 841. The non–Dublin investigations of Baldwin and Robertson had begun in Kerry in September 1879.

11. Ibid.

12. The standard biography is by Thomas, Baron Newton, *Lord Lansdowne, a Biography* (London, 1929). The Marquis of Lansdowne owned, in addition to his English estates, lands in Meath, the Queen's County and Kerry. His Kerry estates, where he resided for two months of the year, consisted of 119,000 acres with 995 tenants. 800 of these tenants held lands of under £10 valuation.

13. The Earl of Dufferin was Her Majesty's Ambassador at St Petersburg. He had formerly held an estate of 20,000 acres in Down, which by 1881 had been reduced to 6,000 acres. See Sir Alfred Lyall, *The Life of the Marquess of Dufferin and Ava,* 2 vols. (London, 1905).

14. On Arthur McMurrough Kavanagh see Donald McCormick, *The Incredible Mr Kavanagh* (London, 1960). The author had access to his subject's diaries and letters which are not now available.

15. Colonel Richard Dease offered technical expertise on the question of debt.

16. Charles Hare Hemphill, (1822–1908), first Baron Hemphill, Chairman of counties Louth, Leitrim and Kerry; Liberal MP for Tyrone 1906, *DNB*, 1901–11, pp. 239–40.

17. Hussey, a notoriously powerful and unpopular agent has left a remarkable testament: *The Reminiscences of an Irish Land Agent, being those of S. M. Hussey* (London, 1904). He had been approached by Froude and Bright to write these memoirs, which were compiled by Home Gordon.

18. Stephen Woulfe Flanagan was closely associated with the committee of landlords then sitting in Dublin. He had been a land judge since May 1869 and worked closely with his junior colleague Ormsby. He owned land in Sligo, Roscommon and Clare where he had granted abatements of 25 to 30 per cent in 1879.

19. John Ball Greene. See the *Journal of the Statistical and Social Enquiry Society of Ireland* to which he was a frequent contributor, often in association with T. W. Grimshaw.

20. See *Minutes of evidence taken before Her Majesty's commissioners on agriculture*, vol. 1, [C 2778–1], HC 1881, xv, 25.

21. Ibid., Paragraph no. 1035 – Evidence of William Bence–Jones (evidence presented in numbered paragraphs).

22. Ibid., Paragraph no. 14,568. Evidence of John Corbett, Deer Park, Lismore. He held 40 Irish acres at £30.10.0 annual rent. Both his father and his grandfather had held the land before him.

23. Ibid., Paragraph no. 14,777.

24. Ibid., Paragraph no. 14,886.

25. Ibid., Paragraph no. 20,928.

26. Encumbered Estates Act Files, National Library of Ireland.

27. From *Preliminary report from Her Majesty's commissioners on agriculture presented to both Houses of Parliament*, [C 2778], HC 1881, xv, 1, pp. 841–8.

28. Ibid.

29. T. W. Moody and R. A. J. Hawkins (eds.) with Margaret Moody, *Florence Arnold-Forster's Irish Journal* (Oxford, 1988). Biographical note on Burke, p. 533.

30. Chief Secretary's Office Registered Papers, Letterbook 1880/1464 p. 35. Dublin, National Archives, subsequently cited as NAD, CSORP.

31. NAD, CSORP Letterbook 1880/1361, pp. 37–8.

32. Ibid.

33. NAD, CSORP 1880/1044, p. 31, 13 January 1880.

34. R. B. McDowell, *The Irish Administration 1801–1914* (London and Toronto, 1964), p. 56, quoting Lord and Lady Aberdeen, *We Twa* (London, 1925) vol. i, p. 250.

35. McDowell, *Irish Administration*, p. 112.

36. See ibid., pp. 114–15. McDowell draws heavily on the *Report of the commission appointed by the Lords commissioners of Her Majesty's treasury to . . . enquire into the condition of the civil service in Ireland; . . . on resident magistrates*, HC 1874 (923), xvi.

37. C. D. Clifford Lloyd (Late Special Resident Magistrate), *Ireland under the Land League: A Narrative of Personal Experience* (London, 1882).

38. Ibid., p. 36.

39. Ibid., p. 51.

40. Ibid., p. 53.

41. Ibid., pp. 56–7.
42. Ibid., p. 48.
43. See also *Constabulary Ireland, report of commission*, HC 1866 (3658), xxxiv, pp. 13–14, quoted in McDowell, *Irish Administration*, on the question of promotion from ranks, p. 140, and *Report on the civil service in Ireland (Royal Irish Constabulary)*, HC 1873 [C 831] xxii, p. 9.
44. On government acknowledgement of distress see debate in the House of Commons, *Hansard*, Third series, vol. CCL, cols. 520–60. Hereafter *Hansard* references are in the form *Hansard* 3, CCL, cols. 520–60, 6 February 1880; see House of Lords, *Hansard* 3, CCL, cols. 487–506, where Lord Emly quoted with approbation the anti–interventionist policies of Sir Charles Trevelyan in 1847–48. He was, Emly claimed, the 'greatest public servant ever'. In the committee stage of the Bill in the House of Commons on 16 February 1880 Edmond Synan proposed an amendment to the Relief of Distress (Ireland) Bill 'that it is inexpedient that any portion of property accruing to the Commissioners of Church Temporalities under the Irish Church Act of 1869 shall be applied towards the temporary relief of distress in Ireland, and that the provisions of the Bill authorising such advances out of such property cannot be satisfied . . . from Imperial resources', ibid., col. 688. At an earlier stage of the debate, on 6 February, the Chancellor announced that the Local Government Board were in 'telegraphic communication' with every part of the country. Additional costs were to fall on the rates. As the Chancellor of the Exchequer said, 'We remember the years 1846 and 1847, and we know at that time a very large amount of public money was *unfortunately wasted* upon works undertaken without due consideration and carried out in a manner which necessarily involved considerable waste. But the question was not one of waste of money. If it were all . . . that £5m or £6m were expended without producing any good results, we might have thought less of the miscalculation; but the fact was a very great evil was done – the people were demoralised and it was found necessary to take towards the end very strong measures in order to check the evils that were occurring.' Ibid., col. 169.
45. See Appendix I for an outline of the historiography.
46. For later interpretations of the intent and consequences of resistance to rent payment see Barbara Solow, *The Land Question and the Irish Economy 1870–1903* (Cambridge, Mass., 1971); Paul Bew, *Land and the National Question in Ireland, 1858–1882* (Dublin, 1978); Samuel Clark, *Social Origins of the Irish Land War* (Princeton, 1979); James S. Donnelly jr., *The Land and the People of Nineteenth-Century Cork: The Rural Economy and the Land Question* (London, 1975); W. E. Vaughan, 'An assessment of the economic performance of Irish landlords 1851–81' in F. S. L. Lyons and R. A. J. Hawkins (eds.), *Ireland under the Union: Varieties of Tension* (Oxford, 1980); L. P. Curtis, 'Incumbered wealth: Landlord indebtedness in post–famine Ireland', *American Historical Review*, LXXV, 2 (April 1980); Samuel Clark and James S. Donnelly, jr., (eds.), *Irish Peasants: Violence and Political Unrest 1780–1914* (Wisconsin, 1984).
47. NAD, Chief Secretary's Office, Carton no. 1. 'Queen vs Parnell and Others. Markings of subsequent use handwritten on unfolioed poster.
48. Ibid.
49. H. C. G. Matthew (ed.), *The Gladstone Diaries with Cabinet Minutes and Prime–Ministerial Correspondence, vol. IX, January 1875–December 1880* (Oxford, 1986), p. 488, footnote 6. The article appeared in *Nineteenth Century*, vii, 389, 493 (March 1880).

50. Information from Henry Boylan, *A Dictionary of Irish Biography* (Dublin, 1968) and McCormick, *The Incredible Mr Kavanagh*.
51. Ibid.
52. Quoted in Mark Bence–Jones, *Twilight of the Ascendancy* (London, 1987), p. 30. For the original letter see A. B. Cooke and A. P. W. Malcolmson (eds.), *The Ashbourne Papers, 1869–1913: A Calendar of the Papers of Edward Gibson, 1st Lord Ashbourne*, Public Record Office Northern Ireland, subsequently cited as PRONI, in association with the House of Lords Records Office (Belfast, 1974). See B. 79/3, p. 138. The letter continued ' . . . If they ['my own men'] had proved themselves true, I should no doubt have missed the interest and employment of a parliamentary life, of which the defeat deprives me, but I should have been quite content to live on and work here among them as heretofore. But now it is impossible. I cannot even contemplate it, and my fixed intention is to shut up everything, appoint an agent and leave the country . . .'.
53. Boylan, *A Dictionary of Irish Biography*.
54. O. E. Somerville and Martin Ross, *Irish Memories* (London, 1918), Preface, 'The tents of the Arabs', Act II, 'Dialogue of the King and Enzarza'.
55. Ibid., pp. 140–152. 'The years of the eighties were years of leanness, "years that the locust hath eaten".'
56. J. L. Garvin, *The Life of Joseph Chamberlain, vol. 1, 1836–1885* (London, 1932), p. 319.
57. Richard Hawkins has discussed the post–hoc self–representations of Chamberlain and Charles Dilke in his article, 'Gladstone, Forster and the release of Parnell, 1882–8', *Irish Historical Studies*, xvi, no. 64 (September 1969), pp. 26–34.
58. *National Library of Ireland*, MS 8501 (7), Lowther to Burke, 30 April 1880, quoted in Moody and Hawkins (eds.), *Arnold–Forster's Irish Journal*, p. 3, note 2.
59. *Hansard*, 3, CCLII, col. 67.
60. See London PRO Cab. 37/2, no. 23, Memo by W. E. Forster dated 10 May 1880, discussed at cabinet of 12 May. This memo incorporated the circular of December 1879 to all Resident Magistrates. *All* recommended some form of renewal of exceptional legislation. Many considered that there should be some restoration of the power of arrest of strangers and suspicious persons out at night, and some application of the Westmeath Act to the western counties. See also Cab. 37/2, *Memo on 1870 Land Act* by William O'Connor Morris, County Court Judge of Kerry, 21 July 1880.
61. Quoted in Matthew, *Gladstone Diaries*, ix, p. 518, Forster to Gladstone, 8 May 1880, Gladstone Papers, British Library, subsequently cited as BL, MS 44544, fol. 5.
62. Ibid., p. 516, Gladstone's notes in cabinet May 5, 1880, 2.30 p.m. Item 21 listed before item 1 in Gladstone's note, Gladstone Papers, BL, Add MS 44642, fol. 5.
63. Matthew, *Gladstone Diaries*, ix, p. 518.
64. Ibid., p. 573. Diary entry 29 August 1880: Cruising around Britain on 'Grantully Castle' he wrote, 'Reached Dublin in time to stop suddenly and go to Christ Church. The congregation all agog. Out of doors an enthusiastic extempore reception. Off before five.' Gladstone returned to ship, to resume reading on the Armenian Church.
65. See cabinet decision as listed in Matthew, *Gladstone Diaries*, ix.
66. Landlord and Tenant (Ireland) Act (1870) Amendment Bill: *Hansard*, 3, CCLII, 31 May 1880, cols. 740–1.
67. *Earl Cowper, KG: A Memoir by his Wife* (London, for private circulation 1913). Forster to Cowper, 18 June 1880, printed letter, p. 368.

68. See *Report of Her Majesty's commissioners of Inquiry into the working of the Landlord and Tenant (Ireland) Act 1870* (known as the Bessborough Commission) *and the Acts amending the same*, [C 2779], HC 1881, xviii; vol. ii, *Digest of evidence; minutes of evidence, part 1* [C 2770–1]; vol. iii: *minutes of evidence, part 2* [C 2779], HC 1881, xiv; vol. iv, Index [C 2778], HC 1881, xix.

69. Modern scholarship insists that eviction figures are deceptive since most of those listed as evicted were readmitted to their farms as caretakers. See W. E. Vaughan, 'Landlords and tenants in Ireland 1848–1904', *Studies in Irish Economic and Social History*, 2, 1984.

70. Frederick George Brabazon Ponsonby, 6th Earl of Bessborough, *Dictionary of National Biography*, subsequently cited as *DNB*.

71. Charles O'Conor of Belanagare, the O'Conor Don, Home Rule MP until 1880, DNB, 1900–11, pp. 36–7.

72. Gladstone Papers, BL, Add MS 44544, Gladstone to Forster, 10 June 1880.

73. On 14 June Gladstone saw Argyll, Granville and Forster. 'Long and anxious conversation with the Duke of Argyll on his letter of resignation.' See Matthew, *Gladstone Diaries*, ix, p. 538, and note 5, also on p. 538: 'Compromise agreed on; Argyll not to resign, the Bill to be limited to 1880–1 and to scheduled districts', and 'Gladstone to reserve our entire freedom for the future' and to 'deprecate unreasonable expectations', Argyll to Sir J. MacNeill on 14 June 1880 in Lady F. Balfour, *Ne Obliviscaris*, 2 vols. (London, 1930), i, pp. 285–7. The 'evidence' of eviction figures solicited from Forster had been central to Gladstone's written appeal that preceded the verbal agreement to withdraw the resignation letter. See again Matthew, *Gladstone Diaries*, pp. 539–40, W. E. Gladstone to Duke of Argyll, 14 June 1880. Gladstone Papers, BL, Add MS 44104, fol. 175: 'Would it be quite equitable to press upon the cabinet the proposition . . . it is notorious that we had determined not to deal with the subject during the present session' (quoting from Argyll's letter of resignation).'

> I aver that the only subject we had determined was *not* to deal with the purchase clauses of the Irish Land Act. We never considered the question of ejectments connected with the present distress in Ireland.
>
> For myself I can most strictly say the proposal of O'Connor Power has had no other effect than to draw my attention to a question which, like many other questions with strong claims, I had not considered and had had no time to consider. I must also say of that question that the evidence in regard to it grows and varies *from day to day*. [my emphasis]
>
> I was under the impression that ejectments were diminishing but I now find from figures first seen on Saturday that they seem rather to increase.
>
> I also find that they are attempted wholesale; and that forty constables fail to give the strength necessary to sustain the law. This state of facts entails on me and I think many colleagues might be disposed to say the same thing the duty of enquiring, where I had not previously known there was urgent cause to inquire.
>
> On inquiry I find reason to believe that many ejectments are on account of an inability to pay rent caused wholly by destitution, that destitution due to the circumstances of the last harvest.

74. Richard Hawkins, 'Liberals, land and coercion in the summer of 1880: the influence of the Carraroe ejectments', *Galway Archaeological and Historical Society Journal*, xxxiv, 1974–75, pp. 40–57.

75. Henry Robinson, 22 March 1880, NAD, CSORP, 1880/13676 quoted in Hawkins, op. cit., p. 41.

76. Burke to Forster, ibid.
77. Letter from the Viceroy to Lord Spencer, 14 June 1880, *Earl Cowper, KG: A Memoir by his Wife*, p. 366.
78. Forster, quoted in Hawkins, op. cit.
79. *Hansard*, 3, CCLIII, 25 June 1880, col. 846.
80. Ibid., col. 852.
81. Ibid., col. 857.
82. Ibid., col. 869.
83. Ibid., cols. 1160–5.

Chapter 2 (pages 31–60)

1. For details of cabinet decision of November 1879 see Nancy Johnson (ed.), *The Diary of Gathorne–Hardy, later Lord Cranbrook, 1866–1892: Political Selections*. In particular the following p. 427: '*Wednesday, 5 November* Lowther not definite enough. Grave difficulties before us but very pressing distress limited and local. The Lord Lieutenant [Marlborough] most lax in his proposals for pauperising further the country. What cure is there for these Irish ills? Lord Dillon's 3,900 tenants under rental each one all paupers in fact, dividing and subdividing. We should go no further than preventing deaths by famine, in the interests of the people themselves. *Friday, 7 November* . . . yesterday . . . the cabinet had two Irish Agricultural Commissioners before it [Baldwin and Robertson], and they gave a most lamentable account of distress on the west coast. Short crops, no fuel, deep indebtedness to shopkeepers. Farms of three or four acres which cannot support a family. What prospect for such a country. The indebtedness has increased since the 1870 Act of evil memory, as it seemed to afford some security. We shall have sore trouble to be firm in non–pauperising, while we prevent starvation. Cross, Beach and I are to meet Lowther and consult. Dined with Cairns, next to Sir Evelyn Wood . . . He admitted there was no excuse for the large demand for troops. *Tuesday, 11 November* . . . to the Irish office yesterday . . . At 1 I met Beach and Cross at Irish Office and drew up an outline of what we agreed upon. This memo formed the basis of the cabinet's decision.'

2. For details of these relief measures see the following:
   – *Correspondence relative to measures for relief of distress in Ireland 1879–80*, [C 2483], HC 1880, 1xii, 187;
   – *Annual report of the Local Government Board for Ireland, being the seventh report under the Local Government Board (Irl.) Act, 35 and 36 Vic., c 69: with appendices*, [C 2363], HC 1878–79, xxx, 1;
   – *Annual report of the Local Government Board for Ireland, being the eighth report under the Local Government Board (Irl.) Act, 35 and 36 Vic., 69*, [C 2603], HC 1880, xxviii,1;
   – *Return of all applications from landed proprietors and sanitary authorities in scheduled unions for loans under the notices of the commissioners of public works in Ireland, dated the 22nd day of November 1879 and the 12th day of January 1880 respectively; with result of applications to the 20th day of March 1880, arranged by baronies*, HC 1880 (154) 1xii, 209;
   – *Return of the loans applied for and granted in each of the various unions of Ireland scheduled as distressed . . . up to 7th February 1880; . . . up to the 29th day of February*, HC 1880 (158), 1xii, 283; *Return of numbers in receipt of relief in the several unions of Ireland on the 1st day of January,*

the 1st day of March and the 1st day of June in 1878, 1879 and 1880 (420 – sess. 2) 1xii, 289;
– *Return showing the unions and electoral divisions scheduled by the local government board for Ireland under the Seed Supply (Irl.) Act 1880*, HC (299 – sess. 2) 1xii, 339.

3. *Hansard*, 3, CCLIII, cols. 217–218, debate on Relief of Distress (Irl.) Act (Commons), 17 June 1880.
4. For Parnell's speech in full see ibid., cols. 217–30.
5. Ibid., col. 225.
6. Ibid., col. 239.
7. Ibid., cols. 240–1.
8. Ibid., col. 303.
9. Ibid., col. 304.
10. Ibid., cols. 304–5.
11. Gladstone Papers, BL, Add MS 44157, Forster to Gladstone, 7 May 1880.
12. Gladstone Papers, BL, Add MS 44157, fols. 132–33, Forster to Gladstone, 6 June 1880.
13. Gladstone Papers, BL, Add MS 44157, fol. 141, Forster to Gladstone, 24 June 1880.
14. Gladstone Papers, BL, Add MS 44157, fol. 142, Gladstone to Forster, 25 June 1880.
15. *Hansard*, 3, CCLIII, cols. 410–11. Relief of Distress (Irl.) Act, 21 June 1880.
16. Gladstone Papers, BL, Add MS 44157, 25 June 1880, Gladstone to Forster.
17. Gladstone Papers, BL, Add MS 44104, fol. 175, 15 June 1880 (see *Gladstone Diaries*), Gladstone to Argyll. See also Gladstone's letter of 10 June to Forster, Add MS 44544, fol. 19, quoted in Matthew, *Gladstone Diaries*, ix, p. 537. Relevant as follows:
    'The enclosed letter states strongly the view of the Duke of Argyll on the land question in Ireland, which is based on the two propositions I have scored on the side. There is no doubt of the stringency of my general pledges in 1870.
    Can you inform us by Saturday by figures not only of the graduated increase of evictions but of the counties and districts in which such increase has taken place? And will this not *confirm or confute* the Duke's statement that they are evictions of men unwilling, not men unable to pay their rent?'
18. *Hansard*, 3, CCLIII, 25 June 1880, Compensation for Disturbance (Irl.) Bill, cols. 844–5.
19. Ibid., col. 845.
20. Ibid., col. 848.
21. Ibid., col. 848.
22. Ibid., col. 849.
23. Ibid., cols. 854–5.
24. Ibid., cols. 855–6.
25. Quoted in T. W. Moody and R. A. J. Hawkins (eds.), *Florence Arnold–Forster's Irish Journal* (Oxford, 1988), pp. 7–8, diary entry for Friday 2 July 1880.
26. *Hansard*, 3, CCLIII, Compensation for Disturbances (Irl.) Bill, 25 June 1880, col. 863.
27. Ibid., col. 864.
28. Ibid., 29 June 1880, cols. 1125 and 1126 respectively for these two quotations.
29. Ibid., col. 1127.
30. Ibid.

31. Ibid., col. 1132.
32. Ibid., cols. 1134, 1136–7.
33. Ibid., cols. 1155–6.
34. For the speech of the Attorney–General see ibid., cols. 1160–5.
35. *Hansard*, 3, CCLIII. State of Ireland Debate, 7 June 1880, cols. 1322–3, 1124.
36. *Hansard*, 3, CCLV, cols. 3–43 for the full text of Cairns's speech.
37. Ibid., col. 101.
38. See H.C.G. Matthew's 'Disraeli, Gladstone and mid-Victorian budgets; *Historical Journal*, 22 (1979), pp. 615-43.
39. *Hansard*, 3, CCLV, col. 101.
40. R. Barry O'Brien, *The Life of Charles Stewart Parnell* (London, 1910), p. 184.
41. *Earl Cowper, KG: A Memoir by his Wife*, p. 368.
42. John Morley, *Life of William Ewart Gladstone* (London, 1912), vol. III, p. 37–40, 3rd edn.
43. J. L. Hammond, *Gladstone and the Irish Nation* (London, 1938), p. 193: 'Thus the effect of the action of the House of Lords can be described very simply. The Government said that it was essential if they were to give Ireland peace that they should be allowed by parliament to enforce a moratorium, to check the power of eviction until they had time to reform the law. The House of Lords refused them that power. The moratorium was in consequence enforced not by British law but by Irish violence. All the misfortunes of the following years can be attributed to this governing fact, for the Government were compelled to address themselves to two problems at once, the problem of enforcing respect for bad law, and the problem of turning bad law into good law.'
44. Alarmingly, Merlyn Rees as Northern Ireland Secretary in the 1970s consulted Hammond 'when in doubt'. Merlyn Rees, *Northern Ireland: A Personal Perspective* (London, 1985).
45. William Ewart Gladstone, 'Mr Forster and Ireland', *Nineteenth Century*, September 1888, review of T. Wemyss Reid, *Life of the Honourable William Edward Forster*, 2 vols. (London, 1888). See draft of article in Gladstone Papers, BL, Add MS 44701, fols. 167–73, for Gladstone's numerous revisions in structuring the 'correct' version.
46. *Hansard*, 3, CCLV, 23 August 1880, col. 1879.
47. Forster to Gladstone, 8 October 1880, Gladstone Papers, BL, Add MS 44157.
48. Forster to Gladstone, 8 October 1880, Gladstone Papers, BL, Add MS 44157.
49. Ibid.
50. Donoughmore to Forster, 8 October 1880, Gladstone Papers, BL, Add MS 44157, enclosed in Forster to Gladstone, 8 October 1880. Also published in full in *Cowper, A Memoir*, pp. 399–400.
51. Ibid.
52. *Report from Her Majesty's commissioners of Inquiry into the state of the law and practice in respect to the occupation of land in Ireland*, HC 1845, (605), xix, 1.
53. Forster to Gladstone, 8 October 1880, Gladstone Papers, BL, Add MS 44157, fols. 152–160.
54. Forster to Gladstone, 10 October 1880, Gladstone Papers, BL, Add MS 44157, fols. 174–7.
55. Forster to Gladstone, 25 October 1880, Gladstone Papers, BL, Add MS 44157, fols. 186–7.
56. Ibid.
57. Gladstone to Forster, 25 October 1880, Gladstone Papers, BL, Add MS 44157, fols. 184–5.

58. Ibid.
59. Forster to Gladstone, 5 November 1880, Gladstone Papers, BL, Add MS 44157, fol. 191.
60. Forster to Gladstone, 5 November 1880, Gladstone Papers, BL, Add MS 44157, fol. 194.
61. Hammond, *Gladstone and the Irish Nation*, p. 195.
62. 'Minute by the Viceroy for the Cabinet, 8 November 1880', *Cowper, A Memoir*, pp. 422–4. See as printed for Cabinet of 9 November 1880 in London PRO Cab. 37/3/62.
63. Hammond, *Gladstone and the Irish Nation*, p. 196.
64. 'Minute by the Viceroy for the Cabinet, 8 November 1880', *Cowper, A Memoir*, p. 424.
65. *Cowper, A Memoir*, p. 423.
66. Ibid., p. 429.
67. Ibid., pp. 434–5, Gladstone to the Viceroy, 24 November 1880.
68. Ibid., p. 437, the Viceroy to the Duke of Argyll, 28 November 1880.
69. Ibid., p. 438, Lord Spencer to the Viceroy, 28 November 1880.

Chapter 3 (pages 61–94)

1. *Report of the Irish State Trials 1880–81, with proceedings preliminary and subsequent thereto, from the 'Freeman's Journal', except the eighth to the eleventh day of the trial, of which the report is special*, (Dublin, 1881), p. 1; *Freeman's Journal*, 2 November 1880. See Appendix II for a full list of charges against the traversers.
2. For the State Trial of O'Connell see Angus Macintyre, *The Liberator: Daniel O'Connell and the Irish Party, 1830–47* (London, 1965). See also Oliver MacDonagh, *The Emancipist: Daniel O'Connell 1830-1847* (London, 1989).
3. *Freeman's Journal*, 3 November 1880. K. B. Nowlan, *The Politics of Repeal: A Study in the Relations between Great Britain and Ireland 1841–50* (London, 1965).
4. Reported by the *Freeman's Journal*. The analyses of the *Freeman's Journal* before and during trial, apart from the report of the court proceedings which are accurate and unbiased, can be viewed as dictated by Land League and Irish Parliamentary Party spokesmen at this time. The newspaper launched a special fund to support the case of 'the Traversers'.
5. William Lane Joynt was closely associated with the Dublin Castle Law Officers, and was usually employed in delicate Crown cases. His handling of the case was made public through the covering letters that he sent to the individual traversers, together with their subpoenas. The name of the firm also marks the papers on which the reports of the RIC are typed and summarised to form the Crown brief. Queen vs Parnell and others, 1880–81, Cartons 1 and 2, NAD.
6. This objection had already been registered by Parnell in a letter written by Valentine Dillon under instructions to William Lane Joynt, dated 9 November 1880. Macdonagh's objection was made at the court of Queen's Bench on 10 November 1880, *Freeman's Journal*, 11 November 1880.
7. Macintyre, *The Liberator*, p. 271.
8. Case brought before the court on 18 November. Reported in *Freeman's Journal*, 19 November 1880.

9.   *Evening Mail*, 3 November 1880.
10. See R. F. Foster, *Charles Stewart Parnell: The Man and his Family* (Hassocks, 1976)
11. *Freeman's Journal*, 19 November 1880.
12. Land League manifesto, 6 November 1880. Published in *Freeman's Journal*, 7 November 1880.
13. For an account of selecting a jury panel see *Freeman's Journal*, 13 December 1880.
14. Account in same edition of scene near courthouse, but more particularly evoked street scenes in account of the first day of the trial proper, *Freeman's Journal*, 28 December 1880.
15. On the developed class interests of sections of Dublin society see Mary Daly, *Dublin, the Deposed Capital: A Social and Economic History 1860–1914* (Cork, 1985).
16. Gladstone had intervened personally by writing to Forster to ensure that the Lord Chief Justice was removed from the case, in view of remarks deemed to be prejudicial to the interests of the traversers.
17. *Freeman's Journal*, 29 December 1880.
18. Ibid.
19. Also First Day, Tuesday 28 December 1880, *Freeman's Journal*, 29 December, *Report of Irish State Trials, 1880–81*, pp. 54–5. Again, see Appendix II.
20. Joseph Lee, *The Modernisation of Irish Society, 1848–1918* (Dublin, 1973), pp. 65–105.
21. Ibid., p. 83.
22. For memos of both cabinet meetings see Gladstone's cabinet memos of 30 and 31 December 1880, Gladstone Papers, BL. Add MS 44642, fols. 118 and 125 respectively, quoted in H. C. G. Matthew (ed.), *The Gladstone Diaries with Cabinet Minutes and Prime–Ministerial Correspondence*, vol. IX, (Oxford, 1986) pp. 655–6.
23. Ibid., 'Introduction', p. l, xxvii. See also Gladstone to Forster, 7 December 1880. Add MS 44158 folio 34 and Gladstone's memo for cabinet prepared on 9 December 1880 cited by Matthew, *Gladstone Diaries*, vol. IX, pp. 632–36.
24. Gladstone Papers, BL, Add MS 44158 fol. 64, printed in Matthew, *Gladstone Diaries*, vol. ix, p. 635.
25. See cabinet memo 13 December 1880, Gladstone Papers, BL, Add MS 44642, fol. 108, quoted in Matthew, *Gladstone Diaries*, vol. ix, p. 639. The document here quoted is Gladstone's own memo of the cabinet of 13 December at which the decisions on habeas corpus and land were made in all but name. He concludes the memo with a signed addendum: 'W. E. G. Essence of the former decision lay in the *combination* of remedy with repression'.
26. For the drastic nature of the Land Act as proposed in mid–December see full text prepared for cabinet of 15 December 1880, Gladstone Papers, BL, Add MS 44625, fol. 19, reproduced in Matthew, *Gladstone Diaries*, vol. ix, pp. 640–1.
27. Gladstone to Argyll, 29 November 1880, Gladstone Papers, BL, Add MS 56446, fol. 3, reproduced in Matthew, *Gladstone Diaries*, vol. IX, p. 625.
28. Gladstone to Forster, Gladstone Papers, BL, Add MS 44158, fol. 15, reproduced in Matthew, *Gladstone Diaries*, vol. IX, p. 628.
29. Gladstone's cabinet memo, Gladstone Papers, BL, Add MS 44642, fol. 125 reproduced in Matthew, *Gladstone Diaries*, vol. IX, p. 656.
30. Ibid. Note scribbled by Forster included, together with Gladstone's response.

31. Gladstone to Forster, 4 November 1880, Gladstone Papers, BL, Add MS 44544, fol. 89, in Matthew, *Gladstone Diaries*, vol. IX, p. 608.

32. Gladstone to Morley, 27 October 1880, Gladstone Papers, BL, Add MS 44544, fol. 83 in Matthew, *Gladstone Diaries*, vol. IX, pp. 604–5.

33. Forster to Gladstone, 7 December 1880, Gladstone Papers, BL, Add MS 44157, fol. 36.

34. Forster memo for cabinet, 15 December 1880, Gladstone Papers, BL, Add MS 44625, fols. 94–6

35. *Hansard*, 3, CCCLVII, col. 483.

36. *Hansard*, 3, CCCLVII, cols. 479–81.

37. *Hansard*, 3, CCCLVII, 7 January, cols. 195–200.

38. T. W. Moody and R. A. J. Hawkins with Margaret Moody (eds.), *Florence Arnold–Forster's Irish Journal*, p. 96.

39. NAD, viii centre CSORP. Queen vs Parnell and others, Box 1, Chief Crown Solicitor's department.

40. Ibid.

41. *Hansard*, 3, CCCLVII, col. 485.

42. NADRP, viii centre, Queen vs Parnell and others, Box 1.

43. See Gladstone Papers, BL, Add MS 44157, Add MS 44160. See also Add MS 44625 for Gladstone's crucial memos on land and habeas corpus, August–December 1880.

44. See T. W. Moody, *Davitt and the Irish Revolution, 1846–82*, for the definitive account of Davitt's early years, pp. 1–23.

45. For the full text of *Paudeen O'Rafferty on the Landlord's Ten Commandments* see Appendix III.

46. Dion Boucicault's *The Shaughraun* was first produced in 1875. In December 1881 the play, featuring Sheil Barry in the role of the informer Harvey Duff, was showing in Dublin.

47. This view is most forcibly put in Paul Bew, *Land and the National Question*, and Samuel Clark, *Social Origins of the Irish Land War* (Princeton, 1979).

48. NAD, Chief Secretary's Office Records, Police and crime division. See *List of persons detained under the Protection of Person and Property (Ireland) Act, 1881*. Also *Arrests under the Protection of Person and Property Act 1881–82* (5 vols.).

49. Moody and Hawkins, *Arnold–Forster's Journal*, p. 84.

50. Ibid., p. 87.

51. Bew, *Land and the National Question*, and Clark, *Social Origins*.

52. See H. O. Arnold–Forster 'The Gladstone government and Ireland', *North American Review*, cxxxiii, no. 301, December 1881, pp. 560–77; and also *The Truth about the Land League . . . by 'One Who Knows'* (London, 1882).

53. In the list of persons detained most of the prominent names encountered in contemporary accounts in *United Ireland* and the *Freeman's Journal* occur.

54. See NAD, Chief Secretary's Office, Registered Papers 1881. 1–47, 210 in vols. viii, 59, 67–70. For individual cases see index to RP 1881 at viii, 59, 71.

55. Categories noted from column marked 'crimes of which detainees suspected' in List of persons detained under the Protection of Person and Property (Ireland) Act 1881 and 1882 (amalgamated).

56. All information derived from above list of persons detained.

57. Charles Townshend, *Political Violence in Ireland: Government and Resistance since 1848* (Oxford, 1983), a highly stimulating and important work that addresses this issue.

58. Ibid.

59. See David Fitzpatrick's review essay, 'Unrest in rural Ireland', *Irish Economic and Social History*, xii (1985), pp. 98–105 for a wider focus.
60. Poster kept in NAD, Chief Secretary's Office, Special Commission, Carton 2.
61. NAD, Chief Secretary's Office Records, *Protection of Persons and Property (Ireland) Act*, Carton 1, see *Minute of Inspector-General George Edward Hillier to all County and Sub-Inspectors*, 12 February 1881.
62. Ibid. See copies of these forms as issued.
63. Ibid., Circular from Royal Irish Constabulary Office, Dublin Castle, issued on 29 February 1881.
64. Ibid. Completed forms dated 22 February 1881, signed by Cork city Sub-Inspector.
65. Ibid. See also *List of persons whose arrest is recommended under the Protection of Persons and Property (Ireland) Act 1881*.
66. Ibid., report by Sub–Inspector attached NB.
67. Ibid., *Protection of Persons and Property (Ireland) Act*, Carton 1. *List of all persons arrested under the Protection of Persons and Property (Ireland) Act 1882* (incorporating 1881 list). List of those recommended for arrest in Mayo published in Donald Jordan, *Land and Popular Politics*, pp. 324-28.
68. Ibid.
69. Ibid.
70. Ibid., County Inspector Smith to Inspector-General's Office, Dublin Castle.
71. Ibid., Harry H. Carroll to Smith.
72. NAD, Chief Secretary's Office Registered Papers, 1881/6, 733, Robert Anderson to Carroll, 25 February 1881.
73. NAD, Protection of Persons and Property Act, Carton 1, Barry to Inspector-General's Office.
74. Ibid., Sub-Inspector to Inspector-General's Office.
75. Ibid., Sub-Inspector to Inspector-General's Office.
76. Ibid., *List of all persons arrested under the Protection of Persons and Property (Ireland) Act 1882* (incorporating 1881 list).
77. See Emmet Larkin, *The Roman Catholic Church and the Creation of the Modern Irish State, 1878–1886* (Philadelphia/Dublin, 1975) for details of Vatican negotiations conducted through Errington. Negotiations were more successful during the Plan of Campaign when the Pope's emissary Persico advised the promulgation of a papal rescript condemning the campaign.
78. NAD, CSO Protection of Persons and Property Act, Carton 1, annotations on Clifden file reveal the disagreement of both the County Inspector and the Resident Magistrate Parkinson with the recommendations of the Sub–Inspector. The list of persons detained under the PPP Act (1882) reveals that none of those listed were detained.
79. For files on earlier activities of John Kelly, the alleged boycotter, see NAD, Chief Secretary's Office Crime Returns 31060/54436.
80. NAD, Chief Secretary's Office, PPP (I) Act, Carton 1, Sub–Inspector to Inspector-General's Office. The Resident Magistrate, Hill, concurred.
81. NAD, Chief Secretary's Office, PPP (I) Act, Carton 1. *List of persons arrested under the Protection of Persons and Property Act (Ireland) Act 1882*.
82. Ibid.
83. Ibid., Sub-Inspector Gort to Inspector-General's Office, February 1881.
84. Ibid., *List of persons arrested under the Protection of Persons and Property Act (Ireland) 1882*.
85. Ibid., Sub-Inspector Galway West Riding to Inspector-General's Office including reports.

86. Quoted in R. Barry O'Brien, *The Life of Charles Stewart Parnell* (London, 1910), p. 224.

87. Henry Jephson was employed as a clerk in Dublin Castle from 1865. He was private secretary to Burke from 1872 to 1880 and was Burke's closest friend. Florence Arnold-Forster quotes him as saying after Burke's murder that 'he should not know Dublin without Tom Burke'. See T. W. Moody and R. A. J. Hawkins with Margaret Moody (eds.), *Florence Arnold-Forster's Irish Journal*, p. 489.

88. Horace West, assistant private secretary to Forster from 1880 to 1882, was the son of Gladstone's secretary Sir Algernon West. He was known as 'the Occidental'.

89. See C. D. Clifford Lloyd, *Ireland under the Land League: A Narrative of Personal Experiences* (Edinburgh, 1892).

90. Moody and Hawkins, *Arnold-Forster's Journal*, pp. 399–400.

91. Ibid., p. 180.

92. For Gladstone's speech on the introduction of the Land Bill on 7 April 1881 see *The Times*, 8 April 1881.

93. See T. A. Jenkins, *Gladstone, Whiggery and the Liberal Party 1874–1886* (Oxford, 1988), for a reinterpretation of 'Whiggery'. See Jonathan Parry, *The Rise and Fall of Liberal Government in Victorian Britain* (London, 1993) for the most recent analysis of the complexities of Liberal politics in this period.

94. Moody and Hawkins, *Arnold-Forster's Journal*, p. 183.

95. John Naish was a law adviser to the Dublin Castle administration from 1880 to 1883. He was made Solicitor-General for Ireland in 1883, Lord Chancellor for Ireland in 1885 and 1886 and Irish Lord Justice of Appeal in 1885 and from 1886 to 1890.

96. Robert Anderson was Home Office adviser on political crime from 1868 onwards. He was seconded to Dublin Castle for intervals throughout the 1880s. In an article in *Blackwood's Magazine* he admitted the authorship of one of *The Times* sensationalist 'Parnellism and crime' articles of 1887. He reflected anecdotally on his time in Ireland in two books: *Sidelights on the Home Rule Movement* (London, 1906), and *The Lighter Side of my Official Life* (London, 1910).

97. See H. O. Arnold–Forster, *The Truth about the Land League . . . by 'One Who Knows'* (London, 1882).

98. See *Report from the Select Committee of the House of Lords on Irish Jury Laws; together with the proceedings of the committee, minutes of evidence, and appendix*, HL 1881 (430), xi.

99. *Hansard*, 3, CCLXVII, 621.

100. Moody and Hawkins, *Arnold-Forster's Journal*, p. 403.

101. Ibid., pp. 475–6.

102. Algar Labouchere Thorold, *The Life of Henry Labouchere* (London, 1913).

103. J. L. Garvin and Julian Amery, *The Life of Joseph Chamberlain*, 6 vols. (London, 1932–69).

104. See his acceptance of the Land League, Leeds speech of 7 October 1882, *The Times*.

105. Moody and Hawkins, *Arnold-Forster's Journal*, p. 116.

106. See Gladstone Papers, BL, Add MS 44158.

107. See T. Wemyss Reid, *Life of the Right Honourable William Edward Forster* (London, 1888), ii, pp. 346–8.

108. *Irish Times*, 8 October 1881.

109. Ibid.

110. For a detailed analysis of the so-called Kilmainham treaty and Forster's role at this time see R. A. J. Hawkins, 'Gladstone, Forster and the Release of Parnell, 1882–88', *Irish Historical Studies*, xvi, no. 64, September 1969, pp. 417–45.
111. Moody and Hawkins, *Arnold–Forster's Journal*, p. 283.
112. *Hansard*, 3, CCLXVI, cols. 286–325.
113. A. B. Cooke and J. R. Vincent, 'Select documents; XXVIII Herbert Gladstone, Forster and Ireland, 1881–82 (11)', *Irish Historical Studies*, xviii, 69, March 1972, p. 75.
114. Moody and Hawkins, *Arnold–Forster's Journal*, p. 419.
115. *Hansard*, 3, CCLXVIII, 202.
116. This and preceding quotations from Herbert Gladstone's diary in Cooke and Vincent (eds.), 'Herbert Gladstone, Forster and Ireland', (ii) *Irish Historical Studies*, vol. XVIII, no. 69, March 1972, pp. 77–8.
117. Ibid.
118. See Patrick Maume's forthcoming article in *Irish Historical Studies* on Parnell and fenianism.

Chapter 4 (95–103)

1. For historiographical debate within this interpretative framework see Barbara Solow, *The Land Question and the Irish Economy 1870–1903* (Cambridge, Mass., 1971); W. E. Vaughan, 'An assessment of the economic performance of Irish Landlords 1851–81', in F. S. L. Lyons and R. A. J. Hawkins (eds.), *Ireland under the Union: Varieties of Tension* (Oxford, 1980); L. P. Curtis, 'Incumbered wealth: Landlord indebtedness in post–famine Ireland', *American Historical Review*, LXXV, 2 (April 1980); Samuel Clark, *Social Origins of the Irish Land War* (Princeton, 1979); James S. Donnelly, jr., *The Land and the People of Nineteenth-Century Cork: The Rural Economy and the Land Question* (London, 1975).
2. Paul Bew, *Land and the National Question in Ireland 1858–82* (Dublin, 1978). The roots of this 'structural' poverty are traced to before the famine. See Joel Mokyr, *Why Ireland Starved: A Quantitative and Analytical History of the Irish Economy 1800–1850* (London, 1983).
3. Barbara Solow, *The Land Question and the Irish Economy 1870–1903*.
4. See E. D. Steele, *Irish Land and British Politics: Tenant Right and Nationality 1865–1870* (Cambridge, 1974). For a detailed discussion see J. P. Parry, *Democracy and Religion, Gladstone and the Liberal Party, 1867–1875* (Cambridge, 1986).
5. *Report of Her Majesty's commissioners of Inquiry into the working of the Landlord and Tenant (Ireland) Act 1870, and the Acts amending the same*, [C 2779], HC 1881, xviii, vol. ii, *Digest of evidence, minutes of evidence, part 2 and Index*, [C 2779], HC 1881, xix (Bessborough Commission), quoted in Solow, *The Land Question*, pp. 27–8.
6. *Royal Commission on the depressed condition of the agricultural interest: Preliminary report*, [C 2778], HC 1881, xv; *Final report*, [C 3309], HC 1882, xiv; *Assistant Commissioner's Reports*, [C 2678], HC 1880, xviii; [C 2778], HC 1881, [C 2951], HC 1881; xvi, [C 3375], HC 1882, i–vi; *Minutes of evidence*, [C 2778], HC 1881, xv; [C 3096], HC 1881, xvii; [C 3309], 1882, xiv; *Digest of evidence*, HC 1881, [C 2778–II], xvi, 1882, [C 3309–II], xiv; *Appendices 1881* [C 2778–II], xvi, 1882 [C 3309–II], xiv.

7.   Paul Bew, *Land and the National Question* is the most original analysis of the question, principally in its emphasis on the class complexities within the tenant position.

8.   C. Ó Gráda, 'Agricultural decline 1860–1914', in Roderick Floud and Donald McCloskey (eds.), *The Economic History of Britain since 1700, 1860 to the 1970s*, vol. 2 (Cambridge, 1981). See also C. Ó Gráda, *Ireland before and after the Famine: Explorations in Economic History, 1800–1925* (Manchester, 1988). For the revised picture see K. T. Hoppen, (1990).

9.   David S. Jones, 'The cleavage between graziers and peasants in the Land Struggle 1890–1910', in Samuel Clark and James S. Donnelly, jr. (eds.), *Irish Peasants: Violence and Political Unrest 1780–1914* (Madison, Wisconsin, 1984). See also for the development of this trend in the 1890s and 1900s Paul Bew, *Conflict and Conciliation*.

10.   *Report of the Royal Commission, appointed to inquire and report to what extent, if any, and in what parts of that portion of our United Kingdom of Great Britain and Ireland, called Ireland, the operation of the Land Law (Ireland) Act, 1881, is affected either by combinations to resist the enforcement of legal obligations or by an exceptional fall in the price of produce; and also to inquire and to report to what extent there exists any general desire among tenants to avail themselves of the provisions of the Purchase of Land (Ireland) Act, 1885, and whether the operation of that Act might be expedited and extended, especially in the congested districts by providing security, through the intervention of Local Authorities, for loans advanced from public funds for the purchase of land, and also to report whether any modifications of the law are necessary.* HC 1887, XXVI (referred to as the Cowper Commission).

Chapter 5 (104–21)

1.   Most of this chapter has been published elsewhere. I have amended the penultimate sentence. See Donal McCartney (ed.), *Parnellism and Power* (Dublin, 1991), pp.102–24. See appendix 1 for the historiography.

2.   See note 10 of 'Introduction' for relevant studies.

3.   A. B. Cooke and John Vincent, *The Governing Passion: Cabinet Government and Party Politics in Britain 1885–86* (Brighton, 1974).

4.   L. P. Curtis jr., *Coercion and Conciliation in Ireland 1800–1892: A Study in Conservative Unionism* (Princeton/Oxford, 1963).

5.   Cooke and Vincent, *Governing Passion*. This position has since been revised by Jenkins (1993) and Parry (1993).

6.   *Special Commission Act, 1888. Reprints of the shorthand notes of the speeches, proceedings and evidence taken before the Commissioners appointed under the above named Act, vols. 1–12* (HMSO, 1989); *Report of Special Commission Parliamentary Papers*, vol. XXVII, [C 5891], (1890).

7.   For a full bibliography of the historical accounts of the Commission see T. W. Moody, 'The Times versus Parnell and Co, 1887–90', in T. W. Moody (ed.), *Historical Studies* (London, 1968), pp. 147–82. For a clear statement of the historical consensus see F. S. L. Lyons, 'Parnellism and Crime, 1887–1890', *Transactions of the Royal Historical Society*, 5th series, vol. 24 (1974), 1223–40. See also Paul Bew, *Charles Stewart Parnell* (Dublin, 1980 and 1991) and R. F. Foster, *Lord Randolph Churchill: A Political Life* (Oxford, 1981).

8.   Sir Joseph West-Ridgeway to Arthur Balfour, 20 February 1889, Balfour Papers, BL, Add MS 49809.

9. For an understanding of Randolph Churchill's position see Foster, *Churchill*, pp. 365–6.

10. *Hansard*, 3, CCCV, 13 April 1886, cols. 1458–64.

11. Ibid.

12. Ibid., 8 April 1886, cols. 1833–85.

13. *Report of the Special Commission*, [C5891], PP 1890, XXVII, pp. 3–5. So legally anomalous was the Commission that Sir Charles Russell had collected 'under nine heads the accusation which *he* [my emphasis] alleged he had to meet'.

14. Report of the Inspector–General RIC, 10 December 1885, Carnavan MSS, quoted in Curtis, *Coercion and Conciliation*, p. 63.

15. Lord Salisbury, 'Disintegration', *Quarterly Review*, 1883. Full reference in bibliography.

16. Nancy Johnson (ed.), *The Diary of Gathorne–Hardy, later Lord Cranbrook* (Oxford, 1981), in particular p. 427.

17. See Foster, *Churchill*, pp. 279–82 for Churchill's relations with Salisbury at this time.

18. *Cowper Commission, . . . to inquire and report to what extent the operation of the Land Law (Ireland) Act 1881 is affected by combinations to resist the enforcement of legal obligations or by an exceptional fall in the price of produce; and also . . . desire among tenants to avail themselves of the Purchase of Land (Ireland) Act 1885 . . . modifications of the law necessary.* HC 1887, xxvi.

19. Ashbourne to Salisbury, 18 July 1886. Salisbury MSS quoted in Curtis, *Coercion and Conciliation*, p. 129.

20. See for example the letter of Jeremiah Leahy, Secretary of the Fieries branch of the National League in Kerry, to his successor John MacMahon. The letter was seized by Sergeant Cornelius McCarthy in the presence of District Inspector Paston Crane – authorised under the Protection of Persons and Property Act 1882, *Special Commission, Proceedings and evidence*, vol. 2.

21. *The Times*, 7, 10, 13 March; 12, 18 April; 2, 13, 20 May 1889.

22. F. S. L. Lyons, *Charles Stewart Parnell* (London, 1971), 'Apotheosis', pp. 422–52.

23. See Leon O'Brien, *The Prime Informer* (London, 1971) for a discussion of Joyce's role, also that of R. A. Anderson, who revealed his authorship of the second 'Parnellism and crime' article in *Blackwood's Magazine* (April, 1910). The first article was by J. Woulfe Flanagan.

24. See West-Ridgeway to Balfour, London, BL Add MS 49812, fol. 77, 30 April 1891. 'I hope the Treasurer means to make the superannuation difficulty all right otherwise you won't be able to do anything for Joyce. I feel rather [indecipherable] about him, for I feel sure that he expects something and there is no doubt that his past services deserve recognition'.

25. Joseph Soames was the legal advisor to John Walter, proprietor of *The Times*. When Edward Caulfield Houston, correspondent for *The Times* in Dublin and Secretary of the Irish Loyal and Patriotic Union, was approached by Richard Pigott and offered the forged letters, he referred the question to George Buckle, the editor, and to J. S. MacDonald, the manager. Soames was the main legal advisor. The conduct of the 'research' into the *Times* case in Ireland was his.

26. Henry Matthew, the Home Secretary who was responsible for the secret service in America (i.e. Gosselin) supplied *The Times* with information about the Land League even before the letters were published. For Matthew's later dealings with Gosselin see Oxford Bodleian MS, English history, Sandars 725 (34).

27. See in particular the debate in the Lords, *Hansard*, 3, CCCXLII, cols. 1362–

1410. Blanche Dugdale and Arthur Dugdale, *James Balfour, I* (London, 1936), p. 148, quotes a letter from the Attorney–General to Balfour: 'The Report is very satisfactory in several aspects . . .'

28. Rudyard Kipling, 'Cleared, in memory of a commission', in *Barrack Room Ballads*, (London, 1892).

29. For example see NAD, Chief Secretary's Office, *Return of Crime in the South–Western Division from September 1887 to February 1892*. Crime was substantially the same at the end of that period as at the beginning, London, PRO Colonial Office 904/62, fol. 44. See also Colonel Turner's reports to Dublin Castle in January 1892. Morley, on the point of dismissing Turner in 1893, noted on his final report that Turner's accounts of 'improvement' did not appear to correspond to the reports of the police through the area. See Turner's letter to *The Times* on the state of Clare, *The Times*, 10 March 1893, Turner to Balfour, 27 November 1890, Balfour Papers, BL, Add MS 49689, fol. 106.

See also Alfred E. Turner, *Sixty Years of a Soldier's Life*, (London, 1912). Returns of boycotting in the south–western division from 1 October 1887 to February 1892 did, however, show a dramatic fall, London, PRO, Colonial Office, 904/62, fol. 46. Figures from January 1890 are, however, suspiciously low. Turner saw the south–west as his private fief. In his letter to *The Times* he noted, in peeved tones, that Mr Morley '. . . did not vouchsafe to ask my opinions, who had been intrusted with the task by his predecessor of super-intending the work of the Crimes Act in Clare and other counties from its com-mencement in 1887 . . . Under the last government the revocation of the Crimes Act was only a tentative measure . . . the change of venue clause should not have been revoked' (i.e. this ensured that trials could not take place in the home county of the accused). See also NAD, CSORP, S 6205, south–western division, 1892, and also CSORP Reports of officers in charge of the Special Crime Department in Ireland on the Administration of the Crimes Act in their area. April 1889: Mr Reeve northern division; Mr Gambell, Clare and Kerry, with observations by Colonel Turner. Also papers on the results of the Crimes Act in the Midland Division, all in Crime Department, Special Branch, Chief Secretary's Office. Success attending the administration of the Crimes Act, February 1889, south–western division.

30. See individual NAD Crime Special Branch S files on individuals and groups, e.g. S 6247 Gaelic Athletic Association branches, 1892; S 6995 for Foreign Office despatches on the Irish Association in Chicago; S 7726 on attempts to heal Nationalist split – sermon, Monaghan. See also NAD Divisional Commissioners' and County Inspectors' monthly confidential reports 1887–92; District Inspectors' Crime Special reports 1887–1898; Divisional Commissioners' and County Inspectors' monthly confidential reports 1892. Also London, PRO, CO 904; Returns of inquiries held under Section 1 of 'The Criminal Law and Procedure (Ireland) Act 1887', *Parliamentary Papers 1893–94*, 215, pp. 355–61.

31. See *Cowper: A Memoir*, pp. 363–505, for an account of the difficulties facing Irish administration in 1880–81, together with a collection of important correspondence, especially with Spencer. See London, PRO, Cab. 39/3/67, memo by Cowper on the state of the country printed for cabinet, 9 November 1880.

32. London, PRO, CO 904/62, fol. 48. This title (presumably devised by Turner) was followed by a statement: 'The following Tabular Statement tells an eloquent tale as to the effects of agitation during the last fourteen years upon some of the worst counties in Ireland, and also as to the results of so-called

Coercion.' The National League was not suppressed in Limerick or most of Cork but it was absolutely suppressed in Kerry and Clare after 1887.

33. MS draft in Davitt's handwriting, Davitt Papers/AV Defence, pp. 228–9, according to Moody, *Davitt*, p. 369. Copy quoted here deposited in NAD, Queen vs Parnell and Others, carton 4.

34. *Kerry Sentinel*, 22 August 1882 – official organ of Land and later National League in Kerry. Edited by Timothy Harrington MP, Secretary of the National League. Despite his involvement in the Plan of Campaign he remained a staunch Parnellite after 1891.

35. *Special Commission, proceedings and evidence*, vol. 2, paragraph 13,324-14,000 for Curtin case.

36. London, PRO, Cab. 37/24/26.

37. Ibid.

38. Balfour to West-Ridgeway, 30 May 1889, Balfour Papers, BL, Add MS 49828, fol. 39.

39. See Balfour/West-Ridgeway correspondence, London, Balfour Papers, BL, Add MS 49811, fols. 160–201, 308 on New Tipperary.

40. London, PRO Colonial Office, 904/20.

41. West-Ridgeway to Balfour, 11 December 1890, Balfour Papers, BL, Add MS 49828, fol. 284.

42. For the best analysis of the Parnellite split see Frank Callanan, *The Parnell Split* (Cork, 1992). See also Callanan's study of Parnell and the hillside-men in McCartney (ed), *Parnell: The Politics of Power* (1991).

Chapter 6 (122–44)

1. Joseph Lee, *The Modernisation of Irish Society 1848–1918* (Dublin, 1973), p. 83: 'The contrasts in the type of agriculture help explain why Kerry lagged 18 months behind Mayo in the agitation calendar.' For the political reasons for the county's centrality in Tory policy–making after 1886, see the next two sections on the contrast between the perspectives and policies of Major General Sir Redvers Buller and his successor Major General Alfred E. Turner. See the propaganda emphasis on Kerry outlined previously.

2. See Charles Melville, *Life of General the Rt. Hon. Sir Redvers Buller* (London, 1923).

3. Major General Sir Alfred Turner, *Sixty Years of a Soldier's Life* (London, 1912).

4. See *Return, for each month of 1879 and 1880, of Land League meetings held and agrarian crimes reported to Inspector-General of Royal Irish Constabulary, in each county*, HC 1881, lxxvii, 793. Also, *Return by provinces, of offences reported to Inspector-General of the Royal Irish Constabulary between 1st January 1880 and 30th November 1880, and cases in which offenders were convicted; were made amenable but not convicted; are awaiting trial; and were neither convicted nor made amenable*, HC 1881, lxxvii 595; ibid., *for period to 31 December 1881*, HC 1881, lxxvii, 607; ibid., *for period to 31 December 1882*, HC 1882, lv, 17.

The impact of policy on the nature of statistics required or demanded by government has been pointed out in the chapter 'Parnellism and Crime'. See in relation to Kerry in the early 1880s the following: *Return by provinces, of highest number of reported outrages in any year between 1844 and 1880; and of same for 1880 and each succeeding year*, HC 1887, lxviii, 27. Significantly, 1887 was the year in which such a compilation was initiated.

5. For Tralee politics see William Feingold 'Land League power: the Tralee Poor Law elections of 1881', in Samuel Clark and James Donnelly, jr. (eds.), *Irish Peasants: Violence and Political Unrest, 1780–1914* (Madison, Wis., 1984).

6. S. M. Hussey, *The Reminiscences of an Irish Land Agent, Being those of S. M. Hussey*, compiled by Home Gordon (London, 1904).

7. Ibid.

8. See *Thom's Official Directory of the United Kingdom of Great Britain and Ireland for the year 1886*, pp. 1088–93 for the county directory of Kerry. Tralee and Killarney had respective populations of 9,396 and 6,589, with Castleisland being the sixth town of the county, with a population of 1,466. Castleisland's notoriety was derived from the surrounding townlands rather than from activities in the town itself. It had, however, an importance disproportionate to its size because two main roads, one to Limerick and thence Dublin, and one to Cork, intersected there. All police reports and evidence before the Special Commission spoke of place in terms of townlands, so there was ample scope for confusion since the number of townlands in the county was 2,716. See also *Census of Ireland, 1881, part 1; area, houses and population, also the ages, civil or conjugal condition, occupations, birthplaces, religion, and education of the people; vol. ii, Province of Munster; no. 3, County of Kerry*, Parl. Papers 1882, [C 3148], iii.

9. Salisbury to Balfour, 22 August 1888. Balfour papers, BL, Add MS 49689, fols. 29–30.

10. See chapter 5 above.

11. See again *Special Commission Act, 1888; reprints of the shorthand notes of the speeches, proceedings and evidence taken before the commissioners appointed under the above named Act*, HMSO 1890, vols., 1–12. *Report of the Special Commission*, [C 5891], Parl. Papers 1890, vol. xxvii. See in particular appendix to vol. 11, pp. 644–64.

12. That part of the Commission's enquiry focused on Kerry can be found in *Special Commission Evidence*, vol. 2, nos. 10,865–21,415. Henceforth references to this source will simply be in the form *Special Commission Evidence*, identified by volume and paragraph number.

13. See Feingold, 'Land League power: the Tralee Poor Law elections of 1881' in Clark and Donnelly, jr. (eds.), *Irish Peasants: Violence and Political Unrest, 1780–1914*.

14. For an analysis of the nature of agricultural decline, with particular reference to falling prices for Kerry goods in the Cork markets see James S. Donnelly, jr., *The Land and the People of Nineteenth-Century Cork: The Rural Economy and the Land Question* (London, 1975).

15 These and subsequent details of acreage and valuation are from *Thom's Directory, 1886*, though frequently the witnesses before the Special Commission provided the details in evidence.

16. See Hussey, *Reminiscences of an Irish Land Agent*.

17. For the evidence of Bennett see *Special Commission Act, 1888; reprints of the shorthand notes of the speeches, proceedings and evidence taken before the commissioners appointed under the above named Act*, vol. 2, nos. 11,492–611.

18. *Special Commission Evidence*, vol. 2, no. 11,512.

19. Ibid., nos. 11,794–908.

20. Special Commission Evidence, vol. 2, nos. 11,937–49.

21. See again 'Landowners in Ireland of 1,000 acres and upward' with their valuation in 1873 listed in *Thom's Official Directory of the United Kingdom of Great Britain and Ireland*, (1887), p. 731.

22. For Culloty's evidence see *Special Commission Evidence*, vol. 2, no. 11,937.
23. Ibid., no. 12,018.
24. Ibid., nos. 12,042–249.
25. For the evidence of Daniel Leahy's widow see *Special Commission Evidence*, vol. 2, nos. 12,319–69. For further details on the amount of police knowledge on the internal politics of the National League see the second section of this chapter on the career of Major General Sir Redvers Buller.
26. *Kerry Sentinel*, 22 August 1882.
27. *United Ireland*, 26 August 1882.
28. *Special Commission Evidence*, vol. 2, nos. 14,389–94.
29. See Hussey, *Reminiscences of an Irish Land Agent*. Hussey himself had quit Kerry in 1884. See also Letterbooks of Maurice Leonard.
30. For Maurice Leonard's interpretation of events see *Special Commission Evidence*, vol. 2, nos. 14,389–15,785. For the first nine months of 1880 Kerry had the highest eviction rate in the country. Evictions in both the second and third quarter of 1880 exceeded the total figures of eviction in 1879.
31. Other accounts of National League Organisation in Kerry, in particular the visits of key speakers and paid organisers can be found in the papers of Timothy Harrington, National Library of Ireland.
32. Special Commission Evidence, vol. 2, no. 14,436.
33. Ibid., 14,466. Placenames are frequently misspelt or mistranscribed in the official record.
34. Ibid., 14,473–90.
35. Since the outrage figures for 1880 were 247 this construction of a pre–lapsarian pre–Land League rural idyll was dubious.
36. For the 24 August 1881 Land League discussion on the tactics to be used in this case see references ibid., 14,503.
37. The types of damage to persons pursued by 'moonlighters' is another anthropological story.
38. *Special Commission Evidence*, vol. 2, no. 14,532.
39. Ibid., vol. 2.
40. Ibid., no. 14,550.
41. For the structure of the Kerry police and details of the District Inspectorate see *Memoirs of a Resident Magistrate (1880–1920) by D. I. P. Crane* (privately printed, 1938), in particular the chapter on his period in Kerry, pp. 88–99.
42. The disappearance of League Secretaries with considerable sums of money to the United States was not merely a figment of the warped official mind.
43. *Special Commission Evidence*, vol. 2, no. 14,579.
44. Ibid., no. 14,582.
45. Ibid., no. 14,585.
46. Ibid., nos. 14,586–91.
47. See Dana Hearne's 1986 Dublin edition of Anna Parnell's *The Tale of a Great Sham*. The central officers of the League, and the parliamentarians who reappeared after Kilmainham were never less than deeply unhappy about the activities of 'the ladies'. They were one of the few subjects on which Charles Stewart Parnell and the bulk of the Irish Catholic hierarchy could intuitively agree.
48. John Moynihan to Samuel Hussey, 12 January 1882, quoted in *Special Commission Evidence*, vol. 2, no. 14,634.
49. See S. H. Melville, *Life of General the Rt. Hon. Sir Redvers Buller* (London, 1913). See also Curtis, *Coercion and Conciliation*, p. 131.

50. On distrust of Hamilton see note 70 below.
51. Gloucestershire County Record Office, St Aldwyn Papers, i.e. Papers of Sir Michael Hicks–Beach, 1st Earl St Aldwyn. All subsequent St Aldwyn references refer to the correspondence of Sir Michael Hicks–Beach and Sir Redvers Buller and are distinguished simply by date. Buller to Hicks–Beach, 2 September 1886. I am indebted to L. P. Curtis's *Coercion and Conciliation* for these references.
52. Ibid.
53. Ibid.
54. Ibid.
55. Buller to Hicks-Beach, 9 September 1886.
56. Ibid.
57. Ibid.
58. Ibid.
59. Buller to Hicks-Beach, n.d., but clearly written in mid–September 1886.
60. Ibid.
61. Ibid.
62. Ibid.
63. Addendum, special query to Hicks–Beach appended to previous letter.
64. Buller to Hicks–Beach, 17 September 1886.
65. Buller to Hicks–Beach, 29 September 1886.
66. Buller to Hicks–Beach, 11 October 1886.
67. Buller to Hicks–Beach, 18 October 1886.
68. Ibid.
69. Buller to Hicks–Beach, 15 November 1886.
70. *Report of the Royal Commission on the Land Law (Ireland) Act 1881, and the Purchase of Land (Ireland) Act, 1885; minutes of evidence and appendices*, [C 4969–1], HC 1887, xxvi, 25. Evidence of Sir Redvers Buller, VC, KCB, Item 16,454, 11 November 1886.
71. Hugh Holmes to Lord Carnarvon, November 1885, quoted in A. B. Cooke and John Vincent 'Ireland and party politics, 1885–87: an unpublished Conservative memoir' (III), Select Document Series, *Irish Historical Studies,* XVI, 64, 1969.
72. Hicks–Beach to Buller, 26 November 1886.
73. For the background to Hicks-Beach's appointment see Cooke and Vincent, *The Governing Passion,* pp. 447–52.
74. Ibid. See also R. F. Foster, *Lord Randolph Churchill: A Political Life* (Oxford, 1981) and his 'To the northern counties station' in Lyons and Hawkins (eds.), *Ireland under the Union* for an analysis of Churchill's attitudes to Ireland.
75. Ibid., pp. 443–4.
76. Ibid., p. 449.
77. Major-General Alfred E. Turner, *Sixty Years of a Soldier's Life*. Turner was an artillery officer who had been military private secretary to Spencer in 1882–4, assistant–military secretary in Ireland in the Carnarvon Tory period of 1885, and private secretary to the Liberal Lord-Lieutenant Aberdeen in the Home Rule administration of 1886. Despite having served in Liberal administrations he was regarded as a 'hard' military man who had played a major role in the organisation of the country into military-style areas under Spencer. Ideologically and practically he was invaluable to Balfour, and was seen as untainted by his former Liberal associations.
78. For Balfour's correspondence with Sir Joseph West-Ridgeway see Balfour Papers, BL, Add MSS 49808–12.

79. Gloucestershire County Record Office, St Aldwyn MS document marked 2455, PC/PP/54.
80. Balfour Papers, BL, Add MS 49820, Turner to Seymour, 16 June 1888. This file is said to be temporarily folioed, therefore only dates are given.
81. Ibid., Turner to Browning, 5 July 1888.
82. Balfour Papers, BL, Add MS 49826, fol. 36.
83. Ibid.

Chapter 7 (145–52)

1. See again L. P. Curtis, *Coercion and Conciliation in Ireland 1880–1892* (Oxford, 1963). See also Andrew Gailey, *Ireland and the Death of Kindness: The Experience of Constructive Unionism 1890–1905* (Cork, 1987) for an excellent account of Tory improvement policies.
2. This emerges particularly clearly in the detailed monthly confidential reports of the Divisional Commissioners and County Inspectors of the Royal Irish Constabulary in the period immediately before the 1892 general election. See London, PRO, Colonial Office, 904, 148, 153, 160, 162. Also in the frenzied *Publications of the Irish Unionist Alliance* for 1894 and 1895, leaflets nos. 166–200, 7th series, and 1–69, 8th series (Dublin, 1895).

   See too the *Eighth Report of the Executive Committee of the Irish Landowners Convention*, submitted on Thursday 26 January 1893, for evidence of the horror of landlords at the constitution and 'language' of the Evicted Tenants Commission.
3. John Morley, *Recollections I* (London, 1917), p. 346.
4. Ibid., p. 348, Morley to Chamberlain, 29 July 1893. Text of the letter: 'The plain truth is that the risk of miscarriage of a settlement [evicted tenants] comes as much from your extreme right as from my extreme Irish left. An almost insuperable difficulty has been created (1) by the resolution passed the other day by the Irish Landowners' Convention, (2) by the line taken by the landlords in the debate . . . If Balfour and you had only stood out against the landlords ultras . . . for it won't be pleasant for you to have to renew coercion the moment you cross the threshold of Dublin Castle.'
5. Sir Joseph West-Ridgeway to A. J. Balfour, 6 May 1894, Balfour Papers, BL, Add MS 49812.
6. Morley, *Recollections II*, pp. 36–7.
7. See Atkinson to Balfour, *Outline of Purchase Scheme*, 23 October 1893, Oxford, Bodleian, Sandars papers, MS Eng. Hist., C 725 (84).
8. *Report of the Evicted Tenants Commission, appointed by Houghton as Lord Lieutenant 'to enquire into and report respecting estates where the tenancy of a holding or of holdings has been determined since the first day of May 1879 and in respect of which holdings claims to be reinstated have been made by the tenants evicted therefrom now resident in Ireland'*, HC 1893–94 XXXI. See also House of Lords debate, *Hansard*, 4, XI, 28 April 1893, 1413–1601.
9. St John Broderick to Arthur Balfour, 3 August 1893, Bodleian, Oxford, Sandars papers, MS Eng. Hist., C 725 (183).
10. *Return to 31st March 1892, of proceedings under Land Purchase Acts, 1885 and 1888; number of applications for advances to 31st December 1891 and total amount; balance of £10m available; number of applications etc.*, HC 1892, (711), xv, 1.
11. *Report of the select committee to enquire into and report upon the principles and practices of the Irish land commissioners and county court judges in carrying*

out the fair rent and free sale provisions of the Land Acts of 1870, 1881 and 1887 and of the Redemption of Rent Act of 1891, and to suggest such improvements in law or practice as they may deem to be desirable, HC 1894 (310) xiii (Morley Commission).

12. There was, however, some difficulty with the 'ultras' in the landlord party, who amended the Bill in the Lords. See correspondence between Balfour and Cranbourne, in particular Cranbourne to Balfour, 10 August 1896: 'The Lords were the principal plank in our platform at the election. They served us well and are our only hope in the future. If they may not substantially amend this Land Bill ... Please be careful not to blunt your tools,' Oxford, Bodleian, Sandars papers, MS Eng. Hist., 729 (59).

13. Moritz J. Bonn, *Modern Ireland and her Agrarian Problem* (Dublin/London, 1906). Translated from the German by T. W. Rolleston.

14. The best overview of these years is provided by Andrew Gailey, *Ireland and the Death of Kindness*. See also R. A. Anderson, *With Plunkett in Ireland: The Co–op Organisers' Story* (London, 1935) and Trevor West, *Horace Plunkett: Co–operation and Politics* (London, 1988). For F. S. L. Lyons they were the years of missed opportunity. See his *Culture and Anarchy in Ireland 1890–1939* (1979).

15. Birrell to Asquith, 20 September 1913, commenting on Sir Louis Dane's *Memo on Ireland*, Oxford, Bodleian, Asquith MS 38, fol. 196.

16. Sir Louis Dane, *Memo on Ireland*, Oxford, Bodleian, Asquith MS 38, fols. 132–43. For the social politics of the Department of Agricultural and Technical Instruction see George Moore, *Hail and Farewell* (London, 1911).

17. For a view which qualifies this significantly see Roy Foster's essay 'Thinking from hand to mouth: Anglo-Irish Literature, Gaelic Nationalism and Irish Politics in the 1890s', *Paddy and Mr Punch: Connections in Irish and English History* (London, 1993).

18. Philip James Bull, 'The reconstruction of the Irish Parliamentary Movement 1895–1903: an analysis with special reference to William O'Brien' (Cambridge PhD). See also Paul Bew, *Conflict and Conciliation in Ireland 1890–1910: Parnellites and Radical Agrarians* (Oxford, 1987).

19. Wyndham/Balfour correspondence, November 1900–1903, Balfour Papers, BL, Add MSS 49803 and 49804. In particular see Wyndham to Balfour, 26 November 1900 for his analysis of the United Irish League, Add MS 49803, fols. 139–44; also *Confidential memo: land legislation for Ireland*, January 1901, Add MS 49803, fols. 165–81.

20. Wyndham to Cadogan (with whom his relations were strained), 13 January 1901, Balfour Papers, BL, Add MS 49803, fol. 161.

21. Wyndham to Balfour, 26 November 1900, Balfour Papers, BL, Add MS 49803, fol. 141.

22. Wyndham to Balfour, Add MS 49803, Balfour Papers, BL, fol. 140.

23. Balfour Papers, BL, Add MS 49803, *Confidential memo*, fol. 179.

Appendix I

For an analysis of these years in works that have a wider focus see Joseph Lee, *The Modernisation of Irish Society 1848–1918* (Dublin, 1973); Nicholas Manseragh, *The Irish Question 1840–1921* (London, 3rd edn, 1975); Patrick O'Farrell, *Ireland's English Question* (London, 1971). The most important recently published works are: Charles Townshend, *Political Violence in Ireland: Government and Resistance since 1848* (Oxford, 1983); and K. Theodore Hoppen, *Elections, Politics and Society in Ireland 1832–1885* (Oxford, 1984).

For classic accounts of British politics in this period from the perspective of 'high politics' see Maurice Cowling, *1867, Disraeli, Gladstone and Revolution* (Cambridge, 1967); Andrew Jones, *The Politics of Reform 1884* (Cambridge, 1972); A.B. Cooke and John Vincent, *The Governing Passion* (Brighton, 1974). See also the following collections of essays: Michael Bentley and John Stevenson (eds.), *High and Low Politics in Modern Britain* (Oxford, 1983) and Michael Bentley (ed.), *Public and Private Doctrine: Essays in British history presented to Maurice Cowling* (Cambridge, 1993).

The following recent studies of Victorian Liberalism are also relevant: the biographies of Gladstone up to the 1860s by Richard Shannon (1982) and H. C. G. Matthew, *Gladstone, 1809–1874* (Oxford, 1986) together with his introductions to subsequent volumes of the *Gladstone Diaries;* T. A. Jenkins, *Gladstone, Whiggery ad the Liberal Party 1874–1886* (Oxford, 1988); Jonathan Parry's studies of the party from the perspectives of doctrine and governance: *Democracy and Religion, Gladstone and the Liberal Party, 1867–1875* (Cambridge, 1986) and *The Rise and Fall of Liberal Parliament in Victorian Britain* (New Haven and London, 1993).

The only comprehensive account of Liberal policy in Ireland, despite its excessive admiration for Gladstone is J. L. Hammond, *Gladstone and the Irish Nation* (London, 1938). L. P. Curtis, Jr, *Coercion and Conciliation in Ireland 1880–1892: A Study of Conservatism Unionism* (Princeton and Oxford, 1963) is the standard work on Conservative policy in these years, but see also Andrew Gailey, *Ireland and the Death of Kindness* (Cork, 1987) and Alvin Jackson, *The Ulster Party* (Oxford, 1989).

Several biographies of English political figures throw a tantalising light on Irish policies. See in particular R. F. Foster, *Lord Randolph Churchill: a Political Life* (Oxford, 1981). The most controversial work on the Irish policies of British governments is A. B. Cooke and John Vincent, *The Governing Passion: Cabinet Government and Party Politics in Britain 1885–86* (Brighton, 1974). For the Irish Parliamentary Party see F. S. L. Lyons, *The Fall of Parnell, 1890–91* (London, 1960); *Charles Stewart Parnell* (London, 1977); *The Irish Parliamentary Party 1890–1910* (London, 1951); *John Dillon: A*

Biography (London, 1968); also Conor Cruise O'Brien *Parnell and his Party* (Oxford, 1957 and 1964); Paul Bew, *Charles Stewart Parnell* (Dublin, 1980 and 1991); Frank Callanan, *The Parnell Split 1880–91* (Cork, 1992); Robert Kee, *The Laurel and the Ivy: The Story of Charles Stewart Parnell and Irish Nationalism* (London, 1993). See also T. W. Moody, *Davitt and Irish Revolution 1846–82* (Oxford, 1981).

In the select documents series in *Irish Historical Studies*, Cooke and Vincent have published two important pieces that illuminate the Irish policies of governments in the 1880s. 'Select documents: XXVIII Herbert Gladstone, Forster and Ireland, 1881–82' (I) and (II) in *Irish Historical Studies,* vols. XVII and XVIII, nos. 68 and 69, September 1971 and March 1972, pp. 521–48 and 74–89 respectively; 'Ireland and party politics, 1885–87: An unpublished conservative memoir', *Irish Historical Studies*, vol. XVI, no. 62, 1968, pp. 154–72; *Irish Historical Studies*, vol. XVI, no. 63, 1969, pp. 321–38; *Irish Historical Studies*, vol. XVI, no. 64, 1969. See also A. B. Cooke and A. P. W. Malcolmson, *Calendar of the Ashbourne Papers 1869–1913*, (PRONI, 1974).

The following articles are important: Roy Foster, 'To the northern counties station: Lord Randolph Churchill and the prelude to the Orange card', in F. S. L. Lyons and R. A. J. Hawkins (eds.) *Ireland Under the Union: Varieties of Tension* (Oxford, 1980), pp. 237–87; P. Davis, 'The Liberal Unionist Party and the Irish policy of Lord Sailsbury's government, 1886–92', *Historical Journal*, vol. XVIII (1975), pp. 85–104; Peter Fraser, 'The Liberal Unionist Alliance: Chamberlain, Hartington and the Conservatives 1886–1904', *English Historical Review*, vol. LXXVII, 1962, pp. 53–78; J. P. Cornford, 'The Parliamentary foundations of the Hotel Cecil' Robert Robson (ed.) *Ideas and Institutions of Victorian Britain* (London, 1967); Richard Hawkins, 'Gladstone, Forster and the release of Parnell 1882–88', *Irish Historical Studies*, vol. XVI, no. 64.

In many cases contemporary accounts or Edwardian biographies and auto-biographies have to be relied upon: A. J. Balfour, *Chapters of Autobiography* (London, 1930); Wilfred Scawen Blunt, *The Land War in Ireland*, (2nd edn, London, 1913) and *My Diaries 1888–1914* (London, 1919–20); Lady Gwendolen Cecil, *Biographical Studies of the Life and Political Character of Robert, 3rd Marquis of Salisbury* (London, n.d.); *Earl Cowper, K G: A Memoir by his wife* (London, privately printed, 1913); Blanche E. C. Dugdale, *Arthur James Balfour* (London, 1936); Michael Davitt, *The Face of Feudalism in Ireland* (London and New York, 1904); Lord Edward Fitzmaurice, *The Life of Granville George Levesen-Gower, 2nd Earl of Granville K. G. 1815–1891*, 2 vols. (London, 1905); A. E. Gathorne-Hardy, *Gathorne-Hardy, first Earl of Cranbrook: A Memoir* (London, 1910); J. L. Garvin and Julian Amery, *Life of Joseph Chamberlain*, 6 vols. (London, 1952–69); Sir A. Hardinge, *Life of Carnarvon*, vol. III 1878–89 (Oxford,

1925); Bernard Holland, *The Life of Spencer Compton, 8th Duke of Devonshire*, 2 vols. (London, 1911); Lady Victoria Hicks-Beach, *The Life of Sir Michael Hicks-Beach, First Earl of St Aldwyn* (London, 1932); Tim Healy, *Letters and Leaders of my Day* (Dublin, 1929); Lord George Hamilton, *Parliamentary Reminiscences and Reflections 1868–1906* (London, 1917 and 1922); Nancy E. Johnson (ed.), *The Diary of Gathorne-Hardy, later Lord Cranbrook 1866–1892: political selections* (Oxford, 1981); Algar Labouchere Thorold, *The Life of Henry Labouchere* (London, 1913); John Morley, *The Life of Gladstone, 1880–1898* (London, 1903) and *Recollections*, 2 vols. (London, 1917); Agatha Ramm (ed.), *The Political Correspondence of Mr Gladstone and Lord Granville, 1876–1886* (Oxford, 1962); Katherine O'Shea (Mrs C. S. Parnell), *Charles Stewart Parnell*, 2 vols. (London, 1914); William O'Brien, *Evening Memories* (Dublin, 1920); R. Barry O'Brien, *The Life of Lord Russell of Killowen* (London, 1922) and *The Life of Charles Stewart Parnell* (London, 1899); Rt. Hon. Lord Peter O'Brien (Hon. Georgina O'Brien ed.), *Reminiscences of Peter O'Brien, Baron, Lord Chief Justice of Ireland* (London, 1916); T. P. O'Connor, *Memoirs of an Old Parliamentarian*, 2 vols. (London, 1929); F. H. O'Donnell, *History of the Irish Parliamentary Party,* 2 vols. (London, 1910).

The development of a popular nationalist consciousness in Ireland remains under-researched. There are no studies of newspapers like *United Ireland*, or references to its iconography. Apart from Townshend's superb study *Political Violence* the papers of the Dublin Castle administration remain relatively unexplored. With the exception of Roy Foster's *Parnell – the Man and his Family* (Brighton, 1976), the late Professor Lyons's biographies, the work of Alan O'Day and Frank Callanan's superb *Parnell Split* (1992), the parliamentary party members remain shadowy. The Irish Unionist Alliance, the Irish Landowners Convention and the Property Defence Association have never been adequately explored. There is a historigraphical consensus that proclaims all of these 'bigger' national questions to be resolved.

Appendix II

Charges faced by the traversers in the case of the Queen vs Parnell and Others

First
> . . . charges that the traversers intending with others to impoverish and injure the owners of farms let to tenants for rent did conspire and solicit and procure large numbers of tenants holding farms at a rent, in breach of their contracts to refuse and not to pay the owner of farms the rents which the said tenants were bound to pay and which the said owners of lands were entitled to be paid under the said contract.

Second
> . . . that the traversers with others having a like intent [i.e. to impoverish landowners] did unlawfully conspire and agree to solicit large numbers of tenants namely those mentioned in the first count, to combine and conspire in breach of their said contracts, to refuse and not to pay their lawful rents.

Third
> . . . that the traversers with a like intent with that stated in the first count namely to impoverish the owners of land did unlawfully conspire and agree by unlawful means to deter and compel them not to pay to the owners of the said farms the rents they were legally bound to pay; and the unlawful means I think I may usefully read to you. The unlawful means are there referred to again and again by threatening to cut off and utterly exclude from all social intercourse and communion whatsoever and from all intercourse and dealings in the way of buying, selling, and other business, and to shun at all time and all places as if affected by a loathsome disease, and to hold up to public hatred and contempt and to subject to annoyance and injury in the pursuit of his occupation and industry, any and every tenant of such farms aforesaid who shall pay the owner thereof the rent which he, the said tenant, shall and might become lawfully bound to pay under his contract of tenancy.

Fourth
> . . . charges a like intent, namely to impoverish the owners of land and that the traversers did unlawfully conspire by unlawful means to deter and prevent the said tenants from paying their lawful rents, and to cause and compel them contrary to their own free will and judgement to refuse to pay their legally contracted rent, and the unlawful means on the fourth I shall read shortly. By threatening and menacing violence and injury to

the person and property of every tenant of any such farm as aforesaid who should pay the owner thereof the rent which he, the said tenant, was and might become lawfully bound to pay under his contract of tenancy. In other words the unlawful means are the social and business excommunication and inconveniences.

Fifth, Sixth, Seventh and Eighth are exactly the same as First, Second, Third and Fourth respectively except that

the persons intended to be impoverished and injured are described not as the owners of farms generally as in the first four counts, but that class of owner who let farms to tenants at a rent exceeding the valuation of such farms respectively as valued under the acts relating to the valuation of rateable property in Ireland, commonly called the Government valuation and also that the tenants in the said counts are the tenants of such farms and not tenants generally.

Ninth

. . . charges the traversers with others intending to impede, frustrate and bring to nought the administration of justice and *the execution of* the writs of fi, fa [sic] and civil bill court decrees issued forth of Her Majesty's court levying of monies adjudged to be due for rent, did unlawfully conspire to solicit large numbers of her Majesty's subjects to combine, conspire and agree by unlawful means to prevent goods and chattels seized under such writs realising such prices as same would otherwise bring, and thereby to impede and frustrate the execution of the said writs; and the unlawful means in that count are stated to be . . . by their agreeing together not to bid for any good of the chattels taken in execution and offered for sale according to the exigency of the said writs of possession and civil bill court decrees respectively, or any of them.

Tenth

. . . charges that the traversers, intending to deter, frustrate, and bring into contempt the administration of justice and the execution of writs of possession and civil bill court ejectment decrees for the recovery of land for the non-payment of rent, did unlawfully conspire to solicit all persons evicted by virtue of said writs from possession of any lands for the non-payment of rent, in disregard of the execution of said writs, and of the court whereout were issued such writs, unlawfully to re-enter upon and retake possession of the lands from which they had been evicted.

Eleventh

. . . charges that the traversers with others intending to impoverish and injure the owners of farms from which any tenant was evicted for non-payment of rent did unlawfully conspire by unlawful means to deter and prevent any person other than the evicted tenants from occupying said farms, and from working for the benefit of the owners upon any such farms; and by unlawful means I may state shortly are threats of social and business excommunication, and damage against every person except the evicted tenant, who shall take or occupy the said farm.

Twelfth

. . . charges that the traversers with others, with the same intention as in the preceding count – namely to impoverish the owner of evicted farms – did unlawfully conspire to solicit large numbers of persons to combine and conspire to deter and prevent any person other than the evicted tenant from taking, occupying, cultivating and working upon said farms; and the means thereto are social and business excommunication.

Thirteenth

. . . charges that the traversers, with others, intending to prejudice in their occupation and obstruct in the lawful exercise of their free will and judgement persons desirous of taking farms of persons who had been evicted for non-payment of rent did unlawfully conspire by unlawful means to deter and prevent all persons, other than the persons evicted from said farms, from taking or occupying the said farms; and unlawful means are social and business excommunication and damage.

Fourteenth

. . . charges that the traversers having a like unlawful intent, did conspire to solicit large numbers of persons to enter into a conspiracy by like unlawful means as in the preceding count to deter and prevent any person other than the persons evicted from any farm from occupying or taking the farm.

Fifteenth, Sixteenth, Seventeenth and Eighteenth as Tenth, Eleventh, Twelfth and Thirteenth with the burden of intent being
to hinder and prevent landlords from letting their lands to the best advantage.

Nineteenth

. . . charges that the traversers unlawfully intending to cause discontent and disaffection and to excite ill-will and hostility between landlords and tenants, did unlawfully conspire to cause and create discontent and disaffection among her Majesty's subjects, and to excite and promote feelings of ill-will and hostility between landlords and tenants, and to excite and promote feeling of ill-will and hostility towards the landlords of Ireland, amongst the rent of her Majesty's subjects in Ireland.

Appendix III

Paudeen O'Rafferty
on the
Landlords' Ten Commandments

Dedicated to Exterminators and Rack-renters, as also to the people who work.

The Creed of the Right Hon. Lord Clan Rack-rent, Earl of Idleness, and Viscount Absentee.

1st. I am the Landlord, thy Master, who paternally condescends to take charge of thy earnings in the shape of rent.

2nd. Thou shalt have no other Master but me, and no other use for thy money than to be duly paid and delivered in at my Rent Office upon every gale day, in order that I may live in a state befitting my rank, and be sumptuously fed and delicately cared for, without stooping to the ignominy of Labour or feeling the hardships of want.

3rd. Thou shalt not speak disrespectfully or with covered head to thy Master, his Agent, Bailiff, footman or dogman, or murmur or complain against the holy doctrine – 'Obey thy Masters'.

4th. Thou shalt keep holy the Sabbath Day (*Laborare est orare*) by labouring to earn thy sacred obligations of Rent, and win for thyself that poverty and self-denial which is essential to eternal salvation.

5th. Honour thy Landlord that thy toil may be long in the land of thy birth, and thy reward at some not distant day the romance of eviction, workhouse luxury, or occidental emigration.

6th. Thou shalt not kill any hare, rabbit, fox, or bird, that may visit thy farms; thou shalt not fish for, catch or eat any creature found in the streams which flow through my fields, or commit the sacrilege of doubting the justice of those laws which give more protection to the game of the field than to those who are moulded in the image of their Creator.

7th. Thou shalt not violate the great moral law upon my estate, which forbids the marriage of thy sons or daughters, particularly thy daughters, until myself or my agent shall first satisfy ourselves that such a step is agreeable or beneficial to myself or my agent.

8th. Thou shalt not steal an idle moment, neither shall thy children, from the blessed occupation of labour in my service, to indulge in the worldly pleasures of reading books or newspapers or to listen to immoral teachings against my sacred prerogative as thy lord and master.

9th. Thou shalt not bear any witness against the difference between my rent and the valuation of that arch-infidel Griffith; neither shalt thou speak behind my back to the evil agents of the National Land League – a society which aims at the destruction of Landlord law and order, and which must plunge its fanatical supporters into eternal peasant proprietory.

10th. Thou shalt not covet a better condition of life or sigh for worldly wealth or comfort in which there lieth both evil to body and soul; neither shalt thou envy my manorial residence, carriages, horses, hounds, or pleasures, but continue to cheerfully toil from early morn till hungry eve, to rest satisfied with thy mud-walled cabin, thy noble rags and blissful ignorance in order that one day thy reward shall be reaped by the appearance at thy door of a legion of spirits in the uniform of the RIC, to conduct thee and thy children to that mansion of penitential bliss which the English Government and myself have created for thy use.

Paudeen O'Rafferty's Opinions upon the Foregoing Creed

God, the Creator of this Universe as well as the land of Ireland, is my only Landlord in Justice, for it was He who made all creatures and all things, whereon they should live, and stipulated the rent to be paid when He declared that mankind should earn its bread by the sweat of the brow.

The Land, like the air, and the sunshine, and the water, is a natural agent created (like them) for the sustenance of the human family and not for the profit and pleasure of a few whom Society may deem exalted and privileged.

God is the essence of Justice and Goodness, and could not, therefore, ordain that a few who pay Him no sacrifice in the shape of labour should own the land, that would be useless without that toil which is essential to the bringing forth of food for the children of men.

The laws which reverse the Divine intentions of the Almighty cannot be of Justice or of Him, and must, therefore, be the offspring of Injustice and of Wrong.

A system which gives to idleness the first claim upon the earnings of industry is a fraudulent and a monstrous one. I toil and sweat – I tramp and suffer – to fulfil my obligations to the cause of my existence; I labour every day in order that my children shall not want, and that I may discharge my duties to those who aid me, in my progress through life, by their labour in supplying me with clothing and such necessaries; yet most of my earnings is not my own – the fruits of my toil are seized upon by another, and in the form of rent I am compelled to pay a tax for living on the earth upon which my Creator placed me, and for using the land which He made for my sustenance.

The supreme God-ordained right of existence is contravened and stamped upon by the arbitrary power of monopoly and wealth, and man's injustice to man has supplanted the eternal law of the Creator in his behalf.

The toiler in the field, the artizan in the workshop, the miner in the pit, the mariner on the sea, the brain-worker at his desk, are all fulfilling the duties of life, and are producing the food and creating the wealth which sustains mankind and upholds the framework of governments and society; yet, another class – the aristocratic caste – does nothing but govern and trample upon the classes which support it in voluptuous use.

To crush the industrious and monopolise wealth, power, pleasure, and honour in this life, the privileged – though idle and morally worthless few – are allowed by passive millions to act as follows:

To govern in every land and make laws for every people – but themselves – to keep.

Armies are organized and officered to conquer and keep under the people who work.

Policemen are to watch, judges to try, and prisons to keep, the toilers who have to support them. A society is empowered to look upon work as menial and degrading, and upon idleness and fashion as ennobling and grand.

And finally,

Religion is expected to preach doctrines to people which make slavery and poverty the chief ends of life, and cowardice and submission to every wrong a passport to everlasting happiness.

I, Paudeen O'Rafferty, farmer, from Krucknaspulugudthawn, in the county of Mayo, enter my solemn protest against the landlord's creed, and to society's injustice against me and my co-workers; and having come to the Phoenix Park meeting to advocate the cause of Land, Labour, and Liberty, and not being able to make a speech, do hereby place my opinion before the people of Dublin City.

(Signed)

Paudeen O'Rafferty

Bibliography

Sources are divided into:
    Manuscript Sources
    Printed Primary Sources
    Printed Secondary Sources
    Unpublished Dissertations
Since Victorian biographies are treated as primary sources, they are included in the *Printed Primary Sources* category of the bibliography. The reports of the *Irish Land-owners' Convention* and the *Congested Districts Board Baseline* reports are listed.

MANUSCRIPT SOURCES

i. Manuscript collections of the papers of politicians

Balfour Papers, British Library, London.
    Papers of Arthur James Balfour, Chief Secretary to the Lord-Lieutenant of Ireland, March 1887 to November 1891.
Campbell-Bannerman Papers, British Library, London.
    Papers of Henry Campbell-Bannerman, Chief Secretary to the Lord-Lieutenant of Ireland, October 1884 to June 1885.
Crewe Papers, Cambridge University Library.
    Papers of Robert Offley Crewe-Milnes, second Baron Houghton and Marquess of Crewe, Viceroy of Ireland, 1892–95.
Gladstone Papers, British Library, London.
    Papers of William Ewart Gladstone.
Harcourt Papers, Bodleian, Oxford.
    Papers of William George Granville Venables Vernon Harcourt, Home Secretary in Liberal administration 1880–85, Chancellor of the Exchequer in Liberal Home Rule administration of 1886 and again in Gladstone's fourth ministry from 1892–95.
Sandars Papers, Bodleian Library, Oxford.
    Papers of J. S. Sandars, Private Secretary to Arthur Balfour. This collection contains a few isolated pieces that illuminate Balfour's Irish career.
St Aldwyn Papers, Gloucestershire County Record Office.
    Papers of Sir Michael Hicks-Beach, Chief Secretary to the Viceroy of Ireland, August 1886 to March 1887.
Salisbury Papers, Hatfield House, Hatfield.
    Papers of Robert Arthur Talbot Gascoyne Cecil, Third Marquess of Salisbury, Prime Minister and First Lord of the Treasury, 1886–92 and 1895–1902.
Harrington Papers, National Library of Ireland.
    Papers of Timothy Harrington, founder of the *Kerry Sentinel*, imprisoned in 1881 and 1883, MP for Meath, 1883–85, and for Dublin (Harbour) Division, 1885–1910.

Secretary of the National League and deviser of 'Plan of Campaign' in 1886. Acted for Parnell as counsel in the Special Commission.

ii. Archives of government and administration

These papers incorporate both published and unpublished material from the Chief Secretary's Office, now divided between the London Public Records Office at Kew and the National Archives, Dublin. The principles of division seem arbitrary, though there is a preponderance of printed papers for the years after 1893 at Kew. These are mainly bound and printed police reports for the later 1890s and early 1900s which were removed in 1922 by the evacuating administration.

National Archives, Dublin

Police reports 1882–1921, very incomplete collection, 5 cartons.
Crime Branch Special Divisional Commissioners' and County Inspectors' reports 1887–98, 10 cartons.
Crime Branch Special Inspector-General's and County Inspectors' reports 1898–20, 15 cartons.
Crime Branch Special 'B' files 1880–83, 2 cartons.
Protection of Person and Property (Ireland) Act 1881, 2 cartons.
Crime Branch Special Reports of District Inspector's Crime Special on secret societies and the operation of the Criminal Law and Procedure (1887) Act 1887–98, 6 cartons.
Queen v Parnell and Others, 1880–81, 11 cartons.
Chief Secretary's Office Law Opinions Entry Book. CSO LB 414, 1881–97.
Chief Secretary's Office Registered Papers, index for 1881 and 1882. CSO CR 175 and CSO CR 180.
Individual registered papers, files listed by year and number, eg. CSO RP 1881/13.
Crime Branch Special 'S' Files: 8116 Criminal history of Clare, 1887–93; 6317 Nationalist associations, 1890–92; 6247 GAA branches, 1892; 6186 South-western division, Royal Irish Constabulary, 1892; 6205 South-western division, 1892, Report submitted to Houghton, 28 January 1893; 6715 Return of enquiries held under the Criminal Law and Procedure Act (1887), 10 May 1893; 8391 Gosselin's précis of police reports on Evicted Tenants' Movement, 1894; 9238 Amnesty movement in Dublin, November 1894; 7828 Established strength of various nationalist associations; 6234 Mallon: Dublin Metropolitan Police: report on.

Public Records Office, Kew

CO 903/3 Irish Crimes Records, 1892.
CO 903/4 Irish Crimes Records 1892–94, Intelligence notes, M series 1–18.
CO 904/62 Containing detailed confidential monthly reports of the south-western division by Major General Alfred E. Turner for 1892.

Printed Cabinet Memoranda

CAB 37/23 Political condition of Ireland, January 1889, no. 5.
CAB 37/23 Secret societies in Ireland and America, April 1889, no. 13.

PRINTED PRIMARY SOURCES

i. Parliamentary Papers

Hansard, debates of Houses of Lords and Commons, third series, 1879–1903.

Return of all agrarian outrages which have been reported by the Royal Irish Constabulary between the 1st day of January 1879 and the 31st day of January 1880, giving particulars of crime, arrest and results of proceedings, HC 1880 (131), lx, 199.

Return (in continuation of the return ordered on the 15th March 1880) of all agrarian outrages . . . between the 1st day of February 1880 and the 31st day of October 1880 . . ., HC 1881 (6), lxxvii, 273.

Return for each month of 1879 and 1880, of Land League meetings held and agrarian crimes reported to Inspector-General of Royal Irish Constabulary, HC 1881, lxxvii, 793.

Return of all agrarian outrages . . . between the 1st day of November 1880 and the 30th day of November 1880 . . ., HC 1881 (6–I), lxxvii, 409.

Return of all agrarian outrages . . . between the 1st day of December 1880 and the 31st day of December 1880 . . ., HC 1881 (6–II), lxxvii, 487.

Return by provinces, of agrarian offences throughout Ireland, reported to the Inspector-General of the Royal Irish Constabulary between the 1st day of January 1881 and the 31st day of December 1881, showing the number of cases in which offenders were convicted; the number of cases in which persons were made amenable but not convicted; the number of cases in which accused are awaiting trial; and the number of cases in which offenders were neither convicted nor made amenable, HC 1882 (72), lv, 17.

Return by provinces, of agrarian offences . . . between the 1st day of January 1882 and the 31st day of December 1882 . . ., HC 1883 (12), lvi, 1.

Return by provinces, of agrarian offences . . . between the 1st day of January 1883 and the 31st day of December 1883 . . ., [C 3950], HC 1884, lxiv, 1.

Return by provinces, of agrarian offences . . . between the 1st day of January 1884 and the 31st day of December 1884 . . ., [C 4500], HC 1884–85, lxv, 1.

Return by provinces, of agrarian offences . . . between the 1st day of January 1885 and the 31st day of December 1885 . . ., [C 4701], HC 1886, liv, 1.

Return by provinces, of agrarian offences . . . between the 1st day of January 1886 and the 31st day of December 1886 . . ., [C 5024], HC 1887, lxviii, 1.

Return by provinces, of agrarian offences . . . between the 1st day of January 1887 and the 31st day of December 1887 . . ., [C 5345], HC 1888, lxxxiii, 399.

Return by provinces, of agrarian offences . . . between the 1st day of January 1888 and the 31st day of December 1888 . . ., [C 5691], HC 1889, lxi, 521.

Return by provinces, of agrarian offences . . . between the 1st day of January 1889 and the 31st day of December 1889 . . ., [C 6008], HC 1890, lix, 795.

Return by provinces, of agrarian offences . . . between the 1st day of January 1890 and the 31st day of December 1890 . . ., [C 6327], HC 1890–91, lxiv, 805.

Return by provinces, of agrarian offences . . . between the 1st day of January 1891 and the 31st day of December 1891 . . ., [C 6649], HC 1892, lxv, 449.

Return by provinces, of highest number of reported outrages in any year between 1844 and 1880; and of same for 1880 and for each succeeding year, HC 1887, lxviii, 27.

Return of crimes against human life, firing into dwelling houses, administering unlawful oaths, etc, Reported by Constabulary, between 1st March 1878 and 31st December 1879; number and names of persons convicted, 1880, lx.1; *for 1880:* HC 1881, lxxvii.1; *for January to April 1885,* 1884–85, lxiv, 357.

Return of offences in each county reported to Constabulary Office in each month of 1880 distinguishing offences against persons, property and public peace; with summary, HC 1881, lxxxvii, 619; *for 1881:* HC 1882, lv.1.

Return of offences reported to Inspector-General of Constabulary between 1st and 14th January 1881, HC 1881, lxxvii, 635; similar *Return in continuation,* lxxvii, 639.

Return of outrages reported to Constabulary during each calendar month from January to March 1882, showing persons made amenable to justice, with results of trials, HC 1882, lv, 61; *for April,* HC 1882, lv, 65.

Return of offences, exclusive of threatening letters and notices for first six months of 1882 and of 1887, and analysis of returns during first and second six months of same years, HC 1888, lxxxiii, 411.

Return of crimes and outrages reported by Constabulary in counties of Galway, Mayo, Sligo and Donegal from 1st February 1880 to 30th June 1880; of meetings for promoting land agitation within same counties since 30th June 1879; of cases in which resistance was offered to police, HC 1880, lx, 291.

Return, for each month of 1879 and 1880, of Land League meetings held and agrarian crimes reported to Inspector-General of Royal Irish Constabulary in each county, HC 1881, lxxvii, 793.

Return of lists of districts proclaimed under the Criminal Law and Procedure (Ireland) Act 1887, showing the portions of the Act so put in force in each proclaimed district, and the date of the proclamations, HC 1887, lxvii.

Memorandum as to the principles upon which outrages are recorded as agrarian, and recorded as such in the returns laid before parliament, HC 1887, lxxxiii, 287.

Memorandum [by A. J. Balfour] as to the principle upon which outrages are recorded as agrarian, HC 1887, lxviii, 140.

Correspondence relative to measures for relief of distress in Ireland 1879–80, [C 2483], HC 1880, lxii, 157–86; *further correspondence,* [C 2506], HC 1880 (9), lxii, 337–38.

Proclamation by Lord-Lieutenant of Ireland, 20 October 1881 relative to association styling itself Irish National Land League, [C 3125], HC 1882, lv, 275–77; [C 3124], HC 1882, lv, 271–74.

Report of Commission of Enquiry as to the rules concerning the wearing of prison dress, HC 1889, lxi.

Annual report of the Local Government Board for Ireland, being the seventh report under the Local Government Board (Ireland) Act, 35 and 36 Vic., with appendices, [C 2363], HC 1878–79, xxx, 1.

Annual report of the Local Government Board for Ireland, being the eighth report under the Local Government Board (Ireland) Act etc., [C 2603], HC 1880, xxviii, 1.

Return of all applications from landed proprietors and sanitary authorities in scheduled unions for loans under the notices of the commissioners of public works in Ireland, dated the 22nd day of November 1879 and the 12th day of January 1880 respectively; with result of applications to the 20th day of March 1880, arranged by baronies, HC 1880 (154), lxii, 209.

Returns of the loans applied for and granted in each of the various unions in Ireland scheduled as distressed . . . up to 7th February 1880; return (in continuation of return ordered on the 10th day of February) of the loans applied for and granted in the various unions in Ireland since they were scheduled as distressed, up to the 29th *day of February,* HC 1880 (158), lxii, 238.

Return of numbers in receipt of relief in the several unions in Ireland on the 1st day of January, the 1st day of March and the 1st day of June in 1878, 1879 and 1880, HC 1880 (420–sess. 2), lxii, 289.

Return showing the unions and electoral divisions scheduled by the local government board for Ireland under the Seed Supply (Ireland) Act, HC 1880 (299–sess. 2), lxii, 339.

Annual report of the local government board for Ireland, being the ninth report under the Local Government Board (Ireland) Act, 35 and 36 Vic. c. 69, [C 2926], HC 1881, lxvii, 269.

Returns of the names of landowners and sanitary authorities who have obtained loans under the provisions of the Relief of Distress (Ireland) Acts, 1880, distinguishing those obtained at the reduced rate of interest, showing the dates of application and of sanction, the amount of the loans, the description of works, together with the dates of first advances and gross amount of money issued on account of such loans, to the 31st day of December 1880 inclusive, arranged by counties and baronies, HC 1881 (99), lvii, 653.

Return showing the amount allowed for relief works in Ireland, the amount authorised to be expended, and the amount expended up to the present date, HC 1881 (274), lvii, 653.

Return of agricultural holdings in Ireland compiled by the local government board in Ireland from returns furnished by the clerks of the poor law unions in Ireland in January 1881, [C 2934], HC 1881, xciii, 793.

Report from Her Majesty's commissioners of Inquiry into the state of the law and practice in respect to the occupation of land in Ireland, HC 1845 (605), xix, 1. (Referred to as Devon Commission.)

Evidence taken before Her Majesty's commissioners of Inquiry into the state of the law and practice in respect to the occupation of land in Ireland, pt. i, HC 1845 (606), xix, 57.

Evidence taken before Her Majesty's commissioners of Inquiry into the state of the law and practice in respect to the occupation of land in Ireland, pt. ii, HC 1845 (616), xx, 57.

Evidence taken before Her Majesty's commissioners of Inquiry into the state of the law and practice in respect to the occupation of land in Ireland, pt. iii, HC 1845 (657), xix, 1.

Appendix to minutes of evidence taken before Her Majesty's commissioners of enquiry into the state of the law and practice in respect to the occupation of land in Ireland, pt. iv, HC 1845 (672), xxii, 1.

Report from the Select Committee on Tenure and Improvement of Land (Ireland) Act; together with the proceedings of the committee, minutes of evidence, appendix and index, HC 1865 (402) xi, 341.

Report from the Select Committee on general valuation etc (Ireland); together with the proceedings of the committee, minutes of evidence and appendix, HC 1868–69 (362), ix, 1.

Two reports for the Irish government on the history of the landlord and tenant question in Ireland, with suggestions for legislation, First report made in 1859; second in 1866, by W. Neilson Hancock, LL D, [C 4204], HC 1868–69, xxvi, 1.

Return by provinces, of highest number of reported outrages in any year between 1844 and 1880; and of same for 1880 and each succeeding year, HC 1887, lxvii, 27.

Reports from Poor Law inspectors in Ireland as to the existing relations between landlord and tenant in respect of improvements on farms, drainage, reclamation of land, fencing, planting etc.; also as to the existence (and to what extent) of Ulster tenant right in their respective districts etc., HC 1870, xiv, 37.

Report from the Select Committee of the House of Lords on the Landlord and Tenant (Ireland) Act 1870; together with the proceedings of the committee, minutes of evidence, appendix and index, HC 1872 (403), xi, 1.

Summary of the returns of the owners of land in Ireland, showing, with respect to each county, the number of owners below an acre, and in classes up to 100,000 acres and upwards, with the aggregate acreage and valuation of each class, HC 1876 (422), lxxx, 35.

Report from the Select Committee on the Irish Land Act 1869; together with the proceedings of the committee, minutes of evidence and appendix, HC 1877 (328), xii, 1.

Report from the Select Committee on the Irish Land Act 1870; together with the proceedings of the committee, minutes of evidence and appendix, HC 1878 (249), xv, 1. (Referred to as Shaw-Lefevre committee.)

Report of Her Majesty's commissioners of Inquiry into the working of the Landlord and Tenant (Ireland) Act 1870, and the Acts amending the same, [C 2779], HC 1881, xviii, 1; . . . *vol. ii;* Digest of evidence, minutes of evidence, *pt. i*, [C 2770–1], *vol. iii:* Minutes of evidence, *pt. ii, appendices*, [C 2778], HC 1881, xiv; *vol. iv: Index* [C 27789], HC 1881, xix. (Referred to as Bessborough Commission.)

Preliminary report from Her Majesty's commissioners on agriculture, [C 2778], HC 1881, xv, 25; *Minutes of evidence taken before Her Majesty's commissioners on agriculture, vol. ii*, [C 3096], HC 1881, xvii, 1.

Copy of a return of the names of proprietors and the areas and valuation of all properties in the several counties of Ireland, held in fee or perpetuity, or on long leases at chief rents, prepared for the use of Her Majesty's government, and printed by Alexander Thom, 87 and 88, Abbey St., Dublin, by the direction of the Irish government and at the expense of the Treasury, HC 1876 (412), lxxx, 395.

First report from the Select Committee of the House of Lords on Land Law (Ireland); together with the proceedings of the committee; minutes of evidence and appendix, HC 1882 (249), xi, 1.

Report from the Select Committee of the House of Lords on Irish Jury Laws; together with the proceedings of the committee, minutes of evidence, and appendix, HL 1881 (430), xi.

Second report from the Select Committee of the House of Lords on Land Law (Ireland); together with the proceedings of the committee, minutes of evidence and appendix, HC 1882, xiv, 1.

Census of Ireland, 1881, part 1; area, houses and population, also the ages, civil or conjugal condition, occupations, birthplaces, religion and education of the people; vol ii, Province of Munster; No. 3, County of Kerry, Parl. Papers 1882, [C 3148], iii.

Report of the Royal Commission on the Land Law (Ireland) Act, and the Purchase of Land (Ireland) Act 1885, [C 4969], HC 1887, xxvi, 1; minutes – referred to as Cowper Commission.

Special Commission Act 1888; reprints of the shorthand notes of the speeches, proceedings and evidence taken before the commissioners appointed under the above named Act, HMSO 1890.

Report of the Special Commission, [C 5891], Parl. Papers 1890, xxvii, 447–640. (Referred to as 'Parnellism and Crime' enquiry.)

Return to 31st March 1892, of proceedings under Land Purchase Acts, 1885 and 1888; number of applications for advances to 31st December 1891 and total amount; balance of £10m available; number of applications etc., HC 1892 (711), xv, 1.

Report of the Select Committee to enquire into and report upon the principles and practices of the Irish land commissioners and county court judges in carrying out the fair rent and free sale provisions of the Land Acts of 1870, 1881 and 1887 and of the Redemption of Rent Act of 1891, and to suggest such improvements in law or practice as they may deem to be desirable, HC 1894 (310), xiii. (Referred to as the Morley Commission.)

Returns showing, for the counties of Clare, Cork, Kerry, Galway and Mayo respectively the number of civil bills in ejectment, on title, for non-payment of rent, or for overholding, entered at quarter sessions for each of the years from 1879 to 1888 inclusive, according to form return no. 1; and of the numbers of writs issued in actions for recovery of rent or possession in each of the counties of Clare, Cork, Kerry, Galway and Mayo in the Queen's Bench, Exchequer and common pleas divisions of the High Court of Justice for each of the years from 1879 to 1888 inclusive, according to the form return no. 2, HC 1889 (211), xi, 1, 417.

Return of payments made to landlords by the Irish land commission pursuant to the 1st and 16th sections of the (Arrears of Rent) Act; and also a return of rent charges cancelled pursuant to the 15th section of the Act, [C 4059], HC 1884, xiv, 1, 97.

Return by province and counties (compiled from returns made to the Inspector-General of the Royal Irish Constabulary) of cases of evictions which have come to the knowledge of the Constabulary in each of the years from 1849 to 1880 inclusive, HC 1881 (185), xxvii, 1, 725.

Thom's official directory of the United Kingdom of Great Britain and Ireland for the year 1886.

Report of the committee of enquiry into the Royal Irish Constabulary, [C 3577], HC 1883, xxxii.

Report from the Select Committee on Land Acts (Ireland); together with the proceedings of the committee, minutes of evidence, appendix and index, HC 1894 (319), xiii.

Royal commission of enquiry into procedure and practice and the methods of valuation followed by the Land Commission, the Land Judge's Court and the Civil-

bill Courts in Ireland under the Land Acts and the Land Purchase Acts, vol. i, report, [C 8734], HC 1898, xxxvi.

Vol. ii: minutes of evidence, [C 8859], HC 1898, xxxv, 41.

Royal Commission on Labour; The Agricultural Labourer, vol. iv (Ireland), [C 6894 – xix], HC 1893–94, xxxvii.

Judicial statistics 1881 (Ireland), [C 3355], HC 1882, xxv, 1.

Report of the Evicted Tenants Commission to enquire into and report respecting estate where the tenancy of a holding or of holdings has been determined since the 1st day of May 1879 and in respect of which holdings claim to be reinstated have been made by the tenants evicted therefrom now resident in Ireland, HC 1893–94, xxxi. (Referred to as Evicted Tenants Commission.)

ii. Published books and articles

Amery, Leo, *The Leo Amery Diaries, vol. I: 1896–1929*, London, 1980, eds. John Barnes and David Nicholson.

Anderson, Sir Robert, 'Parnellism and Crime', published separately as reprint from *The Times*, 3rd series, London, 1887.

Anderson, Sir Robert, *Sidelights on the Home Rule Movement*, London, 1906.

Anderson, Sir Robert, *The Lighter Side of my Official Life*, London, 1910.

Anderson, Sir Robert, *With Plunkett in Ireland: The Co-op Organisers' Story*, London, 1935.

Argyll, George Douglas, 8th Duke of Argyll, 1823–1900, *Autobiography and Memoirs*, London, 1906, ed. Dowager Duchess.

Arnold-Forster, H. O., 'The Gladstone Government and Ireland', *North American Review*, vol. 133, no. 301, December 1881.

Arnold-Forster, H. O., *The Truth about the Land League . . . by 'One who Knows'*, London, 1882.

Bagenal, Philip T., *The Irish Agitation in Parliament and on the Platform: A Complete History of Irish Politics for the Year 1879*, Dublin, 1880.

Bahlman, D. W. R. (ed.), *The Diary of Sir Edward Walter Hamilton, 1880–1885*, 2 vols., Oxford, 1985.

Mr Balfour's Tours in Connemara and Donegal, Dublin, 1890.

Balfour, A. J. B., 'On the 1890 Land Bill', *North American Review*, vol. 151, no. 104, July 1890, pp. 1–13.

Balfour, Arthur James, *Chapters of Autobiography*, London, 1920.

Balfour, Arthur James, *Chapters of Autobiography*, London, 1930.

Bateman, John, *Great Landowners of Great Britain and of Ireland*, London, 1878.

Battersley, T. S. F., *The Secret Policy of the Land Act: Compensation to Landlords, the Corollary of the Act*, Dublin, 1882.

Becker, Bernard H., *Disturbed Ireland: Being the Letters Written During the Winter of 1880–81*, London, 1881.

Birrell, Augustine, *Things Past Redress*, London, 1937.

Blunt, Wilfred Scawen, *The Land War in Ireland*, 2nd ed., London, 1913.

Blunt, Wilfred Scawen, *My Diaries 1888–1914*, London, 1919–20.

Bodkin, Matthias, *MacDonnell: Recollection of an Irish Judge; Press, Bar and Parliament*, London, 1914.

Bonn, Moritz, *Modern Ireland and her Agrarian Problems*, translated from the German by T. W. Rolleston, Dublin, 1906.

Broderick, G. C., *Memories and Impressions, 1831–1900*, London, 1900.

Brooks, John and Sorenson, Mary, *The Prime Minister's Papers, iv: Autobiographical Memoranda 1868–1894*, London, 1981.

Buckle, G. E., *The Letters of Queen Victoria*, a selection from Her Majesty's correspondence and journals between the years 1862 and 1885, published by authority of the King, vol. III, 1879–1885, London, 1928.

Buckland, Patrick, *Irish Unionism*, PRONI, 1973.

Bussy, Frederick Moir, *Irish Conspirators: Recollections of John Mallon, the Great Irish Detective, and Other Reminiscences*, London, 1910.

Cant-Wall, E., *Ireland under the Land Act, collected reports by the Standard correspondent 1881*, London, 1882.

Chamberlain, Joseph, 'A Unionist policy for Ireland', *Birmingham Daily Post*, 1888.

Clark, Alan, *A Good Innings: The Private Papers of Viscount Lee of Fareham*, London, 1974.

Clarke, Sir Edward, *The Story of My Life*, London, 1918.

Cooke, A. B. and Vincent, John, 'Select Documents: XXVIII Herbert Gladstone, Forster and Ireland, 1881–82', parts 1 and 2 in *Irish Historical Studies*, vol. XVII, nos. 68 and 69, September 1971 and March 1972, pp. 521–48 and 74–89 respectively.

Cooke, A. B. and Vincent, John, 'Ireland and party politics, 1885–87: an unpublished Conservative memoir', *Irish Historical Studies*, XVI, no. 62, 1968, pp. 154–72; ibid. XVI, no. 63, 1969, pp. 321–38; ibid. XVI, no. 64, 1969.

Cooke, A. B. and Malcolmson, A. P. W. (comps.), *The Ashbourne Papers, 1869–1913: A Calendar of the Papers of Edward Gibson, 1st Lord Ashbourne*, PRONI, in association with the House of Lords Record Office, Belfast, 1974.

Davitt, Michael, *The Fall of Feudalism in Ireland, or the Story of the Land League Revolution*, London, 1904.

Dublin Mansion House Relief Committee, *The Irish Crisis of 1879–80: Proceedings of the Dublin Mansion House Relief Committee 1880*, Dublin, 1881.

Dun, Finlay, *Landlord and Tenants in Ireland*, London, 1881.

Dunlop, Andrew, *Fifty Years of Irish Journalism*, London and Dublin, 1911.

Dunraven, Earl of, 'Moderate reform in Ireland', *Nineteenth Century*, lix, January 1906, pp. 25–9.

Dunraven, Earl of, 'The Irish Council Bill', *Nineteenth Century*, lxi, June 1907, pp. 133–46.

Dunraven, Earl of, 'The New Irish Land Bill', *Nineteenth Century*, lxiv, December 1908, pp. 1050–66.

Dunraven, Earl of, *Irish Reform Association*, manifesto.

Earl Cowper, *KG: A Memoir by his Wife*, printed for private circulation, London, 1913.

Eversley, Lord, *Gladstone and Ireland*, London, 1912.

Fitzgerald, P., *Recollections of Dublin Castle and Dublin Society*, London, 1902.

Fitzmaurice, Lord Edward, *The Life of Granville George Leveson-Gower, 2nd Earl Granville KG 1815–1891*, 2 vols., London, 1905.

Froude, J. A., 'Ireland', *Nineteenth Century*, vii, 43, September 1880.

Gardiner, A. G., *The Life of Sir William Harcourt*, 2 vols., London, 1923.

Garvin, J. L., *The Life of Joseph Chamberlain*, vol. 1, 1836–1885, London, 1932.

Gathorne-Hardy, A. E., *Gathorne-Hardy, 1st Earl of Cranbrook: A Memoir*, London, 1910.

Gordon, Peter (ed.), *The Red Earl: The Papers of the 5th Earl Spencer 1835–1910*, vol. 1, 1835–1885, Northampton, 1981.

Green, Garrow, *In the Royal Irish Constabulary*, London, 1905.

Gregory, William, *Autobiography*, London, 1894.

Grimshaw, T. W., *Facts and Figures about Ireland*, London, 1893.

Hamilton, Lord George, *Parliamentary Reminiscences and Reflections 1886–1906*, London, 1922.

Hammond, J. L., *Gladstone and the Irish Nation*, London, 1938.

Hardinge, Sir Arthur, *Life of Henry Edward Molyneaux Herbert, 4th Earl of Carnarvon, 1831–1890*, 3 vols., London, 1925.

Harrison, Henry, *Parnell Vindicated*, London, 1931.

Harrison, Henry, *Parnell, Joseph Chamberlain and Mr Garvin*, London, 1938.

Harrison, Henry, *Parnell, Joseph Chamberlain and 'The Times'*, Dublin, 1953.

Headlam, Maurice, *Irish Reminiscences*, London, 1947.

Healy, T. M., *Why there is an Irish Land Question and an Irish Land League*, New York, 1881.

Healy, T. M., *Why Ireland is not Free: A Study of Twenty Years in Politics*, Dublin, 1898.

Healy, T. M., *Letters and Leaders of my Day*, London, 1928.

Hearne, Dana (ed.), *Anna Parnell: The Tale of a Great Sham*, Dublin, 1986.

Hicks-Beach, Lady Victoria, *The Life of Sir Michael Hicks-Beach, 1st Earl of St Aldwyn*, London, 1932.

Holland, B., *The Life of Spencer Compton Cavendish, Marquis of Hartington and 8th Duke of Devonshire*, London, 1911.

Houston, E. C., *Number One's Book*, London, 1894.

Howard, C. H. F. (ed.), *Joseph Chamberlain, a Political Memoir 1880–92*, London, 1953.

Hurlbert, W. H., *Ireland under Coercion: The Diary of an American*, 2 vols., Edinburgh, 1888.

Hussey, S. M., *The Reminiscences of an Irish Land Agent, Being those of S. M. Hussey*, compiled by Home Gordon, London, 1904.

Irish Unionist Alliance, *Publications*, vols. I–IV, incorporating series leaflet publications of the Irish Unionist Alliance, Dublin and Belfast, 1893–94.

Johnson, Nancy (ed.), *The Diary of Gathorne-Hardy, later Lord Cranbrook, 1866–1892: Political Selections*, Oxford, 1981.

Keeton, George W., *Trial by Tribunal, a Study of the Development and Functioning of Tribunal Enquiry*, London, 1960.

Kipling, Rudyard, '"Cleared" – in Memory of a Commission', *Barrack Room Ballads*, London.

Lecky, W. E. H., *Democracy and Liberty*, 2 vols., London, 1896.

Lloyd, C. D. Clifford, *Ireland under the Land League: A Narrative of Personal Experience*, London, 1882.

Lyall, Sir Alfred, *The Life of the Marquess of Dufferin and Ava*, 2 vols., London, 1905.

Lucy, Sir Henry, *A Diary of the Salisbury Parliament 1886–1892*, London, 1892.

Lynch, Pat, *They Hanged John Twiss: a tense and dramatic episode of the Irish Land War*, The Kerryman, Tralee, 1982.

MacDonald, John (ed.), *The 'Daily News' Diary of the Parnell Commission*, London, 1890.

Mackail, J. W. and Wyndham, Guy, *The Life and Letters of George Wyndham*, London, 1925.

Marjoribanks, Edward and Colvin, Ian, *The Life of Lord Carson*, 3 vols., London, 1932.

Matthew, H. C. G. (ed.), *The Gladstone Diaries, ix 1875–1880*, Oxford, 1986; *x 1881–1883, xi 1883–1886*, Oxford, 1990.

Melville, Charles H., *Life of General the Rt. Hon. Sir Redvers Buller*, London, 1923.

Micks, W. L., *An Account of the Congested Districts Board for Ireland from 1891–1923*, Dublin, 1925.

Midleton, K. P., Earl of, *Records and Reactions, 1856–1939*, London, 1932.

Midleton, K. P., Earl of, *Ireland – Dupe or Heroine*, London, 1932.

Mill, J. S., *England and Ireland*, London, 1868.

Mill, J. S., *Chapters and Speeches on the Irish Question*, London, 1870.

Monteagle, Baron, 'The Irish Land Question Today', *Nineteenth Century*, xxxix, May 1896, pp. 756–61.

Monteagle, Baron, 'The Irish Land Bill: the latest, is it the latest?', *Nineteenth Century*, liii, May 1903, pp. 738–46.

Moody, T. W. and Hawkins, R. A. J. (eds.), with Moody, Margaret, *Florence Arnold-Forster's Irish Journal*, Oxford, 1988.

Morley, John, *Recollections*, 2 vols., London, 1917.

Morley, John, *The Life of William Ewart Gladstone*, vol. III, London, 1912.

Nevinson, H. W., *Changes and Chances*, London, 1923.

Newton, Thomas, Baron, *Lord Lansdowne, a Biography*, London, 1929.

O'Brien, R. Barry, *The Life of Charles Stewart Parnell*, London, 1899.

O'Brien, R. Barry, *The Life of Lord Russell of Killowen*, London, 1902.

O'Brien, Peter, Baron, *The Reminiscences of the Rt. Hon. Lord O'Brien, Lord Chief Justice of Ireland*, edited by his daughter, Hon. Georgina O'Brien, London, 1916.

O'Brien, William, *Ireland under Tory Rule*, Manchester, 1889.

O'Brien, William, *When We Were Boys*, London, 1890.

O'Brien, William, *Irish Ideas*, London, 1893.

O'Brien, William, introduction to W. P. Ryan, *The Heart of Tipperary: A Romance of the Land League*, London, 1893.

O'Brien, William, *Mr O'Brien's Position in National Politics: How the Party Pledge was broken and Land Policy Obstructed*, Galway, 1905.

O'Brien, William, 'Was Fenianism ever formidable?', *Contemporary Review*, lxx, May 1897, pp. 680–93.

O'Brien, William, 'Who fears to speak of '98'?', *Contemporary Review*, lxxiii, January 1898, pp. 14–34.

O'Brien, William, 'If Ireland sent her MPs to Washington', *Nineteenth Century*, xxxix, May 1896, pp. 746–55.

O'Brien, William, 'The breakdown in Ireland', 2 parts, *Nineteenth Century*, lxii, July and August 1907.

O'Brien, William, 'The new power in Ireland: a retrospect and a postscript', *Nineteenth Century*, lxvii, March 1910, pp. 424–44.

O'Brien, W. and Ryan, D. (eds.), *Devoy's Postbag*, Dublin, 1948.

O'Connor, T. P., *Sir Henry Campbell-Bannerman*, London, 1908.

O'Connor, T. P., *Memoirs of an Old Parliamentarian*, 2 vols., London, 1929.

O'Donnell, Frank Hugh, *A History of the Irish Parliamentary Party*, 2 vols., London, 1910.

O'Neill, Brian, *The War for the Land in Ireland*, London, 1923.

O'Shea, Katherine, *Charles Stewart Parnell*, 2 vols., London, 1914.

Plunkett, Horace, *Report for the Recess Committee*.

Plunkett, Horace, 'Balfourian amelioration in Ireland', *Nineteenth Century*, lxviii, December 1900, pp. 891–904.

Plunkett, Horace, *Ireland in the New Century*, Dublin, 1904.

Plunkett, Horace, *Noblesse Oblige: An Irish Rendering*, Dublin, 1908.

Plunkett, Horace, *Plain Talk to Irish Farmers*, Dublin, 1910.

Property Defence Association, *Annual Report of the Committee for Years Ending 30 November 1881, etc.*, Dublin, 1881–88.

Ramm, Agatha (ed.), *The Political Correspondence of Mr Gladstone and Lord Granville, 1876–1886*, 2 vols., London, 1962.

Reid, T. Wemyss, *Life of the Right Honourable William Edward Forster*, 2 vols., London, 1888.

Robinson, Sir Henry, *Memoirs, Wise and Otherwise*, London, 1923.

Ross of Blandensburg, John, 'With Mr Forster in Ireland in 1882', *Murray's Magazine*, ii, August 1887, pp. 165–86.

Salisbury, Lord, 'Disintegration', *Quarterly Review*, no. 312, October 1883, reprinted in Smith, Paul (ed.), *Lord Salisbury on Politics, a Selection from his Articles in the Quarterly Review, 1860–1883*, Cambridge, 1972, pp. 338–76.

Selborne, Earl of, *Memorials: Personal and Political, 1865–1895*, 2 vols., London, 1898.

Shaw, Bernard, *John Bull's Other Island*, London, 1903.

Shaw-Lefevre, G. J., *Incidents of Coercion: A Journal of Visits to Ireland in 1882 and 1888*, London, 1888.

Somerville, O. E. and Ross, Martin, *Some Experiences of an Irish RM*, London, 1899.

Somerville, O. E. and Ross, Martin, *All on the Irish Shore*, London, 1903.

Somerville, O. E. and Ross, Martin, *Irish Memories*, London, 1918.

Swinburne, 'The Commonwealth – a song for the Unionists', *The Times*, 1 July 1886.

Thorold, Algar Labouchere, *The Life of Henry Labouchere*, London, 1913.

Trollope, A., *The Landleaguers*, 3 vols., London, 1883.

Tuke, James Hack, *Irish Distress and its Remedies: The Land Question: A Visit to Donegal and Connaught in the Spring of 1880*, London, 1880.

Turner, Alfred E., *Sixty Years of a Soldier's Life*.

Tynan, P. J. P., *The Irish National Invincibles and their Times*, London, 1894.

Ward, Mrs Humphrey, *A Writer's Recollection*, London, 1919.

West-Ridgeway, Sir Joseph, 'The Liberal Unionist Party', *Nineteenth Century*, vol. 58, August 1905, pp. 182–97.

Zimmerman, Georges Denis, *Irish Political Street Ballads and Rebel Songs*, Geneva, 1966.

iii. Other printed primary sources

Congested Districts Board, *Base Line Reports to the Congested Districts Board, 1892–98*, confidential printed reports in one volume kept in Trinity College Library, Dublin.

Irish Unionist Alliance publications.

Irish Landowners' Convention, *Reports of the Executive Committee, Submitted to the Irish Landowners' Convention*, 4th report, 18 December 1889; 5th report, 5 June 1890; 7th report, February 1892; 8th report, January 1893, including appendix separately published as a pamphlet, *Home Rule and the Irish Land Question*, 10th report, January 1895; 11th report, February 1896; 12th report, January 1897, including appendix containing memorandum submitted to government in March 1896, three weeks before introduction of Land Bill, 'Memorandum Relative to the Land Judge's Report' (late Landed Estates Court); 14th report, February 1899, incorporating appendix entitled 'A Memorandum Submitted for the Relief of Irish landlords Submitted for the Consideration of Her Majesty's Government'; 15th report, April 1900, 16th report, April 1901; 17th report, August 1902, 18th report, April 1904.

Full Collection Reports 1–29, 1887–1919, National Library of Ireland 3330941 i8.

Return of the resolutions and statements adopted by the Irish Landowners' Convention on the 10th day of October, 1903; and report of the Irish Land Conference dated 3rd day of January 1903; and minute on the Land Conference Report, adopted on the 7th day of January 1903, by the Executive Committee of the Irish Landowners' Convention, for HMSO Dublin, 1903.

PRINTED SECONDARY SOURCES

Adelman, Paul, *Gladstone, Disraeli and Late Victorian Politics*, London, 1970.

Anderson, Benedict, *Imagined Communities: Reflections on the origin of the Spread of Nationalism*, London, 1983.

Arensberg, C. and Kimball, S. T., *Family Life and Community in Ireland*, Cambridge, Mass., 1968.

Bagenal, Philip A., *The American Irish and their Influence on Irish Politics*, London, 1982.

Beales, D. E. D., 'Gladstone and his diary: "Myself, the worst of all interlocuters"', *Historical Journal*, xxv, 1982, pp. 463–9.

Bentley, M, *Politics without Democracy, 1815–1914: Perception and Preoccupation in British Government*, London, 1984.

Bentley, Michael, *The Climax of Liberal Politics, British Liberalism in Theory and Practice 1868–1918*, London, 1987.

Bentley, Michael (ed.), *Public and Private Doctrine: Essays in British History Presented to Maurice Cowling*, Cambridge, 1993.

Bentley, Michael and Stevenson, John (eds.), *High and Low Politics in Modern Britain*, Oxford, 1993.

Bew, Paul, *Land and the National Question in Ireland, 1858–1882*, Dublin, 1978.

Bew, Paul, *Charles Stewart Parnell*, Dublin, 1980 and 1991.

Bew, Paul, *Conflict and Conciliation in Ireland 1890–1910: Parnellites and Radical Agrarians*, Oxford, 1987.

Biggs-Davison, Sir John, *George Wyndham, a Study in Toryism*, London, 1951.

Black, R. D. C., *Economic Thought and the Irish Question, 1817–1870*, Cambridge, 1960.

Boyce, D. G., *The Revolution in Ireland, 1879–1923*, London, 1988.

Boyce, George and Day, Alan (eds.), *Parnell in Perspective*, London, 1991.

Brady, L. W., *T. P. O'Connor and the Liverpool Irish*, London, 1983.

Brown, Malcolm, *The Politics of Irish Literature: From Thomas Davis to W. B. Yates*, London, 1972.

Buckland, P. J., 'The Southern Irish Unionists, the Irish Question and British Politics, 1906–10', *Irish Historical Studies*, XV, 1967.

Buckland, Patrick, *Ulster Unionism and the Origins of Northern Ireland, 1886–1922*, 2 vols., Dublin and New York, 1972.

Buckland, Patrick, *Irish Unionism 1885–1923, a documentary record*, Belfast, HMSO, 1973.

Buckland, Patrick (ed.), *Irish Unionism II, 1885–1923*, HMSO Belfast, 1973.

Callanan, Frank, *The Parnell Split 1890–91*, Cork, 1992.

Cecil, Lady Gwendolen, *Biographical Studies of the Life and Political Character of Robert, 3rd Marquis of Salisbury*, 2 vols., London, n. d.

Chilston, 3rd Viscount, *Chief Whip, the Political Life and Times of Aretas Akers-Douglas, 1st Viscount Chilston*, London, 1961.

Clark, Samuel, *Social Origins of the Irish Land War*, Princeton, 1979.

Clark, Samuel and Donnelly jr., James, (eds.), *Irish Peasants: Violence and Political Unrest, 1780–1914*, Madison, Wis., 1984.

Clarke, Peter, *A Question of Leadership: Gladstone to Thatcher*, London, 1991.

Collins, Peter (ed.), *Nationalism and Unionism: Conflict in Ireland, 1885–1921*, Belfast, 1994.

Cooke, A. B. and Vincent, John, *The Governing Passion: Cabinet Government and Party Politics in Britain 1885–86*, Brighton, 1974.

Cornford, J. P., 'The transformation of Conservatism in the late 19th century', *Victorian Studies*, VII, 1963–64, pp. 35–66.

Cornford, J. P., 'The parliamentary foundations of the Hotel Cecil', in Robert Robson (ed.), *Ideas and Institutions of Victorian Britain*, London, 1967, pp. 268–311.

Côté, Jane McL., *Fanny and Anna Parnell, Ireland's Patriot Sisters*, Dublin, 1991.

Cowling, Maurice, *1867, Disraeli, Gladstone and Revolution: the Passing of the Second Reform Bill*, Cambridge, 1967.

Crotty, Raymond, 'The Irish Land Question', *The Tablet*, 235, 7 November 1981, 1888–89, pp. 1114–16.

Curtis jr., L. P., *Coercion and Conciliation in Ireland 1880–1892: A Study in Conservative Unionism*, Princeton and Oxford, 1963.

Curtis jr., L. P., 'Incumbered wealth: Landlord indebtedness in post-famine Ireland', *American Historical Review*, LXXXV, 2, April 1980, pp. 332–68.

Curtis jr., L. P., 'One class and class conflict in the Land War', *Irish Economic and Social History*, viii, 1981.

Curtis jr., L. P., 'Stopping the hunt, 1881–1882: An aspect of the Irish Land War', in C. D. H. Philpin (ed.), *Nationalism and Popular Protest in Ireland*, Cambridge, 1987, pp. 349–402.

Daly, Mary, *Dublin, the Deposed Capital: A Social and Economic History 1860–1914*, Cork, 1985.

Dangerfield, George, *The Strange Death of Liberal England*, London, 1936.

Dangerfield, George, *The Damnable Question: A Study in Anglo-Irish Relations*, London, 1976.

Davies, P., 'The Liberal Unionists and the Irish Policy of Lord Salisbury's Government, 1886–92', *Historical Journal*, vol. xviii, 1975, pp. 85–104.

Delaney, V. T. H., *Christopher Palles, Lord Chief Baron of Her Majesty's Court of Exchequer in Ireland 1874–1916, his Life and Times*, Dublin, 1960.

Dugdale, Blanche, 'The Wyndham-MacDonald imbroglio, 1902–06', *Quarterly Review*, January 1923.

Dugdale, Blanche, *Arthur James Balfour*, 2 vols., London, 1936.

Egremont, Max, *Balfour*, London, 1980.

Fitzpatrick, David, 'Unrest in rural Ireland', *Irish Economic and Social History*, xii, 1985, pp. 98–105.

Fitzpatrick, David, *Politics and Irish Life, 1913–21: Provincial Experiences of War and Revolution*, Dublin, 1977.

Fitzpatrick, David, 'The disappearance of the Irish agricultural labourer, 1841–1912', *Irish Economic and Social History*, vol. v, 1980, pp. 66–82.

Fitzpatrick, David, 'The geography of Irish nationalism 1910–21', in C. D. H. Philpin (ed.), *Nationalism and Popular Protest in Ireland*, pp. 403–39.

Foner, Eric, 'Class, ethnicity and radicalism in the Gilded Age: the Land League and the Irish Americans', in *Politics and Ideology of the Civil War*, New York and Oxford, 1980.

Foster, R. F., *Charles Stewart Parnell: The Man and his Family*, 1976.

Foster, R. F., *Lord Randolph Churchill: A Political Life*, Oxford, 1981.

Foster, R. F., *Modern Ireland 1600–1972*, London, 1988.

Foster, Roy, *Paddy and Mister Punch*, London, 1993.

Fraser, Peter, 'The Liberal Unionist Alliance, Chamberlain, Hartington and the Conservatives, 1886–1904', *English Historical Review*, 77, 1962.

Gailey, Andrew, *Ireland and the Death of Kindness: The Experience of Constructive Unionism 1890–1905*, Cork, 1987.

Garvin, Tom, *The Evolution of Irish Nationalist Politics*, Dublin, 1981.

Garvin, Tom, 'The anatomy of a nationalist revolution: Ireland 1858–1928', *Comparative Studies in Society and History*, 28, 1986, pp. 468–501.

Garvin, Tom, *Nationalist Revolutionaries in Ireland, 1858–1928*, Oxford, 1987.

Geary, Laurence, *The Plan of Campaign 1886–1891*, Cork, 1986.

Gellner, Ernest, *Nations and Nationalism*, Oxford, 1983.

Glaser, J. F., 'Parnell's fall and the non-conformist Conscience', *Irish Historical Studies*, vol. 12, no. 46, September 1960, pp. 119–38.

Hamer, D. A., 'The Irish Question in Liberal Politics, 1886–1894', *Historical Journal*, xii, 1969, pp. 511–32.

Hawkins, R. A. J., 'Gladstone, Forster and the release of Parnell, 1882–88', *Irish Historical Studies*, xvi, no. 64, September 1969, pp. 417–45.

Hawkins, R. A. J., 'An army on police work: Ross of Blandensburg's Memorandum', *Irish Sword*, xi, no. 43, Winter 1973, pp. 75–117.

Hawkins, R. A. J., 'Liberals, land and coercion in the summer of 1880: the influence of the Carraroe ejectments', *Galway Archaeological and Historical Society Journal*, xxxiv, 1974–75, pp. 40–57.

Heyck, T. W., *The Dimensions of British Radicalism: The Case of Ireland 1874–95*, London, 1974.

Hobsbawm, Eric J., *Nations and Nationalism since 1780: Programme, Myth, Reality*, Cambridge, 1993.

Hooker, E. R., *Readjustments of Agricultural Tenure in Ireland*, Chapel Hill, NC, 1958.

Hoppen, K. Theodore, *Elections, Politics and Society in Ireland, 1832–1885*, Oxford, 1984.

Hoppen, K. Theodore, *Ireland since 1800: Conflict and Conformity*, London, 1989.

Howard, C. D. H., 'Joseph Chamberlain, Parnell and the "Central Board" scheme, 1884–85', *Irish Historical Studies*, viii, 1952–53, pp. 324–61.

Jackson, Alvin, *The Ulster Party, Irish Unionists in the House of Commons, 1884–1911*, Oxford, 1989.

Jay, Richard, *Joseph Chamberlain, A Political Study*, Oxford, 1981.

Jenkins, T. A., *Gladstone, Whiggery and the Liberal Party, 1874–1886*, Oxford, 1988.

Jones, Andrew, *The Politics of Reform 1884*, Cambridge, 1972.

Jordan, Donald, 'John O'Connor Power, Charles Stewart Parnell and the centralisation of popular politics in Ireland', *Irish Historical Studies*, May 1986.

Jordan, Donald E. Jr., *Land and Popular Politics in Ireland: County Mayo from the Plantation to the Land War*, Cambridge, 1994.

Joyce, William L., *Editors and Ethnicity: A History of the Irish-American Press, 1848–1883*, New York, 1976.

Kee, Robert, *The Laurel and the Ivy, the Story of Charles Stewart Parnell and Irish Nationalism*, London, 1993.

Kinzer, Bruce L., 'J. S. Mill and Irish Land: a reassessment', *Historical Journal*, 27, 1, 1984, pp. 11–27.

Larkin, Emmet, *The Roman Catholic Church and the Creation of the Modern Irish State, 1878–1886*, Philadelphia and Dublin, 1975.

Larkin, Emmet, *The Roman Catholic Church in Ireland and the Fall of Parnell, 1880–1891*, Liverpool, 1979.

Loughlin, J., Gladstone, *Home Rule and the Ulster Question 1882–1893*, Dublin, 1986.

Lubenow, W. C., *Parliamentary Politics and the Home Rule Crisis, the British House of Commons in 1886*, Oxford, 1988.

Lyons, F. S. L., *The Irish Parliamentary Party, 1890–1910*, London, 1951.

Lyons, F. S. L., *The Fall of Parnell, 1890–91*, London, 1960.

Lyons, F. S. L., *Parnell*, Dundalk, 1963.

Lyons, F. S. L., *John Dillon, a Biography*, London, 1968.

Lyons, F. S. L., *Charles Stewart Parnell*, London, 1977.

Lyons, F. S. L. and Hawkins, R. A. J., *Ireland under the Union: Varieties of Tension: Essays in Honour of T. W. Moody,* Oxford, 1980.

McCartney, Donal (ed.), *Parnell: The Politics of Power*, Dublin, 1991.

McCormack, W. J., *Ascendancy and Tradition in Anglo-Irish Literary History from 1789 to 1939*, Oxford, 1985.

MacDonagh, Oliver, *States of Mind: A Study of Anglo-Irish Conflict 1780–1980*, London, 1983.

MacDonagh, Oliver, *The Hereditary Bondsman: Daniel O'Connell 1775–1829*, London, 1988.

MacDonagh, Oliver, *The Emancipist: Daniel O'Connell 1830–1847*, London, 1989.

McDowell, R. B., *The Irish Administration 1801–1914*, London and Toronto, 1964.

Matthew, H. C. G., 'Disraeli, Gladstone and mid-Victorian Budgets', *Historical Journal*, 22 (1979), pp. 615–43.

Matthew, H. C. G., *Gladstone, 1809–1874*, Oxford, 1986.

Moody, T. W., *Davitt and the Irish Revolution, 1846–82*, Oxford, 1981.

O'Brien, Conor Cruise, *Parnell and his Party 1880–1890*, Oxford, 1957.

O'Broin, Leon, *The Prime Informer – a Suppressed Scandal*, London, 1971.

O'Callaghan, Margaret, 'Parnellism and crime: constructing a conservative strategy of containment', in McCartney (1991), pp. 102–24.

O'Callaghan, Margaret, 'Irish history, 1780–1980', *Historical Journal*, 29, 2, 1986, pp. 481–95.

O'Callaghan, Margaret, 'Review of K. Theodore Hoppen, "Ireland since 1800: conflict and conformity"', *Irish Historical Studies*, 27, 1990–91, pp. 285–87.

Ó Gráda, *Ireland before and after the Famine – Explorations in Economic History, 1800–1825*, Manchester, 1987, 1993.

Palmer, N. D., *The Irish Land League Crisis*, New Haven and London, 1940.

Palmer, Stanley H., *Police and Protest in England and Ireland, 1780–1850*, Cambridge and New York, 1988.

Parry, J. P., *Democracy and Religion, Gladstone and the Liberal Party, 1867–1875*, Cambridge, 1986.

Parry, Jonathan, *The Rise and Fall of Liberal Parliament in Victorian Britain*, New Haven and London, 1993.

Philpin, C. D. H. (ed.), *Nationalism and Popular Protest in Ireland*, Cambridge, 1987.

Pinto Duchinsky, Michael, *The Political Thought of Lord Salisbury 1854–68*, London, 1967.

Pomfret, John, *The Struggle for Land in Ireland 1800–1923*, Princeton, 1930.

Pugh, Martin, *The Making of Modern British Politics 1867–1939,* London, 1982.

Shannon, Richard, *The Crisis of Imperialism 1865–1915*, London, 1974.

Shannon, Richard, *Gladstone, vol. I, 1809–1865*, London, 1982.

Smith, E. P., *The Making of the Second Reform Bill*, Cambridge, 1966.

Solow, B. L., *The Land Question and the Irish Economy 1870–1903*, Cambridge, Mass., 1971.

Solow, B. L., 'A new look at the Irish Land Question', *Economic and Social Review*, 12 July 1987, pp. 301–14.

Stansky, Peter, *Ambitions and Strategies, the Struggle for Leadership of the Liberal Party in the 1890s*, Oxford, 1964.

Steele, E. David, 'Gladstone and Ireland', *Irish Historical Studies*, 17 (1970–71), pp. 63–71.

Steele, E. David, *Irish Land and British Politics: Tenant Right and Nationality 1865–1870*, Cambridge, 1974.

Townshend, Charles, *Political Violence in Ireland: Government and Resistance since 1848*, Oxford, 1983.

Tulloch, Hugh, 'A. V. Dicey and the Irish Question, 1870–1922', *The Irish Jurist*, 15, 1980.

Vaughan, W. E., 'Landlord and Tenant Relations in Ireland between the Famine and the Land War, 1850–1878' in L. M. Cullen and T. C. Smouth (eds.), *Comparative Aspects of Scottish and Irish Economic and Social History*, Edinburgh, n.d., pp. 85–96.

Vaughan, W. E., 'An Assessment of the Economic Performance of Irish Landlords', in F. S. L. Lyons and R. A. J. Hawkins (eds.), *Ireland Under the Union, Varieties of Tension: Essays in Honour of T. W. Moody*, Oxford, 1980, pp. 173–99.

Vaughan, W. E., *Landlords and Tenants in Ireland 1848–1904*, Dundalk, 1984.

Vaughan, W. E. (ed.), *A New History of Ireland, vol. 5, Ireland Under the Union, I, 1801–70*, Oxford, 1989.

Vaughan, W. E., *Landlords and Tenants in mid-Victorian Ireland*, Oxford, 1994.

Vincent, John, 'Gladstone and Ireland', *Proceedings of the British Academy*, lxiii, 1977, pp. 193–238.

Walker, Brian, *Parliamentary Election Results in Ireland, 1801–1922*, Dublin, 1978.
Warren, A. J., 'Gladstone, Land and social reconstruction in Ireland 1881–87', *Parliamentary History*, ii, 1983, pp. 153–73.
Warwick-Haller, Sally, *William O'Brien and the Irish Land War*, Dublin, 1990.
Winstanley, Michael J., *Ireland and the Land Question 1800–1922*, London and New York, 1984.
Young, Kenneth, *Arthur James Balfour*, London, 1963.
Zastoupil, Lynn, 'Moral government: J. S. Mill on Ireland', *Historical Journal*, 26, 3, 1983.

UNPUBLISHED DISSERTATIONS

Bull, Philip James, 'The reconstruction of the Irish Parliamentary Movement: an analysis with particular reference to William O'Brien', University of Cambridge, PhD, 1972.
Jones, David S., 'Agrarian capitalism and rural social development in Ireland', Queen's University of Belfast, PhD, 1978.
Kennedy, Liam, 'Agricultural co-operation and Irish rural society, 1880–1914', University of York, PhD, 1978.
O'Callaghan, Margaret, 'Language and religion: the quest for identity in the Irish Free State, 1922–32', University College, Dublin, MA, 1981.
Vaughan, W. E., 'A Study of Landlord and Tenant Relations in Ireland between the Famine and the Land War, 1850–78', Trinity College, Dublin, Ph.D., 1974.
Warren, A. J., 'The Irish policies of the Gladstone Government, 1880–85', University of Oxford, D Phil, 1974.

Index

Abercorn, 1st Duke 46
Act of Union 27
Admiralty, and law enforcement 16
agrarian agitation (*see also* crimes, disorder, outrages) 49, 96
  Buller view 142
  causes 8, 148
  control by Dublin Castle 12, 27, 54, 114
  Forster figures 23-4
  Gladstone view 85, 107-8
  S.M. Hussey view 63
  interpretation by British administration 69-70
  Irish Parliamentary Party dissociation from 108-9
  in Kerry 122-32
  Land League implicated in 76
  language of 20-1
  Parnell Commission view 108-9, 124
  support by population 56, 85
  and Tenants' Relief Bill 109
  interpretation of *Times* 95
agricultural depression 2, 5, 7, 12, 44, 48, 99
  of late 1886 100, 132
  and evictions, Kerry 124
  and tenants' interests 147
  and Tenants' Relief Bill 109
agriculture
  efficiency of 13, 14, 15, 148
  revisionist economic view 97
Anderson, Robert 88
anti-Parnellites 145
Ardwainig 129
Arensberg, C. 6
Argyll, Duke of 27, 34, 35, 59, 71, 88
arms, unlicensed, possession of 23-4
Arms Act (1881) 88
Arms Bill (1881) 78
army (British), in Ireland 25
  against agitation 46, 51

and Buller 133
  in south and west, 'uneasiness' regarding 86
  use to support evictions 25, 38-9
Arnold-Forster, Hugh Oakley (Oakel) 78, 89
Arrears Act (1882) 94, 100, 128
Arrears Bill 106, 109, 113
Ashbourne, 1st Baron 110
'Ashbourne Act' (1885) 99, 100, 135, 136, 138
Athenry 84

Bagenalstown 22
Baldwin, Professor 12, 14, 15
Ballaghantouragh 127, 128
Ballinamore 75
Ballindine 85
Ballinlough 75
Ballydesmond 123
Ballyglass 75
Ballynamanagh 130
Ballyragget 22
Barry, John (MP) 68
Barry, Justice 25, 62, 67
Bauard 131
Beaufort 75
Bell, Alan 84, 85
Bence-Jones, William 13
Bennett, Alexander 124
Bessborough, Lord 26, 40, 71, 85
Bessborough Commission 2, 3, 71, 73, 154
  and Land Bill 1881 52, 73
  Conservative view of 98
  and tenant 'interest' 97
Bew, Paul 78, 82, 149
Biggar, Joseph 3, 20, 33, 53, 54, 62, 63, 68, 89
Birrell, Augustine 148-9
Blennerhasset, Arthur 124, 125
Blennerhasset, Rowland 86, 138

Borris 22
Boycott, Charles Cunningham (Captain)
    61
boycotting 72, 78, 82, 83, 84
    defeat by Balfour 114
    Buller's attempts at suppression 132,
        134, 137, 138
    Buller view 110-11
    Conservatives view 114
    and Curtin murder case 117
    Holmes view (1885) 140
    in Kerry 125, 127
    and non-jury trials 115
    and Plan of Campaign 143
    statistics 5
    and *Times* case 116
Boyton, Michael 54, 62, 63, 68, 79
Brabazon, Frederick George *see*
    Bessborough, Earl of
Brehon Law 57
Brennan, Thomas 20, 54, 62, 63, 70
Bright, John 24, 59
Bright Clauses 24
Broderick, St. John 146, 147, 149
Brosnan, Timothy 127
Buller, Sir Redvers 5, 110, 122, 131-42,
    143
Burke, Thomas Henry 14-15, 17, 23, 87,
    88
    and Carraroe evictions (1880) 28
    warns of Fenians 24
    and prosecution of Parnell 51-3, 58
Bushman 130
butter prices 70
Byrne, G.M. 68

Cahill, Patrick 124
Cairns, Earl 45
Campbell, Robert 84
Campbell-Bannerman, Sir Henry 106
Carleton, William 9
Carnarvon, 4th Earl 106, 109, 140
Carraroe evictions (1880) 26-8, 29, 39
Castleisland 122, 123, 133, 138
Castle Rackrent (Edgeworth) 77
Catholic Church 6
Catholic emancipation 50

Catholics 17, 50, 146
Cavendish, Lord Frederick 93
Chamberlain, Joseph 22, 61-2, 75, 89
    and suspension of habeas corpus 55,
        56, 57, 59, 71
Chaplain, Henry 12, 40, 41
Childers, Hugh C.E. 25
Churchill, Randolph 68, 109, 110, 119
    and Home Rule 142, 146
    view of Land League in Mayo 30, 45
    and Parnell Commission 105
    and Salisbury 142
civil war 45, 86, 87
Clare (County) 82, 83, 110, 111, 132,
    136-7
Claremorris 85
'"Cleared" – in Memory of a Commis-
    sion' (Kipling) 104
Cleary, F.S. 82, 83
clergy 52, 84, 120
Clifden 16, 84
Clifford, Thomas 125-6
coercion
    under Beaconsfield 16
    Carnarvon advises ending of 106
    'coercion and conciliation' thesis 105
    and Conservative administration
        109-10, 113, 114
    and County Inspectorate for Clare 83
    under Cowper 59, 86
    under Forster 52
    under Gladstone 4, 25, 53, 55-7, 88,
        92, 93
    under Hicks-Beach 142, 143
    debates on 114-5
Coercion Act (1882) 71, 128, 139
Commins, A.J. 68
Commission on Parnellism and Crime
    107-21, 122, 123, 124, 132, 144
Commissioners of Public Works 31, 33
common law (of England)
    and property 39, 56, 58
Compensation of Disturbances Bill
    (1880) 2, 25, 27, 28, 29, 30, 33-48
compulsory purchase (of land) 149
congested districts 5, 99, 100, 150
Connaught 45, 52, 58

'conspiracy theory' 4, 9, 48, 49, 59, 69, 72, 73, 76
  and Parnell Commission 113, 122, 123, 124, 132, 154
  and Plan of Campaign 143
  and Richmond Commission 99
  and State Trial 61, 62, 68, 108
  and *The Times* 111-2, 122-8
Conservatives
  economic analysis of 1880's 7
  view of Bessborough Commission 98
  view of Compensation of Disturbances Bill 40, 45-6
  and Cowper Commission 102
  view of Evicted Tenants Bill 26, 29-30
  view of Ireland 4, 95-6, 102-3, 106-7, 109, 142
  view of Irish MPs 119
  and Land Bill (1881) 88, 89
  Marlborough administration 16, 31, 36
  criticism by Parnell 31-2
  policy *see* policy
  recognition of rural poverty 5
  support for landlords 50-1
Constabulary Act 51
constitutional nationalism 119, 120, 121
Cooke, A.B. 105, 106, 140, 142
Corbet, W.J. 68
Corbett, John 14
Cork (City) 81
Cork (County) 52, 82, 132, 133
County Courts 17, 36, 37
  judges 26, 28, 36
County Inspectors 84, 114
Coury, Cummis 84
county (landed) society 50, 51
  source of Justices of the Peace 17
  source of RIC officers 18
Cowen, Joseph 12, 64
Cowper, 7th Earl 24, 28, 46, 49
  Florence Arnold-Forster view 87
  and Land Act (1881) 88
  and situation in Ireland 86
  and suspension of habeas corpus 51, 52, 55-9, 78, 85
Cowper Commission on Land Act (1881) 99-103, 110, 111, 140-1, 142

Cranbrook, Viscount 46, 109
crime (*see also* agrarian agitation; disorder; outrages) 1, 31, 41-2, 45-6, 53-4, 55, 56, 57, 62, 86, 87, 89, 106, 126-7, 128, 147
  alleged, of Land League members 78, 82, 99, 108-9
  categorisation by Hicks-Beach 5
  statistics 10, 47, 70, 75, 94, 106, 153
  and Turner 143
Crime Prevention Bill (1882) 93
Crimes Act 106, 113, 115, 116, 117, 137, 147
Crimes Bill 111, 112, 143
crop failure 44
Cuirnane, John 129
Cullinane, Martin 129
Culloty, John 126-7
cultural nationalism 149
Curtin, John 116-7
Curtin murder case 116, 137
Curtis, L.P. 105, 106

dairy farming 13
Dalton, Joseph 84-5
Daly, John 68
Dane, Sir Louis 148-9
Davitt, Michael 10, 20, 32, 68, 73, 75, 76
  'Charter of the Land League' 115
  and Curtin murder case 117
Dawson, C. 68
Dease, Richard 13
defenderism 8
Department of Agriculture and Technical Instruction 148, 149
Devon Commission 2, 8, 9, 51
Devonshire, 8th Duke 34
Devonshire Commission 34-5, 39
Devoy, John 9
Dicey, Albert Venn 62
Dilke 55, 56, 59
Dillon, Henry Augustus 14
Dillon, John 54, 62, 63, 68, 89, 118, 119
  as anti-Parnellite 145, 146
  detention (1881) 73, 79, 91
  and Parnell Commission 114, 144

Dillon, Luke 63
Dillon, V.B. 63
disestablishment (of Church of Ireland) 50
disorder (*see also* agrarian agitation; crimes; outrages) 2, 16, 17, 23, 52-3, 69
  Forster view 76
  and prosecution of Land League members 57
  control by National League 5
Disraeli, Benjamin 12, 30
Donegal 30, 35, 44
Dowse, Richard 26, 143
Dromahegmon 129
dual ownership 98
Dublin Castle (administration) 16-7, 22, 74, 76
  under Balfour 112, 133
  under Brackenbury 94
  and evictions 25, 26-7
  as interpreter of 'Irish problem' 153-4
  and prosecution of Land League members 51, 63, 78, 90
  difficulty in enforcing law 37-40
  language, concerning boycotting 111
  and London 15-6, 55, 106
  and Parnell Commission 115, 122
  and Peace Preservation Act 12
  and police 2, 10, 17-8, 79, 80, 150
  and public expenditure 24
Dublin Evening Mail 64-5
Dublin Metropolitan Police 18, 62
Dufferin, Earl of 13
Duffy, Gavan 71
Dunmore (Co. Galway) 84
Dunsany, Lord 22

economic depression 2, 12, 44-5, 76, 98, 99
  and Dublin Administration 25
  and Liberal government (1880) 20
  and nationalists 21
Edgeworth, Maria 9, 42, 77
Egan, Patrick 20, 54, 62, 63, 64, 68
Elizabethan settlements 123
emigration 7, 40, 98

Emly, Lord 40
employment 44
Encumbered Estates Act (1849) 14
English law 32, 96, 103
Ennis 83, 84, 136
Evicted Tenants Bill (1893) 25, 146
Evicted Tenants Commission 145, 146
evictions 2, 9, 13, 20, 23, 25-6, 30, 36, 37, 52, 53, 58
  in Carraroe 27-8, 29, 38
  figures interpreted by Dublin Castle 153
  Forster view 72
  in Kerry 70, 124, 125-32
  Liberal view 147
  and Land League members 62
  and police protection 137
  statistics 7, 31, 38, 40, 41, 89

'fair rent' 100
Family, Life and Community in Ireland (Arensberg & Kimball) 155
famine 28, 32
  of 1847 6, 9, 29, 57, 89
farmers *see* tenant farmers
farms (holdings) 6, 29, 30, 37
  1914 ownership 151
  compensation for improvements 37, 97
  in Connemara 27
  purchase rate 1891 147
  rented 13, 15
Farranfore 129
Feingold, William 124
Fenians 9, 24, 78-9, 82, 95
Fieries 127
Finea 75
Finneran, Hubert 84
Fitzgerald, J.D. 62, 67
Fitzpatrick, David 1
Flag of Ireland, The (newspaper) 29
Flanagan, Stephen Woulfe 13
Forster, Florence Arnold- 39, 75, 78, 86-9, 90
Forster, William Edward 29, 39, 74, 84, 88
  and agrarian problems 68-70

as Chief Secretary 15, 21-3, 24, 31
as coercionist 86
and Compensation of Disturbances Bill (1880) 25, 28, 35, 36-7
criticism by press 89
and convictions of Land League members 64
and evictions 27, 28
and Gladstone 34-5, 39-40
and Irish problem 2, 3, 4
and Land League meetings 75
view of land movements 9
and law enforcement 38-9, 40, 90
Liberal colleagues view of 47
and Peace Preservation (Ireland) Act 23
on prosecution of Land League members 46-53, 54, 58
public image 3, 85, 89
on rent increases 37
on Resident Magistrates' reports 115
on suspension of habeas corpus 50-6, 57, 58, 59, 85, 92
on starving peasantry clashes with the law 40
Fottrell, George 100
Franks, D.B. 24
freehold 30
Freeman's Journal 20, 65
Furey, Patrick 85

Galway (County)
detentions under Protection of Persons and Property Act 81-2, 83-5
evictions in 38, 39
law enforcement in 16-17
rent agitation 41, 42, 51, 73
Garvin, J.L. 22, 89
Gibson, Edward 22
Gill, J.H. 68
Gladstone, Herbert 91-3
Gladstone, William Ewart 1, 3, 34, 47, 88
and agrarian crime 107-8
and agrarian reform 95
and Bessborough Commission 26-7
British press influence on 21-2

and Catholic middle classes 146
and Coercion Bill (1881) 70-5
and Compensation of Disturbances Bill 35-6
concessions on property (1870) 39
and Forster 34, 40-1, 88-9
respect for Irish MPs 119
analysis of Irish problem 4
and Kilmainham treaty 91
and Land Act (1870) 96
and Land Bill (1881) 90, 153
on land agitation 12
and land reform 24-5
and Land League prosecutions (1880) 53
and nationalist strategy 109
relations with Parnell 94
on Protestant ascendancy 11
and Relief of Distress Bill 33
and suspension of habeas corpus 55, 56, 58, 85
Gladstone and the Irish Nation (Hammond) 47
Glougherty, Thomas 86
Gods and Men (Lord Dunsany) 22
Goodman, John Fox 66, 67
Gordon, General 62
Gordon, Patrick 54
Gorman, P.J. 62, 63
Gort 24, 87
Gortalea 128
Goschen, George Joachim 12, 107, 146
Goshawk (gunboat) 16
government enquiries
political bias 15
grazier tenants 99, 149
Great Hunger, The (Kavanagh) 6
Greene, John Ball 13
Griffin, Thomas 84-5
Griffith's valuation 102

habeas corpus (*see also* coercion) 64
proposed suspension 49-59, 61, 70-3, 76
suspension 3, 77, 80, 85, 154
no longer suspended 94
Hamilton, Sir Robert 132, 139, 141

Hammond, J.L. 47, 55
Harrington, Edward 122, 128, 129
Harrington, Timothy 63, 82, 122, 124,
    128
Harris, Matthew 9, 54, 68, 82, 84
Hartington, Marquis of 59, 88, 146
harvests 12, 29, 36, 109
Hawkins, Richard 27, 28
Hawthorne, Michael 85
Headford (Co. Galway) 85
Healy, Tim 68, 73, 93, 110, 119, 128
    as anti-Parnellite 145, 146, 147
    and Local Government Bill (1898) 151
Heffernan, John B. 81
Hemphill, Charles Hare 13
Hicks-Beach, Sir Michael 100, 106,
    109-11, 113, 119
    and Buller 132-3, 134, 137-8, 139,
    141, 142
    liberal view of Irish situation 142-3
    and Wyndham proposals on land
    purchase 150-1
Hillier, Colonel (RIC) 46, 81, 82
holdings *see* farms
Holmes, Hugh 140
Home Rule 4, 80, 93, 135
    Churchill and 142
    Conservatives and 95, 102-3, 105,
    107, 118-9, 145
    defeat in House of Lords 108
    and Irish Parliamentary Party 106
    Liberals and 147, 154
    Parnell and 113, 121
    Unionists and 146
Home Rule Bill (1886) 2, 99, 105, 145
Home Rule movement 113
Home Rule Party *see* Irish Parliamentary
    Party
housing (in mud cabins) 27, 66
Hussey, Samuel Murray 13, 61, 70, 87,
    123, 124, 128, 131

Inchicullane 130
industry (manufacturing) 29
'interest' in land 96
    and Land Act (1881) 98, 99
    tenants' inability to sell 25

*Introduction to the Study of the Law
    of the Constitution* (Albert Venn
    Dicey) 62
Invincibles 93
Ireland
    British press coverage 21, 63, 75, 102
    view of Buller 141
    view of Commissioners on agrarian
    trouble 26
    view of Conservatives 102, 106-7
    view of Gladstone government 22-3,
    24-5, 41
    according to Patrick Kavanagh 6
    image projected by Land League 3
    image, in London 2, 88
    independent 4
    and Parnell Commission 113
    as part of Union 31, 88, 95, 102, 105
    as problem to Britain 11, 12, 41
    solving of, by Forster 87
Irish Church Surplus 32
Irish Church Temporalities Commis-
    sions 31
Irish Landowners' Convention (1902) 5,
    151
Irish language 6
Irish Memories (Somerville & Ross) 22
Irish National Land League *see* Land
    League
Irish Nationalist Party *see* Irish Parlia-
    mentary Party
Irish Parliamentary Party 1, 21, 26, 48-9,
    65, 106, 149
    views of agrarian disturbances 27,
    109
    and Home Rule defeat 108
    tension after Kilmainham treaty 113
    and Land League 9
    obstruction policy 73
    and 'New Departure' 95
    view of O'Donnell 93
    and Parnell Commission 108-9, 113,
    114
    and rents 102, 110
    reunification 149
    and Richmond Commission 99
    speeches on Dublin Castle (1881) 74

Irish people
    character 18, 32, 43, 45, 102, 107
    and Compensation of Disturbances
        Bill 40
    English perceptions of 12, 32
    Forster attempts to influence 28
    General Gordon view 62
    hopes, in 1885 119
    Land League address to (1880) 20-1
    Morley view 146
    Parnell alleges lack of sympathy with
        74
'Irish problem, The' 11-2, 19-20, 31, 34,
        41, 42, 47, 48, 60, 80
    Conservative analysis 7
    Dublin Castle as interpreter 153
    compared to Punjab 148
'Irish question, The' 31, 34, 133
'Irish situation, The' 95
    Conservative analysis 151-2
    view of Florence Arnold-Forster 86-7
Irish World, The 108

Jenkinson 94, 118, 134, 136, 137
Jephson, Henry 87
Johnson, W.J. 31, 63, 73, 76, 87
Joyce, William Henry 111
Joynt, William Lane 74, 75
juries
    and Crime Prevention Bill (1882) 93
    Cork, to try Kerry offenders 134
    criminal, and Plan of Campaign 143
    Irish stereotypes 66, 67
    in Land League trial 65-9
jury trials 62, 88
Justices of the Peace 17

Kavanagh, Arthur MacMurrough 13, 21,
        26
Kavanagh, Patrick 5
Keanasup 132
Keane, John B. 5
Kearney, Patrick 85
Kearns, Lawrence 85
Kelly, John 84, 125
Kenmare, Earl of 35, 87, 116, 123,
        127-8, 129-30, 132

Kerry (County) 4, 13, 110
    anti-government feelings 80
    Buller view of 138-9
    County Court judge 135
    disorder in 52, 70, 111
    Land War in 122-32
    moonlighting in 82, 132
    murders in 136
    and Parnell Commission 144
    police in 138, 139
Kerry, Knight of 21
Kerry Sentinel, The 111, 123, 124, 127,
        128
Kettle, A.J. 20
Kildare Street Club 50
Killarney 123, 129, 131, 133, 136, 140
Killasser 75
Kilmainham treaty 4, 79, 90, 100, 106
Kilmallock 88
Kimball, S.T. 6
Kipling, Rudyard 104

La Touche, John 97
Labouchere, Henry 89
Ladies' Land League 87, 131
Lalor, Fintan 95
Lalor, R. 68
land (*see also* 'land question'; land
        purchase) 14, 96
    and Curtin murder case 116
    as economic problem 110-11
    government policy on 95
    'land of Ireland' 5, 6, 21, 153
    Liberals' decision (1881) 153-4
    Parnell policy on 113
    politics of 4, 91
    and smallholders 15, 28
    tenure, and J. Cowen 64
Land Act (1870) (*see also* Bessborough
        Commission) 28, 34-5, 36, 53, 85,
        95
    and agrarian 'reform' 95
    amendments suggested by Forster 34,
        36, 37-9
    effects 14
    and Home Rule cause gains 80
    Irish landlords view 50

and Land Act (1881) 71
land purchase clauses 24, 25, 37, 38
'land question' 28, 36, 39, 40, 89, 105, 109, 145-152, 153-4
problem to Buller 134-5
Land Act (1881) (*see also* Cowper Commission) 4, 71, 88, 89-90, 91, 92, 94
effects on landlords 98
revisionist view 97
land agents 12, 13, 27, 28
and Cowper Commission 139
as Justices of the Peace 17
witnesses to Parnell Commission 124
relations with tenants 129, 136
Land Bill (1881) 4, 71, 84, 88, 106, 151
Land Commission 90, 98, 109, 111, 147, 150
as buffer in purchase of estates 150
and Cowper Commission 100, 102
and rent revision 142
Land Conference (1903) 151
Land Court 91, 98, 111
land law
and Compensation of Disturbances Bill 25
Land League 3, 9-10, 20-22, 29-30, 32-3, 43, 45, 83-4, 85, 86, 87
view of Balfour administration 118
and Compensation of Disturbances Bill 39
Cowper analysis 86
differences in 154
and Forster 47-8, 89
Gladstone tightening of law on (1881) 70-6
in Kerry 125
and Land Act (1881) 90
and landlords 100
language of 3, 76-7
members charged with conspiracy 62-70, 122-32, 153
and 'New Departure' 95
and 'No Rent' manifesto 91
opportunism of 5
and Parnell Commission 113
politics of 6
position on poverty and unrest 32, 76-7

proscription of members 49-50, 51-9
effects of Protection of Persons and Property Act 79, 81-8
suppression 91
and suspension of habeas corpus 92
Land League courts 128-9
Land League of Mayo 9
land purchase 145, 147, 149-50
state-aided 5
land reform 23, 25
and Gladstone 70
and Protection of Persons and Property Act 79
'land struggle' 113, 151
land system, inequities 147
land tenure (*see also* Bessborough Commission) 13, 32
land valuation 13, 26
Land War 1, 5-8, 10, 20, 58, 97
and Evicted Tenants Commission 146
historiography of 105-6
and Home Rule 95
in Kerry 122-32
and 'New Departure' 95
and poor tenants 99
landlord class 5, 70, 99, 145, 151, 152
landlordism 21, 73, 76
landlords 1, 5, 13, 21, 22, 35
absentee 1, 7, 13, 28, 96
Bessborough Commission support 35
British press coverage 21, 74
brutality of 28
Buller view of 136, 137-38, 139, 140
as cause of starvation 21
and Compensation of Disturbances Bill 39, 40, 41
and Conservative Party 146
and Cowper 87
and Cowper Commission 101, 110
economic conditions of 7, 103
and evictions 27-8
Forster view 72
Holmes view of 140
as Justices of the Peace 17
in Kerry 123
lack of capital investment in property 15

and Land Act (1870) 96-7
and Land Bill (1881) 88, 98-9, 140
and land purchase 149-52
and leases 14
Liberal view of 2
and nationalism 151
and Parnell Commission 108
and Plan of Campaign 100-1
and Purchase Act (1896) 147-8
and rent disputes 26
representations to Forster on agita-
tions 49-52
state loans to 31
relations with tenants 9, 37, 96, 118-9,
136
Lansdowne, Marquis of 13, 14, 35, 123,
146
language
of British government 75-6, 80
of Chaplin 40
of Dublin Castle, on boycotting 111
of English government on Land
League 93
of Forster to Gladstone 34
of Irish Parliamentary Party 106
of Land League 3, 8, 10, 20-1, 43, 74,
76-8
of London versus Dublin 15-6, 17, 47
of Parnell Commission 113-4
of police reports on Land League 74,
75
of politics 107
of Tottenham on agrarian crime
statistics 42
law (*see also* Brehon Law; English law;
land law) 1, 3
and boycotting 116
Chamberlain view 61-2
Forster view 38-9, 72-3
Irish system 11
Land League view 65
landlords view 49-50
'ordinary law' 3, 70, 89
and rural society 10
law and order 20, 22-3, 26, 39, 48, 49,
88
and Balfour 4

breakdown 2, 57
and Buller 133
Conservative view 102-3
Forster and 92
and Richmond Commission 99
and Wyndham 150
law enforcement
Balfour view 145
Cowper view 56
by Dublin Castle 16, 25, 48
Hicks-Beach view 110
landlords' view 49-50
Liberals' consciencious view 38
use of police/army 28, 46
by Forster 37-8, 39, 40, 41, 42, 90
Law, Hugh 24, 25, 30, 31, 48, 87
and Compensation of Disturbances
Bill 34, 44
on relief grants to landlords 33
in state trial of Land League members
63
Lays of the Land League 74
Leahy, Daniel 127-8
Leahy, E. 68
Leahy, Jeremiah 130
Lecabane 128
leaseholders
and judicial rents 136
Lee, Joseph 70, 82, 111, 122
Lefevre, Shaw 23, 24
legislation
and agricultural depression (1879) 12
and Bessborough Report 73
and Compensation of Disturbances
Bill (1880) 40-1
effects on Irish society 149
and landlords under Land Act (1881)
98-9
on land purchase 145, 150-1
special *see* special legislation
Leitrim 35
Leitrim, Earl of 35
Leonard, Maurice 130, 131, 132, 133
liberalism 66
Liberals 5, 22-3
Burke (Thomas Henry) view 16, 28
and Compensation Bill (1880) 29, 39-40

concessions to Irish demands 42
and 'conspiracy theory' 69-70, 75
economic principles 45
view of Forster 47-8
and habeas corpus suspension 3, 154
view of Irish Parliamentary Party 75
view of Irish politics 3
and 'Irish problem' 4, 20, 23, 41
and Land Act (1870) 37, 41, 96-7
and Land Bill (1881) 88
and Land League prosecutions 70-1
and landlords 31, 50
and 'ordinary law' in Ireland 56-7
and Parnell Commission 113
Parnell criticism of 31-2
and police reports to Dublin Castle 115
policy *see* policy
and Protection of Persons and Property Act 79
Spencer administration 94
Limerick (County) 110
Lisbawn 130
Listry 128
Lloyd, Clifford 18, 19, 87, 88, 89, 139
loans
to landlords 35, 36
to occupiers, suggested by Parnell 32-3
local government 138
Local Government Bill (1898) 151
Logue, Michael 84
Londonderry, Lord 142, 146
Loughrea 83
Lowther 16, 23

Maam 24
Maamtrasna (massacre) 82, 106
McCabe, Edward (Archbishop) 52
McCarthy, Justin 68
McCoan, J.C. 68
Macdonagh, Francis 63, 65, 67
McDonagh, James 84
McGahern, John 5
McHale, John (Archbishop) 52
Mackey, Sir J.W. 66
McLoughlin, William 63
McTernan, Captain 83

magistracy 17, 18, 19
Mahon, The O'Gorman 68
managed estates 13, 14
Mansion House Relief Committee 35
Mansfield, J.H. 24
Marlborough, 8th Duke 16, 31, 45
martial law 37, 41
Marum, Mulhallen 68
Matthew, Colin 71
Maughantoorig 130
May, George 62
Mayo (County) 9, 30, 41, 42, 44, 45, 51, 70, 73, 122
Mayo, 6th Earl 46, 148
Meehan, Francis (Sergeant) 116
Metje, R.H. 68
Mill, John Stuart 43, 54, 57, 96
Millstreet 82, 132, 133
Milltown, Earl of 100, 141
Molloy, B.C. 68
Molloy, C. 63
Monteagle, Lord 88, 148
moonlighting 82, 109, 110, 113, 128, 132
Morley, John 47, 71, 89, 145-9
    Commission 147
Morris, O'Connor 135, 137
Moylough (district) 84
Mulloy, John 84
Munster 45, 52, 124
Murphy, James 63
Murphy, Patrick 129
Murphy, Patrick J. 81
Murphy, Tom 5

Naish, John 88, 140
Nally, John 54, 62
Nally, 'Scrab' 75
Nassau, William (Senior) 9
Nation, The 63
National League 82, 94, 106, 108, 109, 117
    Buller investigations 133-41
    complaints of boycotting 141
    as criminal conspiracy 5, 122-32, 143
    differences within 154
    establishment, Kerry 129
    and Parnell Commission 112-3

and tenant problems 111
suggested suppression 142
nationalism 5, 89, 90, 96
  and agrarian economic grievances 148-9
  Conservative analysis 151
  and criminality 115-21
  and Conservative strategy 109
  evolution of 118, 119-20
  parliamentary 9
  and Parnell Commission 112, 113, 114
nationalist movement 69
  'nationalist conspiracy' 118
  and Parnell 91
  and Parnell Commission 113
  political manoeuvering 153
  propaganda 20, 21, 102
  and violence 109
Nationalist Party *see* Irish Parliamentary
  Party
nationalists 4, 21, 90
  and agrarian crime 42
  British government relationship 79-80
  Buller view 137-8
  and definition of 'Irish problem' 47,
    57, 76
  and Gladstone 109-10
  and Land League 49
  language of 8
  attitude towards Morley 146
  MPs 3, 7, 89, 94, 98, 149, 153, 154
  and parliamentary obstruction 75
  and Parnell Commission 112, 117-8,
    123
  attitude towards Horace Plunkett 148
nationality 1, 96, 149, 151-2
Nelligan, Chute 100
Nelligan, Colonel 54
neo-liberalism, and Dublin Castle 132-3
'New Departure' 9, 95
New Ross 22
newspapers (*see also* individual names)
  British, and agrarian crime figures 74
  view of Compensation of Disturbances
    Bill 39-40
  Irish 28
  on Ireland and 'Irish problem' 12, 21,
    24

landowners influence 55
London: image of Ireland 74-5, 86, 87
  nationalist 65, 115, 137
  and proscription of Land League
    members 52
  publication of T. Brennan indictment
    63
  Unionist 64, 65
  and violence 62
Nineteenth Century 21, 47
'No Rent' manifesto 91, 92, 93, 128, 129
Nolan, F. 63
Norbury, 1st Earl 9

O'Brien, Charlotte 87
O'Brien, Justice 62, 67
O'Brien, Peter 63
O'Brien, William 80, 87, 114, 118, 128,
  144
  on compulsory purchase 119
  and 'No Rent' manifesto 79
  and suppression of Land League 91
  concern for tenants 119
obstructionism 21, 73, 75
O'Callaghan, Colonel 137
O'Connell, Daniel 62
O'Connor, Charles 26
O'Connor Don, The 22
O'Connor, Father 117
O'Connor, John 83, 117
O'Connor Power 9, 25, 33, 34
O'Connor, T.P. 68, 74
O'Donnell, Frank Hugh 92, 93, 111, 112
O'Hagan, John 25, 87, 91
O'Halloran, Martin 83
O'Keefe, William 36
O'Kelly, J.J. 63, 68, 79
O'Neill, Patrick 81
Orange Order 8, 54
O'Shea, William (Captain) 71, 92, 93
O'Sullivan, Malachi 54
O'Sullivan, Michael 62
O'Sullivan, William H. 20, 68
Oughterard 24, 27
outrages (*see also* agrarian agitation;
  crimes; disorder) 2, 24, 48, 49, 51,
  54, 55, 56, 58, 72, 86-8, 90

Buller view 134, 135
and Forster 92
and Hicks-Beach 5
in Kerry 124
and Land Commission 142

Paine, Thomas 77
Pall Mall Gazzette 71, 89
Parnell, Anna 1
Parnell, Charles Stewart 20, 29, 93, 104, 105
charged with conspiracy 62, 63, 64
detention (1881) 79, 153
Ennis speech (1880) 10
and extremists 120
and proposed action by Forster 50, 54, 55, 57
view of Forster 72-3
view of Florence Arnold Forster 89
relations with Gladstone 93
on government relief grants 31-2, 33
imprisonment 91
and Land League 48-9, 75
and leaseholders 100
and Parnell Commission 112-3
'Parnellism and Crime' articles 111
and rent revision 142
and Tenants Relief Bill 109
trial 67-71
Parnell Commission 10, 20, 104-21, 122, 123
and Conservative government 123
and outrages 132, 142
Parnellism 4, 119, 120
'Parnellism and Crime' articles 99, 111, 119, 122
Parnellite split 119, 146, 149
Parnellites 67-8, 75, 88, 119, 146, 153
'Paudeen O'Rafferty on the Landlords' Ten Commandments' 10, 76, 188-90
Peace Preservation (Ireland) Act 12, 23, 24, 34, 50, 57, 135
peasants 1, 4, 5, 8
view of Dublin Castle 111
fear of eviction 40
mobilisation 105
peasant proprietorship 145, 152

Peel, Sir Robert 54
Phoenix Park murders 93, 106, 111
Pigott, Richard 65, 111, 112
Plan of Campaign 5, 100-1, 114, 119, 143, 146, 147
Plunkett, Horace 148
police (*see also* Royal Irish Constabulary; Dublin Metropolitan Police) 2, 25, 94, 123, 136, 146, 150, 154
against agitation 46, 51
cost 24, 25
and evidence against Land League members 51, 69, 112
Gladstone proposed reduction in numbers 54
in Kerry 139
reforms 17
relationship with magistracy 18-9
on Protection of Persons and Property Act 81
relationship with the people 86, 133
on suspension of habeas corpus 79
use in support of evictions 25, 29, 38-9, 45
police informers 10
policy, Conservative 2, 4, 13, 132
under Balfour 118
on Ireland 105, 120-1, 141-3
on land 101, 145-54
policy, English 5, 10, 21, 46, 115
on agrarian agitation 68-70, 76
on land 95
and political demands 98
from 1879 105
policy, Liberal 2, 4, 105
Conservative view 103
under Gladstone 3, 23, 31, 34, 53-4, 88
on land 147, 153
and Phoenix Park murders 88
population, 5, 7, 14-5
Porter, A.M. 63
Portsmouth, Lord 14
Portumna 84
potato crop 44-5
poverty 3, 5, 6, 12, 27-8, 29, 44, 66
cause of land inequities 147
Land League view 32

and Richmond Commission 97-8
Power, R. 68
press *see* newspapers
propaganda
British 115
nationalist 20, 65, 102
property 14-5, 21, 23, 30, 37, 40, 72
and Balfour 143
and Bessborough Commission 101
and Catholic Church 6
security of 35
status under Land Act (1870) 36, 39, 95
status under Land Act (1881) 4, 98
property rights 25, 35, 40, 41, 50, 59, 95
Conservatives view 151, 154
and Hicks-Beach 110
Protection of Persons and Property (Ireland) Act (1881) 62, 70-86, 91, 130
Protestant ascendancy 11
public expenditure 24
Purchase Act (1896) 147
Purchase of Land (Ireland) Act (1885) 99-100

Queen vs O'Connell 63
Queen vs Parnell and Others 10, 20, 51, 64

Rainsboro 75
Rathmore 128
Recess Committee (1895) 148
Redmond, John 148
Redpath, James 63
Reed, Sir Andrew 139
Reid, T. Wemyss 47
relief agencies 12
Relief of Distress Bill 32, 33, 36
Reminiscences of an Irish Land Agent, being those of S.M. Hussey 61
rents 13, 14, 23, 24, 26, 72, 110, 135
Buller view 140
intimidation against payment 20, 82, 83, 85, 128
Irish Parliamentary Party demands reduction 110
judicial 147, 149

and Land Act (1881) 97-9
and Land League conspiracy charges 62, 108
Morley view 147
non-payment, and evictions 25, 26, 28, 29, 30, 41, 97
and Plan of Campaign 100
unpaid, appropriation by landlords 32
tenant rights under Land Act (1870) 36-8
resettlement proposals 146-7, 149
Resident Magistrates 2, 79, 81, 83, 84, 94, 115
and boycotters 135
Morley interference 145
Reynolds, James 81
Rhattigan, Reverend 84
Ribbonmen 8, 72, 78, 93, 95
Richmond Commission 2, 3, 12-5, 25, 97-9, 154
Rights of Man (Paine) 77
Robertson, Major 12, 14
Robinson, Henry 27
Robinson, Spencer 21
Ross, D 63, 68
Ross, Martin 22
Rosse, Lord 11
Royal Irish Constabulary (*see also* police)
and Buller 133
and Clare Island disorder (1880) 16
constitution 18
in case against Land League members 62-3
impotence of 19
and Parnell Commission 124
place in community 116, 124
and Protection of Persons and Property Act 81
reports to Dublin Castle 10, 114
and *Times* case 122
rural change 79
rural society 5, 6, 57, 65-6, 80, 96
Dublin Castle observations 118
and the law 10
and 'revisionism' 95
Russell, Sir Charles 111, 112, 113, 116

Russell, T.W. 149
Ryan, Michael 85
Ryan, Thady 85

Salisbury, Lord 99, 109-10
  appoints Sir Redvers Buller 110
  appoints Cowper Commission 99-100
  and Evicted Tenants Commission Bill
    146
  appoints Hicks-Beach to Dublin 141
  and Home Rule Bill 145
  on Ireland 11, 100, 142
  and Parnell Commission 113
  and *Times* case 123
Scrope, Paulette 9
secret societies 24, 54, 61, 81, 92, 93
Seebohm, Henry 90
Selborne, Earl of 88
self-government 71, 108, 118-9
Sexton, Thomas 54, 62, 63, 68, 79, 93
Sheridan, Patrick 54, 61, 68
Shaw, William 26
Shawe-Taylor, John 151
sheriff system 140
Sligo (County) 41, 42, 58
smallholders 14, 32
Smith, W.H. 43, 110
Smithwick, J.F. 68
Soames, Joseph 112, 116
social reform 106
society (*see also* county society; rural
    society)
  Dublin 66
  Irish 149, 153
  London 75
Solow, Barbara 7, 97, 98, 101
Somerville, Edith 22
Special Commission into Parnellism and
    Crime (1887) *see* Parnell Com-
    mission
special legislation (*see also* coercion)
    23, 52, 56, 57, 59, 64
  exceptional legislation 35, 36, 42
Spencer, John Poyntz, 5th Earl 24, 25, 28,
    57
  and coercion 57, 59, 88, 93
  and crime reports 115

  as Lord Lieutenant 94
  and Richmond Commission 12, 13
starvation 19, 25, 27, 29, 33, 35, 42
  view of General Gordon 61-2
  image projected by Land League 76
State Trial (of Land League members) 3,
    46, 62-3, 69, 70, 74
stipendiary magistracy 10, 11, 19
  duties and Dublin Castle 17
  reports provided for *The Times* case
    122
Sullivan, Timothy Daniel 25, 54, 62, 63,
    73, 116, 117
Suspension of Rent Bill 42

tenant farmers 6-7, 13, 14, 36, 76
  relations with agents 129
  Buller view 137-8
  and Compensation of Disturbances
    Bill 39
  and Cowper Commission 101
  Forster view 2
  Holmes view 140
  and Land Act (1870) 96, 97
  and Land Act (1881) 91, 98, 100
  and Land Commission 111
  and land improvement 149
  image projected by Land League 3,
    21, 66
  landlord relations 9, 37
  landlord sanctions 25, 28
  and law 61
  Morley concessions to evicted 145
  relief measures of 1879 32
  resistance to rent payment 20, 25, 26
  in south and west 27, 28, 29, 30, 110
  sub-tenants 96
  and Tenants Relief Bill 109
tenant right 96, 97
Tenants' Relief Bill 109, 113
tenure (*see also* Bessborough Commis-
    sion) 13, 32
  as cause of agrarian disturbances 26
  and Bessborough Commission 73
  and Land Act (1881) 100
  security of 25, 35, 74
'Three Fs' 54, 59, 71, 96

Times, The
    interpretation of agrarian outrage 95
    anti-Irish invective 102
    association of Conservatives with 105
    letters criticising Compensation of Disturbances Bill 39
    letter of Gen. Gordon sympathising with Irish people 62-3
    'Parnellism and Crime' articles 111-2, 116
    The Times case 122-3, 124, 127, 128
    Turner praises 143
tithes, abolition 54
Tottenham, A.L. (Colonel) 41-5
Townshend, Charles Uniacke 14, 79
Tralee 123
    Poor Law election 124
Trevelyan, George Otto 106
Truth about the Land League, The (Arnold-Forster) 89
Tuam 85
Tuke, James Hack 29
Tullamore 89
Turner, Sir Alfred E. 123, 143, 144
Tyrone, Lord 101

Ulster, agrarian crime figures 45
Ulster Custom, The 30, 44, 96, 97
Union, The 22, 31, 50, 53, 96, 99

Unionists 42, 141, 145, 146
United Ireland 80, 91, 111, 115, 120, 127, 141
United Irish League 149
United Irishmen 8
United Kingdom 11, 24
    effects of Compensation of Disturbances Bill 40
    Ireland as part of 38, 56, 89, 102
    landlords view 50
    perception of RIC 18
    Tory view of property and 96

Walsh, John W. 54, 62, 63, 68
Waterford, Lady 146
Webb, Alfred 117
West, Horace 87
West-Ridgeway, Sir Joseph 105, 119, 120, 143
Westmeath 12
Westmeath Act 52, 53
'Westmeath crisis' 57
Westport 19
Whigs 25, 35, 47, 51, 88, 105
Whiteboys 8
Woodford 86
Wyndham, George 145, 149, 150, 151

Young Ireland (Gavan Duffy) 71